Hugh and Me

James Owen Colley
with
Adam Berkelmans

Introduction

My name is James Owen Colley, I was born in Oshawa Ontario, Canada in 1957.

On March 1, 1972, when I was 14, I flew across the Atlantic Ocean to spend six months and seven days with my Great Uncle Hugh. This is the story of our adventures as we travelled through 17 countries in Europe, Africa and Asia. It's the story of a naïve Southern Ontario teenager, travelling with his eccentric Great Uncle Hugh who was a well-educated university professor, architect and a social worker. We had many crazy adventures, troubles and experiences that I think you will enjoy hearing about.

A little background on myself and Uncle Hugh will set the stage as to how we teamed up and the circumstances that led to this hilarious story.

My parents, Muriel and John, were hard-working, middle-class folk, and did their best with five children. My father worked at Bell Telephone, and my mother held many jobs over her life. We never had a lot of money but lived a comfortable typical lifestyle in Southern Ontario. As kids growing up in the 60s we experienced life as all kids of this generation. We lived outside, riding our bikes everywhere, playing hide and seek, road hockey, red rover and hopscotch. We stayed outside all day unless we were called or it got dark. We drank from the garden hose when we were thirsty and peed behind trees. Our lives were confined to a 4-block radius and our only connection to the outside world was T.V. where the Ed Sullivan Show and Walt Disney were the highlight of the week.

When I was 10, we moved from Oshawa to Cobourg Ontario, a small town on the north shore of Lake Ontario.

This was a bit of a culture shock to me as things were a lot more relaxed in school and kids' lives. All the kids seemed wild and free-spirited, a sharp contrast to the very disciplined school system in Oshawa. Kids roamed all over the town and out into the countryside, without fear or regard for their parents. I soon adjusted and enjoyed this new freedom.

When I was 13 my mother received a phone call from my grandfather's 60-year-old brother, Hugh, my great uncle. Uncle Hugh was planning a 6-month tour of Europe and had a proposition for my mother. He wondered if my brother Dave, who was 16 and driving, would like to accompany him and help out with the driving and navigating. If he was willing to do this, Uncle Hugh would finance the whole trip . Great Uncle Hugh had suffered a broken neck years before which resulted in him having a fused spine, preventing him from turning his neck. He didn't think he would manage the narrow roads and busy traffic of Europe by himself.

Well Dave wanted no part of it, partially because neither he nor I knew this great uncle at all. He lived in Oregon and we had maybe met him once. Besides, Dave had a girlfriend and other friends who he was reluctant to leave. Dave was also very introverted and wasn't too keen on taking on an adventure of this magnitude.

Unable to change his mind, my mother broke the news to Uncle Hugh, but she had an alternative solution for him to consider. She suggested that he take me, Jim, the 14-year-old. She laid countless praises of me on him, of how outgoing I was, how quick to learn and I'd be an excellent navigator and map reader. Hugh was disappointed that Dave wouldn't come on the trip of a lifetime and was very skeptical about having a 14-year-old, a mere child, accompany him. Hugh had never married and had no experience with children, so he was extremely cautious. My mother was relentless and very convincing and finally Uncle Hugh agreed.

So off to Europe I went, and spent 6 months touring Europe, learning so much about history, architecture, art, cultures, people and myself.

After our amazing trip, I settled back into family and small-town life. I finished high school and soon after I married my high-school sweetheart, Heather. Heather and I never looked back, we got jobs, bought a house, had three children and lived our lives to the fullest with many friends and family around us. I worked as a labourer in a factory making automotive parts for the big three automakers. I became supervisor at age 20 and then materials and distribution manager and finally manufacturing manager, a position I held for over 20 years, until I retired after 38 years of employment.

Heather and I sold our home of 29 years and built a home on a Canadian Shield lake north of Kingston, Ontario. Our children and nine grandchildren visit often. We have a very social life, on a beautiful lake, and as they say, we are living the dream.

I write this book after over 50 years, the stories and adventures we experienced have always been popular with friends and family, who all encouraged me to write this book. My storytelling has always been very good, while my writing skills are limited, making me hesitant about taking on such a large project. I asked my good friend Adam Berkelmans (The Intrepid Eater), who is an amazing writer, chef and a very creative person, if he would help. He agreed and his contribution has been fantastic. I wrote the story and Adam over-wrote the story with great descriptive additions and his fine writing skills turned my story into a fun reading book that I think everyone will enjoy.

While this was over fifty years ago, my memories are vivid and I've told many of the stories over the years. I did keep a diary while we travelled which helped remind me of our daily travel route. I didn't put too much effort in correcting errors in place names and locations. I've probably exaggerated some points and I'm certain that there are discrepancies and errors, but they are all mine and I make no apologies for them. It's taken me fifty years to finally write this, and I wrote it as I remember it.

I hope you enjoy it!

Chapter 1

February 29, 1972

The hour-long car ride to the Toronto International Airport from Cobourg was, for the most part, silent. My father was driving and my mother in the passenger seat, both bundled up against the February cold, with the heater struggling to keep the windows defrosted as we drove down the 401 Highway. Under their coats, my father wore his customary blue pants and brown sweater, while my mother wore an orange and white, flower-patterned dress. Snow-draped farm fields separated by windrows and small woodlots slid by as I gazed out of the backseat window, my physical stillness at odds with my active and apprehensive inner monologue. Just what the hell was I getting myself into?

The fields eventually gave way to warehouses and buildings as we passed through the city of Toronto, the buildings getting taller as we made our way past the downtown core. Having rarely visited the big city, the urban landscape was exciting to see, a local taste of all the great European cities I'd soon be seeing. We made our way through Toronto and out the other side into Mississauga, towards the airport.

Before I knew it, we had arrived, my father struggling to find a decent parking spot close to the terminal. I had just unwittingly witnessed the last glimpse of Canada that I would have for the next long while as we made our way into the busy airport.

My mother began to cry as I went through the process of checking in, but for me, the reality of imminent departure was setting in and unconcealed excitement was mingling with the anxiety over leaving. She patted my shoulder and said, "Don't fall in the lake." This had been a long-standing private joke between us, something akin to, "Don't break a leg!"

My father looked at me and said, "Have fun, see you in six months," and with that, they turned around and walked away. I was now on my own, a 14-year-old country boy from Ontario, heading to a foreign land to connect with my even more foreign Uncle Hugh, whom I would aid by navigating us across Europe.

In truth, I wasn't even supposed to be doing this. Hugh had requested that my older brother David join him in Europe and function as his driver since he was sixteen and had his driver's license. Being a sixteen-year-old with a job, friends, and a girlfriend, David promptly rejected the offer, electing instead to spend the next six months at home. My mother used all of her charm and praises of me to convince Uncle Hugh that I would be a suitable replacement and after much debate Hugh agreed.

The whole reason Hugh needed a driver was due to a neck injury from a train derailment incident; he could barely turn his head and so would have a hard time driving the chaotic roads of Europe. Due to my age, I couldn't drive, so the logic in sending me in my brother's stead seemed dubious. Hugh seemed to think that if he drove, and I navigated and checked his blind spots, that he could make it work. He wasn't too excited about travelling with a fourteen-year-old boy and worried that he'd be acting like a sort of glorified babysitter.

Despite his misgivings, he decided he could use my help and I consequently found myself being packed off to Europe, to meet up with my Great Uncle Hugh; a man I barely knew.

Moving from the check-in counter and making my way through customs, my adolescent mind overlaid the futuristic surroundings with scenes out of Buck Rogers, with yours truly acting as the swash-buckling space adventurer. I found a seat in the departure area and waited for the boarding call, my wild space-pirate imaginings once again settling into nervous anxiety. Where exactly were my parents sending me? What was it going to be like over there? What if I hated it? I could have said no at any time and cancelled the trip, but I knew that this was a once-in-a-lifetime experience and that I'd be stupid not to go. As I sat there though, I quickly lost that bravado and began to really worry.

Anxiety and excitement warred back in forth in my head as I stared out at the planes taxiing on the runway. Finding the plane I'd soon be boarding out of the airport window, I was in awe at the sheer size of it. I had flown once before, but the plane had been much smaller than this trans-Atlantic behemoth. I was excited to see what it was like inside and became impatient to get going.

The boarding call was finally announced over the loudspeakers and I shuffled down the gangway along with the other passengers onto a plane heading to Frankfurt, Germany where my Great Uncle Hugh and I would commence the first leg of our epic journey across Europe and beyond.

There weren't many passengers on the plane and I ended up sitting alone in an empty row, the thoughts swirling around in my head my only company. As the plane shuttled down the runway, I contemplated my destination: a continent I knew next to nothing about. My only concept of anything European came from the few months of grade-nine history and geography at the Cobourg District Collegiate Institute public school, which I had been so recently removed from in order to take this trip. A couple of textbook chapters on the world wars were to be a woefully inadequate primer on the centuries of art, architecture, and culture on that mysterious continent, as my uncle would soon delight in pointing out.

The stewardesses were very friendly, peppering me with attentive questions: So you're travelling alone? Where are you going? How long? Oh wow, aren't you lucky! Are you nervous? You must be excited! What an adventure! Good luck! They asked if I wanted to lie down and sleep since there was no one occupying the seats on either side of me. They kindly removed the armrests, and I lay down across the seats attempting to get some rest on the way to Frankfurt. Sleep was elusive though, my mind pinballing back and forth between nervous excitement and anxious dread. I doubt I slept even ten minutes the whole flight, instead watching the backs of my eyelids as vague impressions of what Europe might be like flittered back and forth.

I arrived at the Frankfurt Am Main Airport, home to the world's first airline as well as the infamous Hindenburg zeppelin airship, at around 8:30 am German time. I was left to my own devices to figure out how to make my way through customs and retrieve my luggage.

The customs officers were terrifying, so stern and officious and matching the vague impressions of Gestapo I had in my head. I handed them my notary-stamped legal document showing that I was given leave to travel in Europe without my parents and that my great uncle was responsible for me. "Where is your uncle?" they asked menacingly, "Why isn't he on the plane? Why isn't he with you?"

I stammered out some answers and they must have taken pity on my pathetic innocence since they let me through without any of the expected torture or violent interrogation I was expecting. Once I eventually managed to make it through customs and collect my luggage, I hesitantly proceeded to the airport lobby. I stopped and stared, absolutely bewildered at the sheer volume of people hurriedly moving back and forth inside what was an absolutely massive space. Not even knowing where to begin to look for my uncle, or how I would ever be able to find him in this press of people, I edged my way over to a flight screen and stood staring at it.

Here I was, a young boy with no instructions on what to do next, with no ability to speak German, no concept of how airports even worked, and no cash, only traveller's cheques. That's right, my parents, inexplicably and bafflingly, had sent me halfway across the world without any cash whatsoever and with no actual instructions beyond, "You'll meet your uncle in the Frankfurt airport, he's flying in from Portland, Oregon." Still staring uncomprehendingly at the flight screen, I felt shock slowly slithering its way down my spine as I failed to decipher it in any meaningful way. Having no idea what to do next, I simply shuffled back towards the wall and out of the way and sat down on my suitcase.

After an hour of sitting there despondently, watching an endless stream of hurrying, faceless humanity, something caught my eye in the press: A Canadian flag on a flight attendant's brooch, shining like a beacon. With a glimmer of hope, I rushed over to the Air Canada stewardess and asked her if she could help me interpret the flight screen. She kindly pointed out my uncle's flight to me and then rushed on. I sagged with dismay as I realized that my uncle's flight had been delayed; I wasn't going anywhere.

I took my customary seat on my suitcase once more and opened a book to bide the time. After waiting for another hour or so, I spotted a pair of Air Canada stewardesses and made my way over to them with the hopes of gleaning some more information. I asked if they knew what the deal was with my uncle's flight and if they had any idea of when he might be arriving. After checking the system, they regretfully informed me that my uncle's flight had been diverted to London and was currently being refused entry to Germany. They must have seen the beginnings of panic on my face as it slowly dawned on me that I was, in truth, completely and utterly alone in a foreign land with no way of helping myself. They sweetly took it upon themselves to ease my distress and asked if I had had anything to eat lately. I told them no, but that I had no money for food in any case.

Looking at each other, they told me to come along and whisked me over into the stewardess lounge for a bite to eat. They sat me down at a table and put some food in front of me; sandwiches with the crusts cut off, cheese, cucumbers, chips, and a very rare treat in my life, a can of Coca-Cola. Now this wasn't so bad! Where minutes before, I had been hopelessly lost in an overwhelming situation, I was now seated in front of a plate of decent food, surrounded by over a dozen beautiful women, all heaping attention on me. My lifted spirits didn't last long though; shortly after finishing my meal, the pair of stewardesses informed me that they had to catch a flight and I couldn't stay in the lounge. Thanking them for their kindness, I made my way back out into the lobby, once again feeling rudderless and glum.

I sat back down in front of the flight screen and watched it until I became sick of reading *delayed, delayed, delayed* over and over again. I felt too distracted to read my book and I was feeling lonelier by the minute, sitting there with no one to talk to. People from all over the world hurried past me, and on towards their destinations, a goofy-looking, long-haired teen sitting on a suitcase was only a momentary blip on their mental radars, quickly forgotten. Becoming fed up with the lack of interest from passersby, I decided to relocate to somewhere new. I had been noticing a constant long line in front of a cigarette machine across the lobby, so I walked over and deposited myself beside the machine.

Now I had a captive audience of Germans, tourists, and airline employees queued up and facing me. Applying my charm, I struck up conversations with those who spoke English as they waited in line. This provided me with a welcome distraction and proved to be more entertaining than staring at the flight screen. I sat beside the cigarette machine for several hours, cajoling people for entertaining comments or distracting small talk. I must have struck quite a pose with my lime-green button-down T-shirt, brown corduroy pants, and hiking boots!

As I wiled away the time, I began to reflect on my life so far and the trouble I seemed to have constantly dealt to my parents. Flashbacks, too many to count, of my parents berating me and telling me that I had pushed them over the limit, or that I was upsetting the family with my behaviour, washed over me. A constant refrain followed me when I was at home with my family, "Jim (I was Jimmy until they were upset at me) you need to grow up, you need to learn how to behave!" My mind began to descend the dark path of paranoia: could this all just be an elaborate scheme to get rid of me? But would they really go through all of that trouble to pay for a flight to Germany just to rid themselves of their troublesome son?

My mind quickly filled in the blanks: well, of course, killing me would have landed them in jail! By sending me to Europe with no money and no return flight, they could wipe their hands clean of me without having ever broken a law! And who was this Great Uncle Hugh anyway? I barely knew this supposed brother to my mother's father! He could be anyone! He was coming from somewhere in Oregon for god's sake. What if it wasn't even him and they had just hired someone to pose as him and take me away to some awful European backwater shithole where I would be forced to slave away for the rest of my life? I wasn't ever going to make it back home to Canada; I might just be alone forever!

The logical part of my brain attempted to wrest the overwhelming paranoia from taking control and calm myself down, but panic was setting in and I was completely losing command of my thoughts. My cigarette machine acquaintances forgotten, I began to move around the airport attempting to come up with some sort of plan. Should I leave the relative safety of the lobby and find somewhere to sleep and eat in Frankfurt? How was I going to accomplish this with no money and no faculty with the language? It was starting to get late; what the hell was I going to do?

It was then that I saw my second beacon of hope: a well-dressed man of about 50, holding a sign that read HUGH OWEN: the name of my uncle! I rushed over to the man and introduced myself as Hugh's nephew. He luckily spoke English well and informed me that he was named Hans, was from the Volkswagen dealership, and had been tasked with picking us up from the airport. He asked where Hugh was and I filled him in with what I had learned about his flight. We went to a help desk where he spoke in German to the staff and ascertained that my uncle's flight was still going to be delayed another four hours if it was even allowed to enter German airspace. He told me not to worry and that he would take care of me for the time being. He asked if I was hungry and I affirmed that I was famished, so he offered to take me out of the airport and to a restaurant. I frowned in suspicion; this was a complete stranger in a foreign land and I was a young boy with zero experience outside my small-town home. After a moment I shrugged and agreed; what else could I do but trust him?

We took off in Hans' Mercedes and drove to a great restaurant where I ate as only a growing 14-year-old boy could eat. Hans recommended the Wiener schnitzel, which was delicious. After the meal, we drove around the rather dour city and did some nighttime sightseeing for an hour or so, then made our way back to the airport. Talking again with the help desk, Hans confirmed that the airline had worked out whatever issue was keeping them grounded in England and that my uncle's flight was on its way to Germany.

My Great Uncle Hugh finally arrived, disembarking the plane exhausted and in a sour mood. Sixty years old, his thick hair, parted on the right, was just beginning to turn grey. Thick sideburns, typical of the times, framed a face that rarely smiled, and when it did, it was strained. Large, expressive eyebrows capable of instantly communicating his temperament graced the bottom of his high forehead, with thick scholastic-style glasses underneath them. Relatively short, at 5'6", he walked with a slow, stiff-necked saunter that I quickly became impatient with. He wore a wool sweater, a tweed jacket, and slacks that didn't match the rest of his clothes. All in all, he looked like a university professor, a job that he had once held in the past at the University of Toronto.

He had no patience for hearing about the trials and tribulations I had just gone through, so we made our way to the Volkswagen dealership to pick up our ride in uncomfortable silence. It turned out Uncle Hugh had purchased a brand-new VW camper van by phone while at home and had arranged for it to be ready for us to pick up once he arrived. When we got to the dealership, there happened to be a German couple in front of us who were taking a long time to work out whatever they were doing. Uncle Hugh was instantly and inexplicably furious, pacing back and forth and fuming. He began to utter insults against Germans under his breath towards the consternated couple.

This was the first glimpse I got to see of my uncle's baffling hatred for the Germans, but it wouldn't be the last. It turned out that he still hadn't forgiven them for what they did during World War II and deemed the cataclysmic destruction dealt to Europe to be their fault. Having had enough of waiting, Uncle Hugh brusquely asked Hans to find us a place to stay for the night and said we would figure out the van the next day. My stomach seemed to be perpetually sinking; is this what the next six months, an eternity for one my age, was going to be like?

Hans found us a nice bed and breakfast to stay in for the night, so we dropped off our belongings there and went for a stroll, looking for something to eat. As we walked down the street, I spotted a likely looking restaurant and suggested we go to it. Uncle Hugh immediately pointed at another restaurant and strongly suggested we go there instead. With the entire awful day behind me, I decided to dig in my heels and stick to my guns, insisting that we go to the one I chose. Eventually, he relented and we entered the restaurant I had chosen and found a seat. This was to be my first lesson in 'winning' with my uncle Hugh: you *could* never win with him!

I ordered cabbage rolls and potatoes and was genuinely impressed with the food, but Uncle Hugh spent the entire dinner berating me about how bad this restaurant was and how awful the choice I made in coming here was. He was disappointed with my selection and his entire night was apparently ruined due to the near-inedible food. After all of the miles he had travelled that day and all of the stress and turmoil involved, this travesty of a meal was to be his terrible reward. The blistering tirade went on and on, as I sullenly ate my perfectly palatable cabbage rolls.

I was very much taken aback by his admonishments. I had of course fought time and again with my siblings but had never received the direct ire of an adult other than my parents, and wasn't at all emotionally prepared for such a tongue-lashing. Dread began to creep back and I asked myself why I was even in this place with this evil-tempered man. I just wanted to go home.

As my uncle carried on with his haranguing, my earlier mulish stubbornness came in to replace the dread and self-pity. I found new depths of strength I never knew I had in me, as my will hardened into something formidable: I was not going to quit. I was going to make it through these six months, no matter how much abuse my uncle heaped onto me. I was no damn quitter and refused to be seen as one. I wasn't going to let this great uncle of mine bully me; he wasn't so tough. The newfound resolve in my eyes showed and my uncle's scolding dissolved into mutterings, then silence. This was how it was going to be.

We made it back to our room and I crawled into bed, over which was draped a large, cushy duvet, as the nice lady who let us into the room called it. This was the very first time I had encountered a duvet, and the thought of sleeping under a massive pillow was very funny to me. In the face of my humour after our uncomfortable meal, Uncle Hugh grumpily corrected me, calling the duvet an eiderdown, which was the British name for them. "Well excuse me!" I thought to myself, "The nice lady called them duvets, so duvets they'll remain!"

The next day, Hans picked us up in his Mercedes and drove us back to the dealership. This time there was no wait at the desk and the brand-new VW camper van that he had ordered was waiting for us. Although Hugh had spent a significant sum of money on this technological marvel of a vehicle, he had proceeded to cut corners when it came to optional add-ons. The van had only the basic necessities and had come with a standard transmission, which Hugh had never driven before. The 1972 Volkswagen Transporter was brand new and still had that new car smell. It was white, with plaid seats and curtains and had a small kitchen with a sink and a small refrigerator located underneath. The side door had a flip-out shelf, and there was storage above, below, and behind the bed in the back of the van.

Hugh received the keys and we got into the van, ready for a whirlwind trip across most of Europe, led by a stiff-necked stubborn old man with his fourteen-year-old navigator, in a standard van he had no idea how to drive.

The trip began in fits and starts, with accompanying sounds of grinding gears, which set our teeth on edge. Our first stop was in Frankfurt: a seven-story shopping centre which was far and away larger than any I'd ever seen before. Hugh parked the van and we went in to go shopping for supplies. I felt like this place must have everything ever made on earth, and I walked around in constant awe.

We outfitted ourselves with pots and pans, utensils and cooking instruments, flashlights, sleeping bags, and other odds and ends. Hugh also purchased a camping stove, claiming it was much cheaper than getting the one that was supposed to come with the VW. His stingy and miserly ways would come to haunt us several times throughout the trip, but at the time, I was just excited to be buying all of this fun stuff.

At one point, as we walked our shopping cart up and down the aisles, Uncle Hugh threw a single pillow in with the other gear. I eyed it, thinking back to our conversation where he said he'd cover food and lodging, but that I was responsible for personal items. He didn't say anything about the pillow or indicate that I should also grab one; it seemed this was up to me.

It was quite the dilemma though, as it was with all of my personal items; I only had $200 in the bank and I knew it wasn't going to go far. Should I spend some of it on something frivolous like a pillow? It seemed like a waste of money, so I kept walking without putting a pillow for myself in the cart.

Fully outfitted, we packed the van, clambered into the seats and set course south for Switzerland, on the first leg of our journey.

Chapter 2

Uncle Hugh was much more amiable than the night before and was obviously feeling the excitement of the commencement of our trip. We set off for Switzerland in a good mood, but that quickly wore off into shock on my part. Uncle Hugh's driving was abominable! I couldn't decide if I should laugh hysterically or pitch myself out of the passenger door in an effort to preserve my life. He had an awful time figuring out how to use the clutch properly to change gears, and every single stop was followed either by the van stalling or great whiplash-inducing leaps forward accompanied by wretched grinding sounds. I figured the brand-new van would be completely destroyed within the day and was terrified to think of Hugh's reaction to that eventuality. His mood worsened with every minute that passed and I began to wonder which was louder: the grinding of the transmission, or the grinding of his teeth as we awkwardly jolted forward.

It was a wonder we didn't hit any other vehicles or pedestrians on the way to the Autobahn and I'm grateful to this day that the citizens of Frankfurt made it through unscathed. I wanted to help or take over, but obviously couldn't, so I navigated us along as well as I could and just grinned and bared the entire situation.

This level of helplessness on my part was prevalent throughout the trip, but seems to be prevalent in the early teenage condition in general, when you're becoming an adult, but aren't allowed to be one. I was only fourteen, so I sat back and allowed the adult to do what he would, despite the insanity of the situation. Finally getting on the Autobahn, the driving blessedly became easier. We glided along, with no obstructions or stops, giving the smoking transmission a break and allowing ourselves to relax a little bit.

Now it was time to do what I was brought on this trip to do: navigate us through the entirety of Europe. Uncle Hugh expected complete professionalism in executing my task and told me in no uncertain terms that he expected perfection. Having an inkling of what would be in store for me if I sent us down a wrong turn, or got us lost, I took my job seriously and studied the map well. I had to know where we were and where we were going at all times with zero room for error. I was to advise the Fuhrer (as I began calling him in my head) of distances to our next stop, turns, bends, rivers, villages, towns, cities, borders, and countries. I also had to be aware of any animals, detritus, or hazards on the road as well as who may have been coming up alongside the van on the left or right. Uncle Hugh couldn't turn his head, remember, so mine remained on a swivel, jumping from the map to the front, to the sides, behind, in the mirrors, back in front, to the map, and repeat. Uncle Hugh would announce that he had to switch lanes, and I would leap up and run to the back of the van to check blind spots, shouting to the front when the coast was clear.

At night, Uncle Hugh would brief me on the route for the next day. I felt like an RAF pilot being briefed on tomorrow's air raids by my commander, "First we will turn left in Mannheim, then a right in Heidelberg, then we strike in Karlsruhe! Bombs away!" I remembered the routes with alacrity and became truly proficient at map reading and navigation. That's not to say that we never became lost. Arguments broke out often, sometimes hourly, about the proper route to take or whether or not a turn should be made.

Stubborn Uncle Hugh, the Fuhrer, the Grand Poobah, the Been-There-Done-That King himself, always knew a better route than what my map clearly showed. As he was wont to tell me, "I've travelled the entire world and all across Europe. I've studied and taught geography and am a well-educated man. I know Europe like the back of my hand!"

"Well sure," I'd think to myself, "that's why you need me here!" If it hadn't been for me, we would have somehow ended up behind the Iron Curtain with no way of getting home. I'm sure we would still be driving around, lost today!

Eventually, he would relent and follow my original instructions, blindly and recklessly switching lanes or making turns. I think that being a bachelor his whole life made him incapable of working closely with someone doing mundane tasks. He'd never had to share anything or put his trust in anyone before this trip, and doing so now was obviously taking a bit of a toll on him. Spending so much time with one person was a completely new experience for him and having this snot-nosed kid confidently giving him instructions must have been a tough pill to swallow.

I had to quickly learn to hold my own with him, not only for my own pride but because I was often right and to give in would greatly inconvenience both of us. The few times I shrugged and allowed him to have his own way, we ended up hopelessly lost, with Uncle Hugh blowing his gasket and generally directing his tantrums at me, despite my lack of involvement in our predicament. Being the snot-nosed kid I was, I would sit back laughing, refusing to redirect us back on course, completely ignoring his apoplexy. Eventually, he would relent and apologize and I would once again become my professional navigator self and put us back en route.

Cruising down the Autobahn, the clutch taking a well-deserved rest, Hugh calmed down once more and we drove along peacefully. I watched the German countryside languidly slide by; a flat landscape dominated by farmland and forest. The forests were similar to what I was used to in Canada, but with a darker, more elemental undertone, and I remember the trees being huge. The farms were different too, despite being familiar. Everything I was seeing just seemed slightly off. Staring out of the window, wide-eyed, I tried to make sense of my new whereabouts and this situation I had found myself in. It seemed like forever ago since I had been watching the farms and forests of southern Ontario out of the window of my parent's car on the way to the airport. I already felt like a different person. I began to realize that I had always maintained a very childish notion of what Europe was like, and now, with the German countryside laid out before me, I had to revisit and revise those notions. I noted that the German people looked just like us and that their fashions were even very similar. Most of the people I had encountered so far spoke English, so communication had been very easy. I was beginning to feel what many intrepid travellers end up feeling: despite where we grew up, we're really all the same.

After driving for about three and a half hours, we made it to Basel, on the Swiss side of the Germany-Switzerland border. Since we hadn't quite gotten ourselves fully prepared and also due to the chilly March weather, we decided to hold off on camping and found ourselves a hotel instead.

The weather was cool and damp as we walked to the restaurant suggested by the hotel's concierge. We sat down to a supper of spring lamb, the likes of which I had never tasted before. I remember enjoying it well enough, but what I remember more so was the wine. Uncle Hugh ordered glasses for both of us, a sweet red Muscat. He enjoyed his wines sweet and grapey without any oakiness or tannins but claimed that he truly enjoyed Muscat because of the rich history the grape had in Europe. He droned on about the grape's arrival in France, brought over from Italy over 2000 years in the past and about its origin on the shores of the Mediterranean in ancient Greece. I thought to myself that he could really overthink things. I loved the wine because it was as sweet as cream soda and it made me feel great. Being allowed to drink wine as a fourteen-year-old was certainly a perk of being in Europe.

Looking back at times like those, I realize that Hugh treated me as an adult contemporary for the most part; much more than I appreciated at the time. Even when he was berating me, it was really more on equal terms, or at least from a boss to a subordinate, than I cared to admit as a teenager. The way I saw it back then was that he was asserting some sort of parental control over me, which could often lead to adolescent rebellion on my part, but I now see that that wasn't necessarily the case.

I thoroughly enjoyed our dinner and left the restaurant with a pleasant buzz, which lingered on as we continued to explore the city a bit. Basel was full of amazing sights and I walked around wide-eyed like the country boy I was; I had never seen anything like this in my life. A medieval city, Basel was filled with ancient architecture, forbidding Gothic churches, ornate fountains, crenellated stone gates, statues, and houses and buildings designed in the striking south German/Swiss style. Unsullied white walls and brightly-hued roof tiles and shutters contrasted with ancient grey stone foundations and cobblestones.

Professor Hugh the Architect led the way, pointing out and instructing me on the architecture as we strolled through the streets in the deepening dusk. "That one has Gothic influence," he'd drone on, "and that one Norman influence. That one was built in 1530, and that one sometime in the 1600s." His surprising depth of knowledge was issued out to me in a monotone and I took it all in with silent astonishment as he went on and on. I was utterly entranced, and the combination of his never-ending lecture, the beautiful and novel surroundings, and the wine left me in an agreeable dreamlike state.

As the evening drew to a close, we exchanged some traveller's cheques for Swiss Francs and went to bed early, knowing we'd be travelling to Geneva early in the morning. We were going to Geneva specifically to visit some of Uncle Hugh's friends, the Freis, and I was already excited to see someone new. I was also excited since I'd been promised a trip to the store to purchase some running shoes. So far, throughout this whole trip, I had only had my hiking boots to wear. I'd worn them on the plane, in the van, and during fancy restaurant dinners where they were ill-matched with my suit.

Looking back, it seems odd to me now that I had been sent across the world without some normal shoes. I remember in grade six I had gone through a similar situation. Back then we were always sent to school well-dressed; in dressy button-up shirts, slacks, and dress shoes. On one particular day, I arrived at school done up as usual and joined in for track and field events taking place that morning. The day started with the long jump and several running events, which I enthusiastically joined in, alongside my schoolmates in their t-shirts and runners. I never thought anything of it, but when I got home for lunch, my mother was aghast at the condition of my shoes and clothes. Demanding an explanation, I told her about track and field day to which she demanded to know why I had never told her about it.

Lacking any running shoes to speak of, I hadn't really thought about it, to be honest. My parents constantly complained about expenses and money and the lack thereof. Raising five kids was expensive so we generally didn't get any of the extra luxuries in life, though we always had a nice enough home and a comfortable life free of actual poverty. I never complained about the lack of these luxuries, which many of my peers possessed, I just grinned and bared it, not even asking for things when I really needed them. That attitude extended to running shoes on track and field day apparently, and so I had scuffed up my nice dress shoes.

She immediately called my grandfather and he picked me up and drove me to the Oshawa Mall where he bought me a pair of PF Flyers at Kresge's, a five-and-dime store that shut its doors in 1980. I was so excited; not only did I now proudly own a pair of navy-blue high-top canvas and rubber-soled runners, but I also had a, literally, once-in-a-lifetime opportunity to hang out with my grandfather. Driving to and from the store, I sat beside him in the car and he spoke and talked directly to me, rather than broadly to the pack of children I usually belonged to. It made me feel strange, honoured, and somehow manly and I cherished the fleeting moments, feeling that I now saw the man in a different light. This was to be the only few moments I ever spent alone with my grandfather.

He dropped me back off at school and wasn't I proud to come trotting back home that evening in my new runners with three ribbons from track day. "Run Faster, Jump Higher" indeed. Maybe I wasn't such the klutz my parents insisted I was. Maybe I just needed proper shoes!

Echoes of the excitement from that day followed me into my dreams as I fell asleep looking forward to once again getting a nice pair of running shoes the next day.

After a short three-hour drive, we arrived in Versoix, a town outside of Geneva and the second most populous city in Switzerland. The massive majesty that is the Alps surged upwards behind the town, creating a magnificent backdrop. I had seen the Rockies on a family trip to British Colombia as a child, but these mountains seemed different – clean and fresh with villages hugging tight to them, unlike the isolated and craggy mountain wilderness of the Rockies.

The mountains rose around valleys and villages, appearing close and rather squat, but as you neared them, they never seemed to get any closer and their impressive size became more and more apparent. The town of Versoix itself was at the bottom of one of these mountains, hugging the shores of Lake Leman, a glistening azure lake, reflecting the mountains and ancient buildings of the town in its still waters.

We drove down the main street searching for the Freis' house, eventually finding it and parking on the street. The Freis lived in a beautiful old building that clung to the shore of Lake Leman, where the Rhone River spilled into it. It was sandwiched between the shore and the main thoroughfare in the town. It was obviously a house that belonged to a family of wealth.

We were welcomed through the front door by the entire family: Mr. Frei, a large man with broad shoulders who carried himself with such confidence that I couldn't help but picture him as a chivalrous medieval knight; Mrs. Frei, a striking woman who looked as if she should be gracing the silver screen, yet approachable and down to earth; and two daughters, Anne and Barbara, sixteen and thirteen respectively.

The friendly welcome washed over me, but I only really had eyes for the two girls. Even though I had only been in Europe for a few days so far, the prospect of spending some time with people my own age, let alone pretty girls, very much appealed to me. The girls were exceedingly approachable and we became fast friends within minutes of our introduction. The arrival of a boy their age on their doorstep, arriving from far-flung Canada, was likely equally exciting to them. Anne was the older of the two and seemed very mature with an air of European sophistication. She was clearly very intelligent and had a great sense of humour that had us all in stitches on more than one occasion. Her short auburn hair was a stark contrast to Barbara's long sable locks. Like her older sister, Barbara was also very pretty, though due to some initial shyness, she let her sister take the lead. She had a sweet, innocent look on her face, while her eyes twinkled in a mischievous and alluring manner. I must say I was downright smitten!

The girls took me aside and we spent the afternoon getting to know one another. They spoke excellent English as well as German, French, and Italian, which left me in awe and feeling somewhat like a country bumpkin. They were very chatty and knowledgeable about a wide variety of things, which made for easy and enjoyable conversation, a nice change from Uncle Hugh.

The next day, we all went to the open market located in the town square for shopping and sightseeing. This was another new and eye-opening experience for me; so much to see and gawk at! The hectic pace of the colourful market had me entranced and I tried to capture it with the old camera Uncle Hugh had given me at the outset of the trip. To my chagrin, the camera refused to work properly and wouldn't take a picture.

I was beside myself. I needed this intensely colourful and exotic experience to be captured on film and became very anxious to do just that. No matter who tried to make the camera function properly, it just refused to work. I declared that I wanted to buy a new camera since this one was so problematic. Mr. Frei kindly took it upon himself to take me downtown by train in order to find a camera store. We chatted on the train ride there, his large stature at odds with a gentle soft-spoken voice that left me feeling very comfortable in his presence. He had a very fatherly air about him and I found myself really liking this man.

At the camera store, my eyes quickly grew larger than my wallet, as I looked through showcases full of beautiful, high-tech photography equipment. I wanted the perfect camera and he and I looked and looked for just the right one. Eventually, reality caught up with me and it became apparent I was in over my head looking at professional gear. I only had $200 to my name, and that needed to be budgeted for the entire trip. I wisely narrowed my search to cameras that I could actually afford and eventually found an awesome Kodak cartridge-load camera with an adjustable lens for the acceptable price of $35. They wouldn't take my old one in as an exchange, so it got left behind in Switzerland.

My new camera would prove to take excellent pictures and many of my photos surpassed Uncle Hugh's in quality, even though his were taken with a high-end Nikon 35mm. Uncle Hugh would always take forever to take a picture and every occasion he stopped to do so would make for a maddening series of events. First, we would have to scope out the view, walking up and down, back and forth, searching for the perfect angle. Once found, he would often question himself, "Is this really the best viewpoint?" and we would have to start all over, usually ending right back where we'd stopped the first time.

Next, I'd be sent to go digging for the light meter he kept in a special case, which he would then use to take several light readings. With this invaluable information now at hand, it was time to hem and haw about aperture settings on the camera. These had to be perfect and would often be narrowed down with further light meter readings. Having everything in order, it was now time to take a peek through the viewfinder and line up the target in question. Often not completely satisfied, Hugh would then start the process all over again, searching for a new spot altogether. When he was finally satisfied that everything was completely and unconditionally perfect, he would snap the photo, with smug self-assurance that this was an award-winning picture worthy of gracing the slick pages of National Geographic or Time magazine.

I on the other hand, having never really had a camera or taken pictures before, would simply see something that interested me, raise the camera and snap off a picture. Perhaps I had a natural eye or was pre-disposed to an aptitude for photography, but my pictures would often come out looking just as good or even better than my great uncle's. He even begrudgingly admitted this on a few occasions, which gave me untold amounts of Shadenfreude-esque glee after all of the ridiculous posturing from Photographer Extraordinaire

Uncle Hugh. When this happened, he would frown in a consternated manner and utter, "I just can't understand it, nor believe it. How does he do it?"

His picture-taking became more and more of an annoyance over the trip and was very difficult for the fourteen-year-old boy I was to restrain myself. The tedium of plodding through his picture-taking process became increasingly difficult; all I wanted to do was run ahead and explore, not stand around waiting for this wannabe professional photographer on a mission from God to personally photo-document the entirety of Europe. I swore at the time that Uncle Hugh was expecting to be showered with praise and glory at the inevitable mind-numbing slide show he would show off to his contemporaries after the trip, but would be sorely disappointed when he turned off the projector and found everyone fast asleep.

I know now that I was being unfair to the man, as I often was, but a country boy cast into this strange and wonderful new world, at times terrifying, with a strange old man, couldn't be expected to remain patient. Uncle Hugh, for all of the flaws I saw in him, was a highly educated and knowledgeable person and was trying his best to cram as much information into my empty skull as he could. I was quickly developing into the man I am today and a trip like this provided a developmental fast track of sorts, where everything I saw provided illumination and mental expansion. While I don't believe I was conscious of this at the time, I see now that I was developing traits and maturing into certain attributes that I think my mother saw in me from the beginning. I feel that her decision to send me haring off across Europe with her uncle was influenced by many of these traits; she must have recognized the beginnings of them before I left. Otherwise, her motherly instincts may have sought to protect me from such an extended and extraordinary peregrination.

After only a short time in Europe, I was learning how to stand up for myself, how humour could be used to break down anger and tough situations, and how to handle stressful circumstances. Most importantly, I was learning to be confident in myself. Up until that point, I had never been a confident child; with my family, or at school with my peers. I had come from a large family with English values, where children "were to be seen and not heard". I had never been allowed or able to express myself in a normal way. When I finally did it was negative, in the form of talking back or flouting rules, which caused fights with my parents and siblings. I was more used to being sent to my room, grounded, or being hit with the "black stick" than I was to confidently expressing my needs.

In today's world, my father would have been sent to jail and us kids bundled away by Children's Aid, but back then a strapping across the ass with the black stick was a matter of course in our home and in most others. I don't recall it ever being overly painful or having developed any emotional scars from the corporal punishment. In fact, my siblings and I look back on it wryly and have gotten a little sentimental about the black stick my father always kept close at hand to whack us with.

While I was accustomed to my parents' disciplinary techniques, I quickly learned in Europe that Uncle Hugh would never raise a hand against me. Oh, he had plenty of his own unique ways to castigate me, whether it be the silent treatment, blistering scolding, or outright antagonization; psychological weaponry I was not at all used to. Probably the most infuriating thing he would do was ridicule where I came from. When piqued by something I'd said, he would look at me and say something like, "Look how beautiful this place is, nothing like your home in Ontario. So dull, boring, and flat there... completely uninspiring. Such an ugly place you came from, I don't know how you can stand it."

Having left my home for this journey, I had developed a deep pride for it and simply fumed when Uncle Hugh spoke like this. As the trip went on and he hurled more and more slander at where I was from, it planted a deep seed of resentment for the man, which has admittedly never gone away. What really ground my gears was that he was so quick to debase my homeland in private, but was quick to tell locals in whatever country we were in that he was a Canadian, from Ontario. When I confronted him about this, he replied that no one in Europe liked Americans and that he didn't want anyone to judge him for being one. He had even bought Canadian stickers for the windows of the van and a flag to hoist when we stopped at the campgrounds for the night. This hypocritical semblance of patriotism really irked me, as he never let up on Ontario when we were alone.

Drawing strength from my newfound confidence and conviction, I slowly learned to deal with and even counter his mildly abusive antics. I was not used to the psychological warfare he employed and was doubtless too young to fully comprehend what was happening. I just thought he was a strange, mean, 60-year-old man who delighted in deliberately getting under my skin and offending me. When I fought back or instigated a quarrel, he would never yell at me or tell me to stop. He would simply stop talking to me for hours or days or would give it back to me in his own infuriating way. It took me nearly fifty years to realize what was actually happening in our dysfunctional relationship: we were acting like spouses!

In retrospect, he was treating me like an adult, and while I never realized it, was giving me a certain amount of respect. Since he had never had a partner or spouse, I had taken the place of one in our tumultuous existence together. Like an old pair, tired to death of each other, we traded barbs and scorn one minute, then moved past it and relied on each other in a mutually amiable domesticity.

Before I had joined him on this trip, he had lived a life alone, never having had feelings for, or need for anyone else. He had never had to rely on anyone else or ask anyone for their opinions, thoughts or viewpoints. He was free to get up when he wished, eat when and what he pleased, and come and go whenever and wherever he wanted.

Living a life like this meant that he was always right, with no one to dispute the veracity of any of his claims. He lived a peaceful and quiet life, where there was never a need to share any of his thoughts. He took great joy in learning and discovery, whether through school, reading, travelling, or even the fleeting joys of a flower opening, a sunset, or a moving opera. His contemporaries and friends were like-minded educated people who could discuss the finer points in life with him. He had never had to listen to a baby crying, a child screaming, or a teenager bitching and questioning his authority.

I must have been terrifying to the man in some ways; a complete enigma, full of hormones, vigour, and worst of all, *personality*. I don't think that he had ever expected an actual human to join him on this trip as a navigator, one with an identity, opinions, feelings, and actual value. It must have been a strange experience for him when he realized that I actually spoke and thought for myself. I'm sure he thought to himself many times as we drove from city to city, "What a mistake it was bringing this kid along. Why won't he just sit, behave, shut up, and navigate like he was supposed to?"

We were both moving through uncharted waters and were constantly jostling for position, and though it was within his power, he never strove to pull rank and set me straight once and for all. The reason for this, I believe, was partly due to his discomfort and ineptitude at dealing with a child, and partly due to his belief that he could easily defeat me through his superior intellect. We continued to squabble throughout the entire trip, but mutual respect and admiration slowly grew between us, even if it was dysfunctional and qualified by misgivings I still hold to this day.

I took it as a sign of his growing appreciation of me that there began to be instances of affection and even praise, especially in front of new people we met. Times when we were confronted with a new person to impress, Uncle Hugh would take on the form of a proud parent and sing my praises: Jim said this, or did that; he even noticed this or that! "Jim," he'd say, "tell them about our adventures in the desert, or at this or that hotel."

This certainly wasn't every time we met someone new; Uncle Hugh was just as likely to begin a story of one of our adventures and when I chimed in he'd admonish, "You always get to tell it, it's my turn now, be quiet."

Back on the train with Mr. Frei, we headed back to the market to meet up with everyone. I showed off my new camera and took a roll of film's worth of pictures. We had unfortunately run out of time though and I never got to buy the running shoes I was so excited about.

We went back to the house for dinner and I was shocked to see that hot dogs were on the menu! I guess that things here weren't really that different after all. After dinner, we all sat down in the family room and

Uncle Hugh got Mr. Frei to drag out the projector and screen so he could show us all his slides from the United States. After that, we went to bed and once again I was treated to a fabulous mattress with a huge fluffy duvet. It was like sleeping under a cloud; I was totally hooked on duvets and have loved them ever since.

When I awoke and came downstairs the next morning, I was told that one of the girls had gone out to get us a special breakfast. My interest piqued, I eagerly awaited her return to see what she brought home for us. She came back with crescent-shaped pastries that almost looked like bowties. I was told they were called "crossance". Eaten with butter, they were revelatory; so fresh and flaky and delicious. Who would have ever thought something like this existed?

After breakfast, Mr. Frei drove the girls, their affectionate tan Labrador retriever, and me a few miles outside of town and down a bucolic country road. We kept driving until we were in the midst of a forest, and then he stopped and let us out, saying, "I'll see you later!"

We intended to walk back to the house cross-country, through forest and farm fields, until we arrived back in Versoix. We took our time, meandering through the countryside, throwing sticks for the dog and laughing at his antics. We eventually reached a creek and followed it along its bank for over a mile, until we reached a fallen tree blocking our way. The bank past the tree began to get prohibitively steep for walking, so we decided to cross the creek and walk along the other bank. There were several large stones in the creek and if one leapt from one to the next, they could cross it without getting wet. I went first, showing off my prowess to the two girls. Barbara crossed next and made it to the other side fine, but Anne fell into the creek halfway across, losing one of her shoes in the ordeal. The Labrador, responding to some inner instinct, leapt into the river to retrieve the shoe, but instead of bringing it back to us, it went and dropped it back into the creek further downstream, where it was washed away for good.

We were all doubled over in fits of laughter, despite the creek being frigidly cold, seeing as it was still only March. Anne was sitting on the ground, soaking wet, and said, "I think I discombobulated my ankle!"

This just egged on all of our hilarity and had us in tears, repeating "discombobulated" over and over. For years afterwards, whenever we communicated, that word would be brought up.

Barb and I helped Anne limp the rest of the way home on an ankle that seemed to have only been twisted and not discombobulated at all.

We arrived back at the house and the girls pulled a special Swiss machine out of the cupboard. Plugging the machine in, they fed small pieces of cheese into a hopper at one end of the machine and after a few suspenseful moments, the cheese would be discharged out of the other end, perfectly melted. What a wonder!

We dug around in the fridge and pulled out all of the cheese we could find; probably a whole pound of mixed Gruyere, Emmentaler, and Raclette. Eventually, they all ended up going into the machine and then coming out melted, to be scooped up with bread, crackers, or often just our fingers. It was a lot of fun but left me backed up for days afterwards.

Mr. Frei drove us into Geneva that evening to see a movie in the theatre, which happened to be in German. I can't remember much of the movie, but I remember the girls whispering the translation, word for word, to me throughout the entire movie.

When we got home that night, we found a newly purchased copy of the Jesus Christ Superstar record in the family room, which we played over and over, traipsing around the room and singing the songs at the top of our lungs. Every rendition became more and more dramatic as the night wore on and we got to know the words.

I eventually crawled into my fluffy duvet, exhausted and glowing from such a perfect day.

I awoke early the next morning and offered to go fetch breakfast for everyone. After being given a set of directions to the local patisserie, I made my way out into the town, alone for the first time since the airport. I found the bakery easily and gestured to the croissants behind the display case, using held-up fingers to show how many I wanted. I arrived back at the house with breakfast for everyone, feeling like a real Swissman and proud that I was able to contribute something to this lovely family.

Reluctantly leaving the Freis, especially after hugs and kisses from the two girls, we hit the road after breakfast.

Chapter 3

We started our day's drive by meandering through picturesque Geneva, the azure Lake Leman shining blue, with a backdrop of snowcapped mountains framing the scene. We crossed the Swiss-French border at some point and decided to stop in Annecy, a beautiful small town at the foot of the mountains that was crisscrossed by charming canals. After strolling around and soaking in the beautiful old town, we decided to get back on the road. The way out was blocked by a large group of demonstrators who were holding up traffic and waving around signs. Uncle Hugh told me they were protesting nuclear weapons, which was quite typical at the time, with the Cold War in full swing.

I muttered something to the effect of, "We're never getting out of this mess."

Uncle Hugh looked to me and with an air of great and weary wisdom said, "Oh Jim, don't be so pessimistic! We'll get through at some point."

I looked straight ahead, knowing that he was just parroting Mr. Frei. Despite having eyes trained on the Frei girls the entire visit, I had at several points, noticed Uncle Hugh and Mr. Frei in deep and serious conversations. I had overheard one in particular where Mr. Frei had said something like, "I'm very optimistic on the outcome of [...], while many of my colleagues are very pessimistic."

Uncle Hugh had sagely raised his eyebrows, seemingly very intrigued by his comments. He seemed to be analyzing the words when he replied, "So you were really in favour of [...] and felt very OPTIMISTIC about it... Hmm, that is very interesting. And you say your colleagues were dead set against it, eh? Very PESSIMISTIC. You don't say! Hmmm. Well, I'm OPTIMISTIC as well and I wholeheartedly agree with you. Damn those PESSIMISTS."

It sounded like Uncle Hugh was trying the words on for size and very much liked how they fit. Maybe he felt words like that would help present himself as more educated or intelligent. Either way, for the next 6 months I was bombarded with OPTIMISMS and PESSIMISMS whenever I voiced concern about something:

"Jim, don't be so PESSIMISTIC, we will surely find a campground at some point. I'm being OPTIMISTIC, you just have to try harder."

Or:

"Yes dear [British person who we met at the American Express office], we were very OPTIMISTIC when travelling in Morocco. It was a very positive experience; no room for PESSIMISM!"

Or:

"Mr. Waiter, oh Mr. Waiter! I'm not feeling all that OPTIMISTIC about your menu, I don't see anything I like."

To which I quipped, "Oh, don't be so pessimistic."

He'd scowl, puff up his chest and say, "I am not pessimistic James. It's not MY fault that this restaurant is sub-standard in their wares!"

The waiter rolled his eyes, shaking his head at this strange man from who-knows-where. Probably an American!

Uncle Hugh prided himself on his education and considered himself an intellectual – and rightly so, considering his ample schooling, work, and world experience. Sometimes proud intellectuals can come across as snobbish though and he was no exception. His over-use of optimism and pessimism tended to make him come across as arrogant and priggish to people we met. Perhaps he was a little of both of those things in truth.

I endured his ham-fisted use of vocabulary like I endured most of his quirks; as much as it irritated me, I smiled and ignored it, or when cornered, used it as ammo against him. I didn't know what a synonym was back then, but I wish I could have offered him some alternative words to use. It's amazing how often optimism and pessimism can be used as descriptive verbs!

"The ocean looks so blue and optimistic today!"

"Wow, those clouds coming in from the mountains are looking quite pessimistic..."

"I've never seen such optimistically built Roman buildings!"

"That wind coming off the Sahara is very pessimistic in its ferocity and is causing quite the dust storm!"

I guess that is how great and highly educated intellectuals amuse themselves: find new words and use them in aggravatingly inventive ways.

Eventually, the protesters were dispersed by the police and we continued on our way, Uncle Hugh sending me a knowing glance and nodding to himself.

Departing Annecy, we headed towards Valence, France, where we were to find a hotel for the night. After a three-hour drive, we found a hotel and dropped off all of our gear. We strolled around the downtown area and I was once again in awe of the churches, fountains, and old stone buildings that characterize so many European cities. Eventually, I became inured to these things as I saw city after city full of them, but at this time they were still very new to me.

We had dinner at a lovely bistro downtown, where I tried the steak frites, as well as crêpes smothered in chocolate for dessert. My mother needn't have worried about whether or not I'd be eating well on this trip!

The next morning, we set back out, heading south, with Barcelona, then Jàvea, where we planned to meet up with Hugh's cousin Richard, as our next major destinations. First though, we had to make a scheduled stop in Montpellier France, just off the coast of the Mediterranean Sea. Uncle Hugh had to find a Volkswagen dealership to get the first scheduled oil change done on the van, and Montpellier was the only town on the route to Spain that had one.

The whole way there, Uncle Hugh conversationally taught me about Montpellier and its fascinating history. Once a city boasting a rich Jewish culture, it became known as a place that not only tolerated but also flourished due to the mix of Jewish, Muslim, and Christian elements living there. The city was famed for learning and boasted one of the oldest universities in the world, as well as the oldest medical school anywhere. This school, which is still running to this day, taught such illustrious students as Nostradamus himself.

I found myself completely ensorcelled by his description of the city as we made our way there and couldn't wait to see it. Little did I know how badly we'd both be wishing to see Montpellier fading in the rearview mirror in only a few hours from that time.

Clouds rolled in as we got closer to our destination and a miserable icy drizzle began to fall as we entered the city limits. The gloomy skies set the proper mood for what was to come, and we found ourselves reduced to a sullen hush despite our earlier animated conversation.

The streets of Montpellier were, like in many medieval cities, cramped and twisted, forming contorted knots through the city that were a nightmare to circumnavigate. Our nerves were on edge as I tried to follow the directions we had to the Volkswagen dealership through the drenched tangle of one-ways, alleys, pedestrian streets, and drivable lanes with confusing signage. After driving around for what seemed like forever, we finally gave up. The directions we had been given were no good and we couldn't for the life of us find the dealership.

We began asking for directions from pedestrians, all wearing dolorous frowns from the soaking drizzle. After asking three separate people for directions, we found ourselves even more lost, in a maze of tight cobblestone alleyways that the van could barely squeeze through. Adding on to it all was the growing ire from fellow motorists who showed their displeasure at our blundering by using their horns without restraint.

As if the world was conspiring against us, we found ourselves in a neighbourhood where the streets were awfully hilly. Uncle Hugh had been improving at using the clutch throughout the drive so far, but he still had a hell of a time getting started again once stopped on a hill. As fate would have it, we encountered a red light smack dab in the middle of the steepest hill we had found so far and I couldn't help but let out a long gust of breath, predicting what would happen next.

The light turned green and Uncle Hugh very slowly and deliberately eased off the clutch to change gears. Stall! Gritting his teeth and visibly trying to remain composed, he started the van and tried again. Stall!

Again. Stall!

Again. Stall!

Again! Stall!

It seemed there would be no way to ever get off that hill. The light turned red again, matching the colour of Uncle Hugh's flushed face. Collecting himself, he stared straight ahead and waited for the light to turn green.

Stall! Stall! Stall!

Uncle Hugh had begun a descent into pure and unadulterated panic, his ineffectual attempts at moving forward reeking more and more of desperation. People on the street had forgotten their tasks and destinations and had simply stopped on the sidewalks to stare at us, some even laughing and jeering. Horns blared behind us as we lurched forward and rolled backwards. Sometimes we'd gain a little ground in a momentous forward lurch, and other times we'd stall without having moved an inch.

Gone were my smart-aleck remarks and know-it-all grins; I prayed fervently to the VW god, "Please, please let us get off that damned hill!"

The light turned green once more and Uncle Hugh, in a fit of final desperation, cranked down on the break, yanked back on the stick and let go of the clutch. We took off to the sound of our gears rending themselves apart, grinding and squealing horrifyingly. But we were moving!

Uncle Hugh sped away as fast as he could, leaving the bemused citizenry behind. I like to think that they gave us a big cheer before going on with their days.

With frayed nerves and high blood pressure, we continued through the city, still hopelessly lost. Uncle Hugh pulled off the main road and onto a small side street to get out of traffic and calm his nerves a bit. As we crept down a narrow alley, the buildings began encroaching, first taking over the increasingly narrower sidewalks, and then butting directly onto the street itself.

We came to a right-hand bend in the alley that looked to me to be a straight-up 90° turn, with the single-lane road continuing around the corner. We paused briefly before the turn, considering our options, but the only possibilities were to back out down the entire laneway, and out onto a busy street, or to attempt the turn.

Uncle Hugh inched forward, taking it as slow as he was able. Tortoise-like, we crawled into the corner, our left front fender grinding into the building in front of us, and the rear left fender grinding into the building behind us. This couldn't be good. He attempted to jockey the van back and forth in order to slip out, but that did nothing but jam us in even tighter, scraping and denting the week-old van. Remember that Uncle Hugh couldn't at all turn his neck through all of this!

His face showing signs of sheer panicked exhaustion, with hysteria beginning to close in, Uncle Hugh leapt out of the van's sliding door (his own was pressing up against the building) and went haring down the street in search of someone who could help. Uncle Hugh, the Know-It-All, the Dignified Scholar, the Man-Who-Knew-Europe-Inside-Out, was so frayed at the edges that he actually gave up and went seeking help from a stranger.

Eventually, he found someone willing to pluck us out of this nightmare, a likely-looking blue-collar man, who agreed to help. The man climbed into the driver's seat and, apparently using some sort of dread witchcraft, easily maneuvered the van out of its wedged predicament. Tossing the keys back to my uncle, the man sauntered away like it was nothing.

The clouds parted and the rain stopped, and the dealership was exposed to us by a shining ray of light, which lit up the building like a glowing beacon of salvation, emancipating us from this never-ending nightmare of Montpellier. After we had covered what felt like every square inch of the damned city, we had finally found it.

Relieved and completely spent, we flopped down into the chairs in the waiting room and stared at the ceiling, unable to articulate what we had just gone through. Montpellier wasn't done with us yet though.

The manager came in with the reluctant approach of a mechanic with bad news. Unsurprising to me now, but shocking to us back then, the clutch had been completely burnt out, effectively making the van inoperative. The entire thing needed to be replaced. I wondered whether I should call up the people at the Guinness Book of Records to see if we should be awarded the record for the fastest anyone had ever fully burnt out a clutch. We'd only been driving the van for a week, and some of that time it had been parked across from the Frei's!

Unfortunately, there was no award for such a stunning accomplishment, just a massive bill that broke Uncle Hugh's budget as well as the last remnants of his good cheer.

Leaving the van at the shop, we found a hotel close by, and a restaurant where we had a nice meal accompanied by copious amounts of wine to wash down the disastrous day we'd just been through. I shook the whole thing off easily since I was only along for the ride, but the insidious claws of depression left their mark on Uncle Hugh who slumped down in his bed with nary a good night.

The next day, we retrieved the van and hightailed it out of Montpellier; showering the city with curses and vowing never to return to that devil's den again. If there had been a website like Trip Advisor back then, I'm sure Uncle Hugh's scathing review would have been so blistering and caustic that the mayor would have felt it necessary to step down and resign.

Chapter 4

We followed the Mediterranean coastline through the French towns of Narbonne and Perpignan that morning, and shortly found ourselves approaching the France-Spain border in the foothills of the Pyrenees.

For some reason, likely from watching television, I had expected Spain to be a backward, medieval country with nothing to see but desert and cacti. Imaginings of a depopulated, arid landscape with the silhouette of a worn-down man with his donkey plodding into the sun, bounced around my head, but the reality was a far cry from that.

I was pleasantly surprised to glimpse modern homes from the well-paved highway we were on, backed by magnificent vistas of oceans, forests, and mountains. The land was arid, but in a sun-drenched Mediterranean way, the light-hued soil boasting splashes of green from pines and well-ordered rows of olive trees. It was a very beautiful place and my eyes remained glued to the window, soaking in the impressive scenery.

Not even an hour past the border, I heard sirens and looked out of the back window of the van. Two police officers on motorcycles that read Guardia Civil were behind us, red and blue lights blazing. I told Uncle Hugh to pull over and he found a likely spot a little further up the road.

I watched out of the rearview mirror as the police dismounted their motorcycles and removed their helmets. They were dressed identically, leather-clad from head to toe. They donned caps and made a show of removing pistols from gear bags on the bikes and holstering them at their hips. They deliberately walked up to Uncle Hugh's open window, tall leather boots ominously clicking on the pavement.

He greeted them in English and asked if he had done anything wrong to have been pulled over. After a few uncomfortable moments of them simply glaring at him, one harshly demanded why he had crossed over the solid line a little way back. Uncle Hugh stuttered that he wasn't aware of having crossed any line, but if he had then he was very sorry about it.

Faced with more stony silence and a Clint Eastwood-like stare from the officers, just daring him to draw his non-existent gun ("...you've got to ask yourself one question: 'Do I feel lucky?' Well, do you, punk?"), Uncle Hugh looked to be falling to pieces.

"Do you want to go to jail?" murmured one of the cops.

"Pardon me?" Uncle Hugh stammered.

"JAIL." he repeated menacingly, "Do you want to go to jail?"

"Certainly not!" Uncle Hugh exclaimed nervously, "Isn't there some fine I can just pay to avoid all of this? I'm very sorry if I did anything wrong, I certainly didn't mean to!"

After another tortuously long pause, one of them sighed, shaking his head, "Well, we normally don't let people off the hook like this, but if you give us the money to pay the fine, we can take care of it all at the station and let you carry on."

"H-how much is the fine?"

"100 dollars," the officer replied curtly.

Uncle Hugh stared owlishly at the cop as he raised his open hand to the window, waiting for cash. He turned and dug around for his wallet, emptying it into the officer's waiting hand.

Without another word, both cops turned on their heels and walked back to their bikes with the ransom money, put their helmets on and roared past the parked van. I stared wide-eyed at Uncle Hugh as he started up the van and pulled back onto the highway. He was visibly shaking and driving so slowly and deliberately that I could think of nothing else but a dog slinking away with its tail between its legs.

After a while the shock wore off and Uncle Hugh began cursing the crooked cops as road warriors, bandits, thieves, and thugs, displaying a brave affronted attitude that was completely absent during the confrontation.

"If it weren't for Cousin Richard," he said, gaining momentum, "I'd turn this damn van around and leave this dangerous, lawless country full of scoundrels behind!"

Despite his bluster, his eyes flicked constantly to the rearview mirror, and he continued driving like a blind, aged grandmother while motorists impatiently passed us. Instead of hightailing it out of Spain, we continued onwards down the well-paved highway, past the modern-looking houses and pine trees at a snail-like pace.

With the wind taken out of our sails and the sunny day dimmed due to our encounter with the police, Uncle Hugh decided we would find somewhere to stop and stay for the night, despite it only being shortly after noon, and then start fresh again the next day. We began the search for a likely campground where we could spend the night.

I was excited, as this would be the first time we actually camped in the six days since leaving Frankfurt. My family had done some camping back home, but this felt very different and new. We eventually spotted the universal tent symbol for a campground and turned off the highway, diligently following signs into the countryside. Still reeling from the "terrorist actions perpetrated by the Spanish Gestapo", Uncle Hugh was driving extremely cautiously, endeavouring not to make a single mistake. Unfortunately, driving very slowly and deliberately can also draw attention, and in our case, it certainly did.

"Uhh, Uncle Hugh," I said, pointing towards the flashing lights behind us, "you'd better pull over again." I swear he must have popped a vein in his forehead.

As the officer walked up to the window in what seemed like a déjà vu moment, Uncle Hugh slumped down, looking broken and defeated. Tears welled in his eyes as he glanced at his empty wallet sitting on the console. He rolled down the window once again to ask what he did wrong, looking like a whipped dog.

This time the cop looked much less fearsome and politely inquired whether we were lost. Nodding, but fearful to speak, Uncle Hugh must have been a pitiful sight to see. The pleasant-looking man patiently waited until Uncle Hugh finally spilled out that we were just following the signs to the campground but were having a hard time making it there. The officer smiled, gave us detailed instructions on how to get to the campground, bid us a good day and good luck and took off.

"Well, I guess they're not ALL crooks," Uncle Hugh muttered. The helpful actions of this policeman seemed to balance out the crime of the last ones and we got back on the road with a renewed sense of goodwill and adventure. Uncle Hugh sat up straighter and drove normally again and we made it to the campground shortly thereafter.

The campground was surprisingly modern and even had a huge swimming pool. We found a site amongst some European tourists from all over the continent. Some friendly Dutch travellers camping in the site next to us struck up a conversation once we had set up camp. We quickly befriended them and spent the evening chatting over generously poured glasses of Spanish red wine. We also got to use the stove and brand-new camping dishes for the first time and enjoyed a lovely dinner with the Spanish sunset filtering through the trees.

Glowing from the wine and good company, Uncle Hugh turned to me at one point and decreed, "See? Look at how things turn out when you remain OPTIMISTIC!"

I stared back incredulously at him, but he had already turned away to continue his conversation with the Dutch couple.

We woke up the next morning to rain pounding on the van's roof and decided to get going first thing. Despite it being a 500km drive to Cousin Richard's house, we both decided it would be better to do the entire drive straight through rather than find a sodden campground to stay in on the way there. 500 kilometres didn't actually mean much to me at the time, as this trip to Europe was my first introduction to the metric system. I found myself constantly misjudging how long it would take to get to places and had a hard time converting miles to kilometres in my mind when we first started. I can't say I had even heard of the metric system before being in Europe. I'm sure some teacher somewhere had attempted to impart the knowledge into my ungrateful head, but like most youth, lessons like that went in one ear and out the other.

Uncle Hugh was happy to fill me in on everything I'd missed, however, coaching me through the entirety of Metric Studies in a matter of three or four hideously boring hours. It wasn't fair that he had me as a captive audience, captive being the operative word since I was stuck beside him in a moving vehicle, making me listen to all of this metric math nonsense. Geesh! Why did I need to know all of this stuff? His scholarly ministrations eventually wormed their way into my stubborn fourteen-year-old head though and I began to grasp this newfangled measurement system relatively early on in the trip. My comprehension of the metric system and my map reading skills seemed to grow by the day until I felt thoroughly competent in a matter of weeks.

As we neared Barcelona, signs to the famous Basilica de la Sagrada Familia, tempted us to drive into the downtown core to see it, but due to the miserable weather and the fact that we had lost so much time the day before, we decided to skip it and keep plodding on towards Jàvia. Though I never actually got to see the Basilica, I know an astonishing number of facts about it. Uncle Hugh took it upon himself to impart every single thing he knew about the place to me as we slowly wended our way through the busy Barcelona traffic.

The impressive and apparently breathtaking Basilica de la Sagrada Familia was under construction at the time, as it had been for the last 89 years, and still is 50 years later as this is being written. Uncle Hugh droned on about every single detail of its construction, giving me what seemed like a day-by-day account of every single one of the 89 years of its existence. While I am still awed today by Uncle Hugh's impressive breadth of knowledge and I respect the years of education and experience that led to it, the man had no skill whatsoever in conveying it in an interesting manner. There were no Cole's Notes or tidy Reader's Digest essays; Uncle Hugh opened his mouth and a monotonous river of knowledge came tediously pouring out, usually to the dismay of any bystanders.

An entire University degree's worth of knowledge would be thrown at you in a matter of 30-60 minutes, imparted in a dispassionate monotone that proved hard to pay much attention to. As Uncle Hugh went on and on about the Cubist spires, ornate façades, and hyperboloid structures, I did what I usually did and let my mind drift as I stared out of the window at the surrounding city.

It's funny how grim rainy days can mar the beauty of the land- and cityscapes that would usually be breathtaking on a nice day. The repetitive scenery of Barcelona and beyond through Valencia seemed to blend into an endless dreary indistinguishable sameness, much like a wrap-around backdrop in an old Hanna-Barbera cartoon – wait, didn't we already pass that bush, tree, and rock? The traffic was heavy all day and progress was slow. The day lives on in my memory as lasting forever, most of it stuck in traffic amongst rain-washed cars bled of colour, dirty trucks belching diesel fumes, and fancy cars cutting in and out, fruitlessly trying to jockey themselves into a better position. I felt that Europe had lost its lustre that day.

Arriving in Jàvea in the early evening, we drove through the centre of town, which seemed to me more like a backwater village after the bustle of Barcelona and Valencia, looking for Cousin Richard's street. The main street was lined with little shops, but they seemed more like drivesheds in an industrial part of town than the downtown boutiques Uncle Hugh assured me they were. We turned onto a side street, which was lined with orange trees. The smell! The heady fragrance of fresh orange blossoms immediately filled the van and improved my dreary mood markedly. I had never smelled anything like this exotic citric perfume before and found it intense and intoxicating.

Finding the house where Richard was staying, we parked and got out of the van. Richard and a friend of his named Graham came out to meet us, showering us with enthusiastic handshakes, hugs, and inquiries as to our drive. We grabbed our stuff and followed him up to the house which had white stucco with terracotta tiles; very typical for the area, identical, in fact, to every other house on the block. The steps up to the front door were tiled and there was a large veranda. We piled into the house and sat down for some refreshments.

Richard, a distant relation of mine who I believe was my grandfather's cousin on his mother's side, was a retired Englishman, who, along with his friend Graham who was also English, made money by tending rich seasonal homes along the oceanfront and some on the street we were currently on. Many rich folks owned summer or winter homes in Jàvea and paid Richard and Graham decent money to maintain their homes in their absence.

Richard happened to already have houseguests staying over, so he put us up in a neighbouring home that he was watching. The house overlooked an orange grove, and standing on the veranda, all you could see were orange trees for miles. The air was electric with the cloying scent of orange blossoms and it really made me feel like I was indeed on the Spanish coast and nowhere else on earth.

That night, we sat around with Richard and his company drinking and chatting. We drank some sort of Spanish liquor, which was quite tasty, and finished the night with brandy. I was flying high by the time we went to bed and slept like a log.

After a hearty and welcome breakfast of side pork and eggs that helped soak up the aftereffects of the night before, we hit the town and strolled the sidewalks, checking out the shops. One store we stopped at appeared to sell mostly farm equipment, but I was surprised to find a nice pair of runners in the back that fit me perfectly. They were black high tops with white stripes, and I excitedly put them on, carrying around my hikers for the rest of the morning and walking on a cloud.

Returning to the villa, Uncle Hugh announced that he needed a nap, so Cousin Richard and I went for a long walk up into the hills surrounding Jàvea while he lay down. We took a long gravel road that looked to be quite new and was lined with beautiful large villas, all in different stages of construction. Making our way to a high point in the hills, we turned around and enjoyed the sweeping vista of orange groves and the Mediterranean coastline. Richard and I talked and talked the entire walk and a bond quickly grew between us.

The next day Uncle Hugh decided that he needed a new pair of pants, or trousers as he insisted on calling them, so we returned to the downtown core to do some more shopping. After what seemed like hours of hemming and hawing, he decided on a pair of pants, the only ones he liked. Unfortunately, they were way too tight for him and so had to be let out at the waist. The shop owner informed us that the pants wouldn't be ready for two days, so it looked like we were staying put a little longer than we had intended.

That evening, we sat around drinking and looking at old family photos of long-dead relatives in England, none of whom I'd heard of before. Despite that, it was a great evening, full of laughter and reminiscing, though I mostly remained silent. It made me thoughtful about where I'd come from and helped to expand my thoughts beyond my own little self-important teenage bubble. I began to feel a connection to my distant relatives in a way I never had before and wondered what traits of mine may have come from them as Richard and Uncle Hugh pointed to black and white photos claiming that I looked just like this or that person.

The next day we spent driving around the countryside, stopping at several small identical villages along the way. We got out at each one and explored, the villagers staring at us as if we had fallen from the sky. The children clambered to get into every picture we took and followed us as we poked through the dusty streets.

The day after that was spent driving to and exploring an old abandoned castle in a place called Denia. This was the first medieval castle I had ever visited and I absolutely loved exploring every inch of it, climbing up the walls and standing sentry on the ramparts, overlooking the harbour below. I peered out of arrow slots, gazed at imaginary hostile troops through the crenellations, and stood alone at the gate, staunchly defending the castle against the implacable enemy.

There was an open market in the courtyard selling anything and everything imaginable; I had never seen anything like it. I wanted to buy everything in sight and pored over merchant's wares, searching through all of the strange curiosities for some priceless trinket that may have belonged to the castle's original defenders. We sat in an outdoor restaurant and enjoyed Cokes in the sun. It all felt very alien to me, completely and utterly European, and I loved it.

Sadly, it was time to leave the next day. I had a hard time saying goodbye to Richard, as we had grown quite close over the last few days. He suggested we exchange something personal that would remind us of each other. I had very few belongings and so gave him a pair of socks. It was an odd gift, but Richard one-upped me by giving me a pair of gloves that he had shot with a shotgun. Now, that was a very odd gift and totally useless since they were torn to shreds, but I thought of him for years after every time I looked at the silly things.

Perhaps due to our reluctance to leave, Uncle Hugh and I didn't get too far that day and ended up stopping in the nearby town of Puerto Lumbreras for the night. Located in a region of arid but pretty rolling hills, the town was home to a Parador's hotel. Parador's was a chain of high-end hotels that Uncle Hugh had been reading about in a set of beautiful, glossy brochures that he had picked up somewhere. He had learned in the brochures that each hotel in the chain was different from the next – some were actually located in retrofitted old castles! These hotels located in ancient buildings and castles were all magnificently restored and luxurious. He would show me a picture of a room in some Spanish castle and sigh wistfully, shaking his head.

Unfortunately, the Parador in Puerto Lumbreras was a more modern example; beautiful, but not very unique. Even though the expensive hotel wasn't located in a castle like many of the others, Uncle Hugh HAD to stay there. I was left a little mystified as to why, since there wasn't actually anything special about this particular hotel, and the prices were quite high. I guess he just wanted to say that he got to stay at a Parador's, no matter what type it was. I also got the feeling that the ones in castles were a lot more expensive than the one we'd stayed in and were probably out of his price range.

Since it was still quite early, we went down to the lounge for drinks, which was quite lovely. Despite not being in a restored castle, this hotel was far fancier than any other I'd been in before and I was suitably awed. While having a few drinks in the lounge, we ended up meeting two couples from New Jersey, a couple from somewhere in England, and four Canadians. We got to swapping stories, and before long, the drinks were flowing and everyone was mixing and enjoying themselves. Uncle Hugh and I found ourselves having a great time chatting to our newfound friends. Two of the gentlemen I was speaking to even left to retrieve books from their rooms which they gave to me to read.

Nights like this were very typical everywhere we ran into English-speaking tourists all across Europe. The English speakers were drawn to one another and often sought each other out to engage in conversation with someone other than their travel partners or the locals. It didn't matter where in the world they were from – whoever spoke English in the group became immediate friends. I feel that it may be because English speakers tend to be quite weak at speaking other languages and secretly believe that everyone should have to learn English. They are even annoyed with non-English speakers when they struggle with the language.

While travelling, I noticed English speakers from across the world rudely demanding service in English, even though they were visiting a non-English speaking country. The same went for back at home. We expect non-English speaking visitors to know and use perfect English if they want to come visit our country. If they don't already know English, then they have no business coming at all! This struck me as very unfair but, like most English speakers, not enough so that I went and learned new languages.

The next morning, we checked out of the hotel and made our way to the beautiful medieval city of Granada. The city is home to a fabulous castle called the Alhambra, which was built between the 12th and 14th centuries. It was a lavish fortified palace, built for the Moorish royalty who occupied the region at the time. The Moors, who ruled much of Spain for nearly 800 years, were Muslims from North Africa and much of the architecture and art in Granada displays that influence.

It was raining when we arrived so Uncle Hugh decided we would stay in a hotel again rather than camp. He had already picked one out of his "Europe on $5 a Day" guidebook, probably feeling the pinch from staying in such a pricey hotel the night before. He was always looking to cut corners and save money but often didn't want to sacrifice his own comfort to keep things cheap. Cold and rainy days like the ones we were often experiencing that March would push him to splurge on hotels more often, despite wincing at the cost.

The budget hotel he found was right up the street from the Alhambra, which was perfect. We signed up for a downtown night tour and "Gypsy Show" at the front desk and we set out to join the tour group. The tour was excellent, informative and entertaining, but the Gypsy Show left something to be desired and was quite underwhelming. It was very amateur and lowbrow and was obviously set up for basic tourists. It reminded me of a low-end holiday movie from the 1960s, with California girls dressed up as Gypsies. I didn't mind watching the girls so much, but their singing and dancing weren't cutting it. Uncle Hugh suggested we leave and find entertainment elsewhere, and I agreed that we should go find something better.

Walking down the beautiful ancient streets, we spotted a lively-looking nightclub that was below street level and resembled a cave. Descending through the mouth of the cave, we entered a festive barroom and were delighted to see scantily clad women in traditional Spanish costumes dancing on a stage. We ordered drinks at the bar and found some seats with a good view. The girls danced beautifully, the music pumped, and the drinks kept coming. The whole bar felt electrically charged and everyone was having a great time, swaying and clapping to the music – even Uncle Hugh. This was the authentic experience we were looking for!

I could have stayed all night, but eventually, Uncle Hugh decided we should go. We staggered back up the street to our hotel, where we slept with pleasant dreams of Spanish dancers, before waking up groggy and with headaches in the morning.

Beautiful morning sunshine soon washed away our hangovers as we explored the grounds of the Alhambra. The expansive gardens outside the gates were incredible: impossibly lush and verdant. Thousands of rose bushes and orange trees perfumed the air with their heady scents, and a forest of perfectly manicured English elms left me bewildered by their beauty.

The castle itself was equally impressive: magnificent carved stonework, elegant courtyards with fabulous fountains and topiary, sweeping vistas from the ramparts, and a never-ending parade of gorgeous halls, rooms, and arcades. I was so absorbed with the striking beauty of the place that I didn't even mind Uncle Hugh's ceaseless commentary on the historical significance of every piece of art and architecture that the castle had to show.

I had never experienced anything like this place, and I was in total awe that a place with such rich history could exist in the world without me having ever having heard of it. How many other places like this existed in the world? It made me feel tiny and insignificant while at the same time awakening a need to experience more. Until I left on this trip, I had relied on Hollywood to show me the world, but I was beginning to realize that Hollywood only showed the world through an Americanized lens. To see a whole new perspective right in front of me left me with much to think about.

After a long day of walking and exploring, we finally got to rest our weary feet and sat down at a nice outdoor restaurant on the street. We split a delicious chicken paella and a bottle of Spanish wine and quietly enjoyed the evening, people-watching and sipping the wine.

The next day we were bound for Gibraltar, but first, we detoured down a rocky road that slowly wound its way up to the mountaintop town of Ronda. Ronda is another ancient city of Moorish construction that straddles a massive and deep gorge called El Tajo. A stone bridge named the Puente Nuevo crossed the gorge, connecting the two sides of the town. On one side of the bridge was the New Town, built by the Moors in the 15th century, and on the other side was the Old Town, predating even the Romans.

The bridge was very impressive, but Uncle Hugh was having a hard time getting the proper viewpoint for a picture of it in its entirety. He had gone through his picture-taking rigmarole several times before giving up in a huff. Looking down at the sides of the gorge, we noticed that there were houses built on the very edge, further into town, that likely had a perfect view of the bridge. We pegged one out in particular that had a balcony clinging right on the cliff ledge and made our way towards it. We snaked our way through the city, constantly losing sight of it and nearly giving up before seeing suddenly reappear in the distance. We eventually arrived at the house and Uncle Hugh confidently strode up to the door and knocked without any hesitation. Nothing was going to stop him from getting the perfect picture.

A matronly woman answered the door with a confused expression and Uncle Hugh, adopting his very best dignified British manner, asked, "Madam, may we take a picture of the Puente Nuevo from your balcony? We would be most appreciative."

She seemed to understand what we wanted and ushered us in while showering us in an unrelenting Spanish prattle. She guided us to the patio and Uncle Hugh visibly inspected it, nodding in approval, as if he were thinking of purchasing it. I fervently prayed that he wouldn't take an hour to set up a perfect shot while this poor, generous, bewildered woman waited for us to get out of her house. He must have felt some sense of urgency because he blessedly forewent with his usual routine and took the picture in under ten minutes. Nodding that he was happy, the woman, still uttering a constant stream of indecipherable Spanish, began to lead us back to the front door. As we were walking through the house, a small boy of about six years old walked to the front door, blocked it, and held out his hand. He seemed to want payment for the opportunity to take the picture. His Royal Highness Uncle Hugh shouldered past the boy as if he didn't exist and with a kingly wave of his hand called back without looking, "James, be a good man, and look after that boy would you?"

He could be so exasperating! I gave the boy a couple of the pesetas I had in my pocket and ran to catch up with Uncle Hugh, who hadn't stopped to wait for me.

Uncle Hugh's lofty airs quickly dissipated once we were back in the van and leaving the city. The road was extremely windy and dangerous, full of gorges and terrifying drop-offs. Uncle Hugh was driving down the incredibly steep mountain road white-knuckled, with a face pale and ashen, but I was having the time of my life! My blood was pumping and I was letting out "whoops" as we twisted our way past hairpin turns and cliff edges with no guardrails. By the time we returned to the less harrowing main highway, Uncle Hugh was drenched in sweat and shaking. I was grinning ear to ear.

Our plan was to drive to Gibraltar and see The Rock, but as we neared, we encountered a roadblock set up by British soldiers. They explained to us that no one was allowed to pass due to fears of Spanish invasion. See, Gibraltar was and still is considered to be a British Overseas Territory. Spain contested the British rule, stating that Gibraltar belonged to them, despite it being in British hands since 1704. In 1967 a referendum was held and the populace voted overwhelmingly to keep British rule. This sparked a lot of contention with Spain, so Britain sent soldiers in to guard their assets, while Spain closed its borders down and terminated all communication with the region. No one was allowed in or out of Gibraltar via Spain until 1985 when the borders opened back up.

Apparently, Uncle Hugh's encyclopedias weren't up to date, so he was completely ignorant of the situation. Shaking our heads in disbelief, we turned back towards the main highway and drove towards Algeciras, where we were to depart on a ferry to the mysterious continent of Africa.

Uncle Hugh figured we could use a bath and a bit of luxury before we got to Africa, so he booked us into the impressive Queen Alexandria Hotel in Algeciras. The hotel's foyer boasted huge marble pillars and an impressive floor also made from marble. Every detail of the hotel spoke of an elegance and grandeur that belonged to another time, a time before post-war brutalist and nouveau architecture.

While I was staring wide-eyed around the massive lobby, Uncle Hugh nudged me and told me to go retrieve our bags while he went up to the room. I realized he was trying to pull a fast one on me when a bellboy stopped me at the door, offering to take the luggage up to the room for me. Now, I was no fool and I'd seen some movies; I knew that bellboys expected a tip for their service! He went to grab the bags out of my hands, but I shrugged him off, trying to barge past him. There was no way I was going to let Uncle Hugh win and dip into my minimal funds to pay this kid to do something I was very capable of doing myself.

I told him exactly that and tried to move past him again, but he had the doorway blocked. Reaching for the bags again, he grabbed a hold and we started a gentle tug-of-war, with me insisting that I didn't need his help and him pretending he didn't understand what I was getting at. I reefed on the bags so he had to let go or risk breaking them or falling over. Hounding me to the elevator, the unrelenting bellboy stuck to my back like glue, making passes for the bags every time I tried to shoulder him away. I think he was having a great time, but I was starting to lose my temper.

I finally made it into the elevator and turned to glare at him as the doors closed in his smirking face. By the time I made it up to the room, I had become quite cross with Uncle Hugh. The man had plenty of money for this posh hotel room, but apparently was too cheap to tip a bellboy, so left me to do it for him. I thought he had bought the camper van so we could save money by camping anyway; what were we even doing in this fancy place?

I won the now customary coin toss to see who would get ready in the bathroom first, then went in to get dressed up, still stewing about the bellboy. The suit I had with me was a sleeveless jacket with matching pants and I had a navy-blue embroidered shirt on under it. I felt quite impressive in it, like a real worldly man, despite the suit likely being only suitable for a fourteen-year-old.

As Uncle Hugh took his turn in the bathroom, a lengthy process, I called to him that I was going downstairs and left without waiting for a response. I was in no mood to wait around for the man while he got ready.

I made my way down to the lounge and was greeted by a raucous group of about ten people, all laughing and sitting together on couches and chairs. They immediately beckoned me over and introduced themselves to me. It was a mixed group of travellers hailing from the UK, U.S.A., and Australia. They treated me royally, inquiring what I'd like to drink. I never told them my age and thought that I must be really pulling off the suit, for them to be offering me drinks. I asked what they recommended and one asked if I'd ever tried a crème de menthe. I said no, so they passed me one from the bar. Delicious! I quickly finished it and they continued to offer me a variety of drinks I'd never heard of.

The alcohol loosened me up and made me forget all about my bad mood. I felt like I fit right in with this disparate group of tourists and quickly became comfortable among them. We were all fast friends, laughing and joking with each other.

I saw Uncle Hugh come out of the elevator into the lobby. He was dressed in his drab green suit, with his hair slicked up like he was going to be attending an audience with the Queen herself. He walked slowly, staring straight ahead, in a manner that came off as decidedly snobbish.

I called over to him and introduced him to my newfound friends. He responded coldly, putting on his best English airs, and looking down his nose at everyone like they were all the most basic of commoners. Manners aside, these people were all successful and professional people, so his treatment of them confused everybody. His boorish behaviour quickly put a damper on everyone's evening and the laughter and joking quickly faded away. Before long, everyone was leaving, going back to their rooms or out to their vehicles to find a better party elsewhere. Some came back out with treats for me - a jar of peanut butter, which I'd intimated that I'd had an intense longing for, and a stack of paperback books. After that, it was just Uncle Hugh and me left in the lounge; both of us scowling.

I knew what had happened. If it had been Uncle Hugh who had come down first and introduced me, he would have been on cloud nine, expressively telling stories and being the centre of attention. But since I was the one getting the attention and making friends, the miserable old badger would rather scare everyone off than let me have my moment.

Sitting there in silence thinking about it, I began to perk up a bit. Here I was, in Europe for only nineteen days so far and I was already hobnobbing with elite globetrotters, swapping stories with educated and charming folks who I had no exposure to back at home. This was a journey of awakening for me; I wasn't just Uncle Hugh's little helper. I was truly getting a sense, not only of my new self but of the petty man I was travelling with, and I vowed to refuse to let him and his churlish behaviour ruin my adventure. I was going to enjoy myself no matter what it took.

Chapter 5

Early the next morning, we drove the camper van onto the ferry and then climbed up to the upper deck. We were off to Africa!

Never in my life had I even imagined that I'd find myself going to Africa. What would it be like? My imagination was running wild with confused Hollywood images of lions, jungles, and loincloth-clad native inhabitants. Tarzan movies had been my only real exposure to anything "African" and it showed in my expectations of what I'd find there. I prepared myself for the dark and wild continent as shown to me in the movies.

While I was leaning on the taffrail towards the stern of the ferry, lost in my imagination, a young Moroccan man of about twenty joined me and struck up a conversation. His name was Karin, and he was from Tetouan, about an hour from the port of Ceuta, a city on a small piece of Spanish land across the Strait of Gibraltar and our ferry's destination. It turned out he needed a ride from Ceuta to Tetouan, so I hesitantly asked Uncle Hugh if we could take him.

Astonishingly, Uncle Hugh replied with an easy, "Sure!"

After eighty minutes, the ferry ride was over and we pulled up to the dock in Ceuta, Gibraltar's twin city. Deciding not to tarry, we all jumped in the camper van and drove off towards Tetouan. Before long, we passed Spain's border and were in Morocco. I was in Africa now, but it sure didn't match the Africa I had in my head.

Karin acted as a guide as we drove down the rustic highway, pointing out the sights and answering my incessant questions. People were walking everywhere, and there were more donkeys than I had ever seen. The thing that stuck out to me most was the attire that the locals wore. It looked decidedly Arab to me rather than African and also looked unbearably hot. Karin called the clothing djellabas, but to me, they looked more like heavy-duty housecoats or robes. It was so hot outside, I couldn't imagine wearing something so dark and heavy. I asked Karin why they wore them and how they could stand it? He explained that thousands of years ago, his people had figured out that if you dressed in heavy clothing, and drank hot tea or coffee, you heated your body and the air felt cooler. He said that he always noticed that Westerners dressed scantily and drank cold drinks, yet they always complained about the heat.

I frowned to myself trying to make sense of that, but it just didn't compute. I thanked him for the explanation but informed him that I wasn't too keen on trying it out myself.

We dropped a grateful Karin off in the gleaming white port city of Tetouan and then went looking for a campground for the night. We found a likely spot pretty easily, but soon came to regret our choice when we were instantly mobbed by a group of boys who begged us for money. As we set up camp and made dinner, the harassment from the boys was relentless, with many trying a different tack every time.

"Sirs, you need someone to guard your car!"

"Sirs, you need a guide? I can guide you anywhere in Morocco!"

"Sirs, please spare some food for my family to eat!"

"Sirs, I can help carry!"

"Sirs, please, we need money!"

"Sirs! Sirs! Sirs!"

It was downright irritating and didn't cease until our lights went off for bed. The next morning they were waiting for us and started up right away. We gritted our teeth and packed up the van in silence. On to Fes!

The six-hour drive to Fes from Tetouan took us away from the coast and south towards the centre of the country. We had plenty of opportunities to look around and soak in the exotic countryside. Arid sun-baked hills and lush valleys full of plantations, orchards, and forests dominated the region. Each town and village looked identical to the last, full of squat clay brick structures with very little wood involved in the construction, as wood was very scarce in Morocco. Towns perched atop hills with commanding views of the surrounding countryside often had buildings resembling castles, with multiple red clay towers vying for superiority in the otherwise uncrowded skyline. Though much smaller than the European castles I had seen in France and Spain, the way the castle's towers contrasted against the dark rocky hills in the background really impressed me.

A funny thing happened while we were driving through a dusty little village not too long into our journey to Fes. A scruffy, rather dirty old man sitting on his haunches on the side of the road made a strange gesture with his hands. He put a finger from one hand into the closed palm of his other hand and moved it back and forth. It seemed like he was looking at me as he did so.

As we went through another village half an hour later it happened again - another scruffy old man, squatting in the dust, making the exact same gesture as before! Once again, it felt like he was looking right at me when he did it, not at Uncle Hugh or at the van in general.

I'd never seen anyone make a gesture like that before and it left me feeling confused. Why were they looking at me when they did it? I thought about it a lot, keeping those thoughts to myself and not sharing them with Uncle Hugh. I continued to think of what it might mean and was devastated as I came upon a likely answer, feeling my naivety fall away. I was a young boy with long, shoulder-length hair, wearing Western-style clothes that were probably relatively foreign to these men. I think they thought I was a girl. I think the gestures were obscene and that they wanted to have sex with me!

I was shocked and appalled and had a hard time putting my thoughts in order. The thought of these disgusting predatory men so blatantly showing their nefarious wishes and intents left me so unnerved that I began to feel panicky inside. When it happened again I swore that it was the same guy, who had somehow gotten ahead of us and was waiting for me. I started seeing him everywhere I looked, "Oh no, there he is again! He's following me!" I would think to myself.

I suffered in silence even though this same thing continued the entire time we were in Africa. I was too embarrassed to talk to Uncle Hugh about it and felt like he would laugh off my worries, or judge me for bringing up something so sexual in nature. Adolescence is such an awkward time for discussing such things. If he had been able to overhear my thoughts, he would have heard me screaming in panic every time we passed through a village and I saw a man on the street looking at me or making that gesture.

I thought about hacking off my long hair in an attempt to look manlier to them, but never followed through, probably due to that strange teenage apathy that rears its ugly head in response to problems. It left me scared though, and I felt like I eventually didn't even want to look out the window anymore. The thought of being outside and alone in one of the villages simply terrified me. I became a bit obsessed with this "guy" who followed me and was a bit relieved once we were back in Europe when it abruptly stopped.

Nothing ever came of it in the end, but it left an indelible impression on me and gave me some insight into how women must feel as they encounter things like this daily!

Arriving in Fes late in the afternoon, we decided to look for a place to set up camp right away and found a campground just at the edge of the city. The campground was mostly filled with English-speaking tourists, who were all very welcoming and friendly. Once set up, we thought we'd head downtown to check out the medina. Most North African towns and cities have a medina, a historical walled-in section of the city, often sporting fountains, mosques, and narrow twisting streets. Due to the maze-like nature of these streets, medinas are usually closed off to car traffic, which allows them to become busy pedestrian areas, full of hawkers, bazaars, and merchants.

The medina in Fes is one of the largest in the world and attracts a lot of locals and visitors alike. As soon as we neared its walls, we were surrounded by another group of aggressive young boys.

"You want a guide?!"

"NO."

"Hire me! Hire Me!"

"NO!"

"Hire me as guide, I show you!"

"NO, NO, NO!"

The incessant chattering tirade of the boys followed us into the medina, unrelenting.

"Sirs, sirs, hire me and I guide you!"

We continued to simply say no as we elbowed our way through them and into the narrow streets. Uncle Hugh noticed a shop that advertised city guides on a poster beside the door. Thinking that a legit guide might be worth it to lose these annoying kids, we entered the shop to the sounds of wailing and hollering from the boys, insisting that we were crazy and making the wrong choice.

We were set up with a young man, probably around nineteen years old, by the name of Abdul who was very well-dressed and pleasant. He drew us into the labyrinthine streets and alleyways, which were all crammed with everything imaginable: pots and pans, clothes, spices, rugs, jewelry, tools, skinned goats, rabbits, chickens, and who knows what other types of animals. This, coupled with the throng of humanity, the cacophony of braying animals and peddlers calling out their wares, and the press of carts, wagons, horses, and donkeys nearly overwhelmed me, but it all felt so exciting and exotic that I just kept gawking and taking it in. This felt more like Aladdin or Ali Baba and the Forty Thieves than the Africa I was picturing on the ferry ride over.

Abdul led us through the crush, and we walked and walked, the medina never seeming to end. We were constantly harangued and accosted by shopkeepers shouting at us to try their products, but Abdul told us not to engage. He said that if we started talking to any of them, they would never stop talking and would be impossible to get rid of. Anyone who became overly belligerent was confronted by our guide, who told them to back off. We were very relieved that we had hired him, as I feel like we would have been bullied and pushed around so much without him that we'd have to leave.

He brought us to secret courtyards, majestic fountains, beautiful gardens, and fascinating homes inlaid with the most dazzling mosaics. Uncle Hugh was thoroughly enjoying himself. He oohed and aahed constantly, and began walking with his hands held together before his face and sighing, a habit he displayed when he was truly enjoying himself. He looked to be on the verge of giggling, drawing his hands to his mouth and ecstatically sighing every few moments. I think he was able to absorb everything around him at times like this and fix every detail into his encyclopedic mind.

We walked and walked, and I feel like we got to see everything the medina had to offer. We poked our heads into mosques, not being allowed to enter due to our beliefs, looked into souks or small markets, and strolled up residential derbs and dead ends to see the houses. We got to see the Chouara tannery, which was jammed full of huge vats full of dye. Workers would climb into the dye pits with fabrics and leathers, physically pushing them under the dye, and then wringing them out. This resulted in people who were stained the colour of the dyes they worked with. It blew my mind to see a place full of blue, red, and yellow people, who likely remained that colour for the rest of their lives. It just added to the bewildering exoticness of the place.

I had it in my head that I'd like a better hat than the one I had on, so I kept my eye out for a likely souk or shop that carried them. I eventually saw one I liked, so I stopped and removed it from the hook to check it out. The shopkeeper beamed with avaricious anticipation.

"Twenty-five dirhams!" he shouted, which was equivalent to about five Canadian dollars at the time.

Knowing what was expected of me, I countered with, "Ten dirhams!"

He feigned a heart attack, gripping his chest and mewling pathetically. "You're trying to rob me blind!" he gasped, "This fine hat is worth no less than twenty dirhams!"

"Ten," I said, "and no more!"

He pouted and shook his head no. The haggling went on until I got him down to twelve dirhams, at which point he swapped out the hat I wanted for a warped and ugly hat he had sitting behind him.

"No way buddy!" I cried and snatched the hat I wanted out of his hands and passed over the twelve dirhams.

He growled and muttered to himself, then turned away and began calling to new customers, dismissing me entirely. I felt so proud that I had navigated such an intense exchange on my own and was now the owner of a sharp new hat!

Abdul took us to a small restaurant in a little grove of palm trees where we had some cooling mint tea, poured into small cups out of an ornate metal teapot from a ridiculous height. The tea was wonderful, and it was nice to sit in a cool spot out of the press of people and chat with Abdul while enjoying the sights around us.

That afternoon stands out as a very enjoyable one for both Uncle Hugh and me. I feel like we both completely immersed ourselves in the time and place that day and made the right decision to hire a guide, which allowed us to do so.

We headed back to the campground for the night and went to bed rather early after chatting with some of our neighbours. We wanted a good rest before our journey to Marrakesh the next day.

The scenery on the way to Marrakesh from Fes was outstanding as we were driving through the Moyen Atlas mountain range. Moyen means middle, which points to the fact that this mountain range was one of three in Morocco, and obviously the one in the middle. The Moyen Atlas range had many peaks over 2000 meters high, which were still holding onto snow as we drove past them. The colours ranged from brown to emerald green when they weren't completely obscured by fog patches, which we drove through often. Uncle Hugh was nervous while driving along these narrow winding mountain roads with such low visibility, but luckily there were very few other vehicles on the road; that is of course if you don't count donkeys!

We made it to the great city of Marrakesh seven or eight hours after leaving Fes and immediately began looking for a campground to get set up in. After searching fruitlessly for several hours, we gave up and booked a hotel for the night. The hotel turned out to be quite lavish and plush, and I didn't mind missing a night of camping at all.

While cooking dinner at the campsite in Fes, Uncle Hugh had accidentally broken the top off the camp stove. I considered uttering an "I told you so", referring to the well-built VW stove that Uncle Hugh passed up for the cheap one he'd bought in its stead, but I wisely kept it to myself. Uncle Hugh thought we should replace the part for the stove right away, so we headed downtown to find one.

We tried three different stores in the modern downtown core, but they all turned us away, telling us to try the Medina for things like that. Uncle Hugh was hesitant to venture into the medina without a guide, considering what had happened to us the day before, but there didn't look to be any other options. We steeled ourselves and marched into the medina like crusading knights on a quest. It was a scarier experience navigating a medina by ourselves, but after asking a few locals, we were directed to a shop that could accommodate our needs.

The shopkeeper said he could repair the stove and to return in a couple of hours. We walked around, trying to stay near the shop, and checked out the sights. We tried several tasty treats from food vendors, including lamb brochettes, grilled over coals on skewers, and sfenj, which were Moroccan donuts fried in oil right on the street.

Walking back into the shop at the appointed hour, the shopkeeper told us that the part he had didn't fit so he had ordered another, which was on its way. He said to come back in a couple of hours and it would be ready. Frustrated, we walked around some more, but the narrow and twisting streets were beginning to lose their charm. We headed out of the Medina and thought to find some entertainment on the outside where the streets were less busy and overwhelming.

Outside of the medina walls, there were jugglers, snake charmers, fire-eaters, dancers, and just about every sort of street performer you could possibly imagine. We stopped to watch a storyteller since he had the biggest crowd surrounding him out of all of the performers. A hat was presented to us to drop coins into, but we shook our heads no. This caught the attention of the storyteller and he began to direct the crowd's attention to us. They all began to laugh and stare and jeer as he moved towards us, doing coin tricks and clearly mocking us in Arabic.

Wanting this to stop, I dropped a few coins into the hat. The performer announced something to the crowd, switching back and forth from Arabic to English.

I finally got the impression that he thought I was a girl, due to my long hair. I firmly told him that I was not a girl, but a boy. He didn't understand, so I had to explain it to him slowly, with the entire crowd still watching. Once he finally got the point, his eyes went wide, and then he started laughing. He turned to the crowd and explained it all in Arabic, then turned back and planted a big kiss on my cheek. The crowd roared with laughter as my face turned bright red. It was funny, but still quite embarrassing and I wanted nothing more than to move on and escape.

I later learned that due to local customs and religious views, he only kissed me because I was a boy. He would have never dishonoured a woman by kissing her in public. I guess I should consider myself lucky.

It was out of the frying pan and into the fire as I quickly made my escape from the storyteller, right into another scam to remove me from my money. A man had a small set-up with a ball and cup game that he easily fished me into. I felt pretty smart as I chose the right cup several times. The man even began to begrudgingly hand over money that I had won from him by guessing right. I lost it all in the next moment of course, when he sprung the trap and pocketed the ball. He demanded one hundred dirhams, an amount that I'd hardly agreed to. Both Uncle Hugh and I shook our heads and said no, refusing to pay him. He became angry and started shouting so we decided to hightail it out of there, only to realize that a crowd of angry locals had surrounded us. They began yelling and jeering, their faces twisted in anger. I was absolutely terrified and didn't know what to do, as I didn't have enough dirham to pay the man. Uncle Hugh stepped in and paid him, and then we fled back into the dubious safety of the medina, towards the shop where the owner had our repaired stove waiting for us.

Figuring we had had enough adventure for the day, we headed back to the hotel to shake off the afternoon and relax a bit in the luxurious room. It's funny how cities can develop such character in the memory of travellers, as if one good or bad experience can completely define a city's identity. In my memory, Fes is a wondrous, exotic place while Marrakesh is dark and malevolent. Hardly fair, but with only one afternoon to judge by, I wasn't a fan of Marrakesh!

We left the city early the next morning, ready to drive over the Haut Atlas range to the southeast. As the name implies, the Haut Atlas range is the highest of the three Atlas ranges in Morocco, with peaks over 4000 meters. The scenery on the drive was breathtaking; snowcapped mountains with red rock outcroppings and ridges dominating the view. Single homes and small villages dotted the landscape, many of which our route took us through.

Uncle Hugh stopped the van often to take pictures of the gorgeous vistas, and lovely terraced villages with their squat squarish buildings built out of mud or red rock. Every single time we stopped the van and stepped out, a crowd of children would appear out of nowhere, their hands full of odds and ends they'd try to sell us. They'd push woven grass animals in our faces and when we refused to buy, they would demand money or cigarettes from us. Some of the kids were selling chunks of blue quartz, which they claimed came from nearby mines. Uncle Hugh would always look longingly at the quartz, wanting to purchase some to bring home, but we decided that the rocks looked a little too blue to be real.

Eventually, he was worn down after seeing fifty such rocks pushed into his face over the morning. He bought a large specimen from one of the children and gasped with pleasure as he held it up to the light. He seemed very happy with his quartz as we drove away, that is until he noticed the blue smears on his hands holding the steering wheel. We had been duped yet again!

Uncle Hugh was crestfallen and dejected. All of these hustlers and hucksters were not leaving a good impression and Uncle Hugh was beginning to develop a less than amiable impression about Moroccans and the Arab people in general. Already prone to racism, as seen with his interactions with the Germans, it wouldn't take much more to push him right over the edge into hostility for the entire race.

Crossing over the mountains, the leeward side became arid and desert-like, a dustbowl full of grit and scrub brush. There was still beauty to be found though, including at the campground we found for the night in Ouarzazate. Our campsite faced a hill on which sat a towering castle made of red mud. The crenellated towers reached up into the sky, while the crumbling walls created heaps of scree, forming a skirt around it. The castle has featured prominently in many movies over the years, including Lawrence of Arabia, The Man Who Would Be King, and The Last Temptation of Christ (as well as The Mummy, The Gladiator, Kingdom of Heaven, and Game of Thrones well after my visit there). I plunked a chair down next to the van and stared at the castle, imagining being part of a besieging crusader army, until the sun set behind it.

The next day we took a side trip, 120 kilometres south of Ouarzazate to the town of Zagora, which sat on the edge of the vast Sahara Desert. The road into Zagora was lined with Kasbahs, or small castles or keeps, and we stopped continuously at these picturesque sites for photos. The town itself was beautiful with gardens, palm groves, date fields, and the Draa River lazily flowing through the center of it. The greenery was refreshing after so much rock, and it contrasted very nicely with the red mud buildings.

We stayed in Zagora for the night, then made our way to the source of the Blue Spring, where there was a beautiful swimming pool built by the French Foreign Legion. It was a lush oasis, full of water and vegetation. There was a campground close by where we washed the camper van, and then we spent the day swimming and relaxing in the cool water.

Berber children continued to harass us constantly, which was beginning to really wear us down. They always wanted us to give them something or to buy something from them. I was far too naive to realize that pestering tourists was probably the only way they could survive. I didn't want to give them any of my swiftly diminishing money, so I began to braid snakes out of reeds to trade for the woven grass animals they had. Some of the children asked me how I braided the snakes, so we sat down together and I showed them how to do it. I was proud to give them the lesson and I fantasize today that their grandchildren are pestering tourists, trying to sell them woven reed snakes.

One thing that really stood out to me about the place was the toilet situation. They had the funniest toilets that I had ever seen, and upon seeing them, I laughed and laughed until I cried. There was a long building set away from the pool area on a patch of hard-packed earth. Inside were six stalls; each perched over a small creek that ran through the middle of the building. Inside the stall, there was nothing but a hole in the floor, where you could see the creek flowing under it. You squatted over the hole to do your business, letting the creek take care of everything. You definitely didn't want to be in stall #6 on a busy day, as stalls #1 through #5's special tributes would be passing close beneath you. I wouldn't ever want to live downstream to wherever that creek flowed!

After swimming for the day, we headed back to the campground and met a Canadian couple named Pat and Mira, who were from Victoria B.C. They were a lovely couple, and we were excited to discover that they were also travelling in a VW camper van. We spent the night chatting about our adventures, but a day spent swimming in the sun had us all pretty tired, so we turned in for the night earlier than usual.

We decided to spend the next day with our new Canadian friends and whiled away the morning checking out the town of Erfoud. We strolled around the open market and then stood to watch the hustle and bustle of the donkey and camel market. I was very excited to see camels up close for the first time, such strange creatures!

We agreed that it would be fun to drive into the Sahara a little bit, so we all jumped into Pat and Mira's camper van and ventured out towards the desert. On the edge of town, there was a young man in nice business casual clothes standing on the side of the road, holding his thumb out for a ride. Pat stopped, but the man only spoke French. Luckily Pat understood enough to communicate with him and make out what he was saying. He told us he lived about twenty miles into the desert and if we were to give him a ride to his home, he'd be honoured to have us over for tea.

This was exactly the experience we were looking for, so we invited him into the van and continued along the desert road. Assad told us he was an intern at the local hospital and was going home for a few days' vacation. The main road petered out into small sandy tracks leading every which way. All there was for as far as the eye could see was sand and black rock, with no discernable landmarks or points of interest. Luckily, we had Assad in the back giving us directions.

"A gauche!" he'd call, "A droit!" and Pat would swerve left or right, religiously following his directions.

I quietly followed the proceedings with growing alarm; how were we going to find our way back?

There were huge ruts and hidden ravines that Assad skillfully guided us through as only someone who had spent their whole life driving these roads could. After twenty miles of bewildering twists and turns through the Sahara, we finally arrived at Assad's home, an impressive Kasbah that looked more like a castle than a house.

We pulled through the first gate into a huge courtyard studded with palm trees and lush greenery. I was amazed to see it had a river flowing right through it, creating a tranquil, verdant oasis. I tried my best to hide the grin that came to my face when a thought entered my head, "*I hope this isn't the same creek from the pool bathrooms!*"

As soon as we exited the van, we were surrounded by hundreds of chattering people that had seemingly appeared out of thin air. Hordes of children clamoured for pictures, excited and giggling. We stood there bemused, wondering whom we had picked up.

Assad shooed away the kids and then led us down a long hall with vaulted ceilings. I noticed that there were doors on either side of the hallway that were numbered as if we were in an apartment building or motel, only the numbers weren't in any particular order or sequence. We'd pass number 4, then 26, then 39, then 3, and so on until we eventually came to Assad's door, where he stopped and opened it, welcoming us in.

He asked us to be seated on the rug in the sparsely furnished living room, which had a couple of chairs and a small table but was otherwise bare. He then laid out some dates and cups of soured milk for us in the center of the rug. The dates were quite nice, but I found the sour milk to be disgusting and hard to choke down. Despite being from a backwater Ontario town, I knew enough to show my manners though and smiled reassuringly to Assad while I sipped the revolting liquid. He smiled back, pleased, and went into the kitchen to prepare the ubiquitous mint tea served everywhere in Morocco.

Quickly stuffing some dates into my mouth to hide the taste of the drink, our Canadian friends murmured that it was a great honour to be served dates and sour milk, which made me very happy that I had partook and hadn't made a scene.

Assad came back in with the tea and we lounged on the rug, chatting and sipping the delicious brew. The whole time we stayed in the apartment we could hear the chatter of the other people in the compound as well as the giggling of children as they peered into a 4-foot by 4-foot square cut into the ceiling above the living room. They must have climbed onto the roof to get a better look at the foreigners.

We left the apartment and were given a tour of the Kasbah, which was made up of halls and antechambers all connecting to small courtyards, which were then connected by halls and antechambers to the main courtyard we had arrived in. I felt just as lost and bewildered as I had getting through the desert to get here. We met pretty much every soul who lived there, shaking hands or touching our hearts while slightly bowing. We were then brought out for a walk outside in the desert, which I was relieved to do after meeting so many instantly forgotten people.

Assad's Kasbah was perched on the edge of a sand desert, straddling the transition from black rock to the reddish sands of the Sahara. Assad told me to remove my shoes, as it would be difficult to walk in the sand with them on. I did so and we walked up and down the steep dunes, exploring the peaks and valleys of sand. At one point we crested a rise and came across a herd of camels left to roam around, but with their feet hobbled so they didn't get too far. I walked around, happily absorbing the vastness of the desert, until I stepped on a thorn with my bare foot, which pulled my attention away from the astounding landscape pretty quickly. No stranger to thorny intrusions, Assad had me sit down and removed the thorn for me in an efficient manner.

As we wandered back towards the Kasbah, Assad asked us if we'd like to visit his grandmother for tea. We gladly accepted and everyone piled back into the van, Pat following Assad's directions further and further into the desert. We went at least another 20 miles deep into the Sahara and finally found what could have been a mirage in a movie but was in fact a true oasis in the middle of the sandy desert. When we pulled up to it, we could see down the edge of a dune to the bottom where Assad's grandparents' home sat amongst gardens and crops. It was the only house down there, which meant that this old couple lived very isolated from everyone else.

We met his grandmother outside the house and learned through Assad that his grandfather, a hundred-year-old man, was out tending the crops. After having tea, and a bit of an awkward chat with Assad relaying one-word answers back from his grandmother, we urged Assad that we should return since it would be dark soon. He asked us to leave him there, so we got back into the van with some trepidation, not sure if we could ever find our way back to the town. Driving slowly and attempting to trace our way back, with everyone in the van pitching in and offering their memories of how we had gotten there, we eventually made it back to the Kasbah. From there, we miraculously wound our way back home in the dusky light, avoiding the myriad obstacles, tire-puncturing rocks, van-swallowing ravines, and axle-bending ruts that would have left us stranded in the desert for who knows how long.

With sighs of relief, we pulled back into the campground in Erfoud and stumbled out of the van, Pat needing to pry his stiff fingers from the wheel. We had made it! Within moments, children trying to sell us painted rocks and grass animals swarmed us, yelling and pushing items into our faces. I must say, it was almost welcome at that point.

That special day lives on in my memory as being one of the most magical of the trip. Debriefing with Pat and Mira over dinner in the campground that night, we all agreed that special opportunities like that didn't show up every day and that this was one we'd never forget. Assad, his family, and the vast Sahara Desert had won us over.

The next day the four of us piled into our van and went to see Ksar es Souk, a town just north of Erfoud, which was renamed Errachidia a few years later in honour of the King's youngest son. The town was built around a large market, or souk, which was the main draw. After our troubles in the markets in Marrakesh, I knew Uncle Hugh would be just as happy to never see another souk again, but he put on a brave face for Pat and Mira and agreed to go. He wore a fixed sickly smile as we exited the van and walked into the massive market. Luckily, a soldier approached us and struck up a conversation. He eventually offered to act as a guide and we agreed, despite having a few misgivings about his intentions. He was a man of his word though and asked for nothing, guiding us all around the market. The fact that we had a soldier leading us around must have given the people in the market the impression that we were important people and so we were left alone the whole time. Uncle Hugh's rictus grin eventually relaxed into a natural one and we began to have a good time.

The market was absolutely full of food, all laid out on the ground on blankets, with vendors squatting next to them hawking their wares. There were hardly any women in the market and those who were there were completely covered head to toe in fabric. These heavily veiled women bustled with speed and efficiency, while the men seemed to take their time getting around.

I saw my filthy old friend a few times, leering at me from the crowd. I shuddered and tried to ignore him, sticking closer to Pat and Uncle Hugh, but I could feel his eyes on me everywhere we went in the market. I was happy to leave and go back to the relative safety of the campground, where we spent the rest of the afternoon and evening watching Uncle Hugh's slide collection and playing cards. I kept winning at the card games, which meant that Uncle Hugh kept losing, and that earned me many a nasty sneer throughout the evening.

It was time to say our goodbyes to Pat and Mira the next day since we were heading back to Fes. While driving back, we realized our water supply was getting dangerously low, so we kept our eyes open for a BP station to refill our jugs. British Petroleum stations in Morocco were all mandated to drill deep wells for their water supply, even if they were in the city and had access to municipal water pipes. They had filling stations outside of the main building meant for tourists and this certainly saved us from drinking from a contaminated water supply, a perennial problem that existed in the region at that time. We also needed to get our engine compartment lock fixed as someone had tried to break into it while the van was parked in Ksar es Souk.

We wondered what anyone wanted under the hood of the VW and could only come to the conclusion that they were planning on stealing the engine, or a major component of it. Wouldn't that have been great? Stranded in a desert town with no engine?

We were unsuccessful in finding a petrol station that day, but our path took us back to the campsite we had stayed in on the way to the Sahara that had the huge castle on the horizon. I was happy to camp here again and spend the evening once again reenacting battles on the ramparts from my camp chair.

The next day was April Fool's Day and I had plans to really get Uncle Hugh with a good prank. I woke up extra early and quietly stuffed my sleeping bag with clothes, then crept out of the van. I went for a long walk circling the campsite from afar and keeping my eye on the van. I thought Uncle Hugh would never wake up, but eventually, I saw him climb out of the van and close the door as slowly and quietly as he could, which told me he had fallen for the ruse and thought I was still sleeping. He lit the stove and started brewing some tea. I circled around one last time, and then boldly strode into the campsite and right up to him. Boy was he ever confused!

Startled, he looked at me, then the van, then back at me and stammered, "Wha-? How? What? Where did you come from?"

"Oh, I've been up for hours," I proclaimed, "Did you sleep well?"

"Well, uh, well yes. I thought you must have been very tired to sleep in so late so I didn't want to disturb you."

I opened the van door and pulled the clothes from my sleeping bag. "APRIL FOOL'S!" I crowed.

I had no idea how he would react to something like this, even after all of the time we had spent together on this trip, so I was ecstatic when he clapped his hands and roared with laughter.

"You sure got me, my boy," his name for me when he was pleased with me, "That was a good one!"

I don't think anyone had ever played an April Fool's prank on him before and he was secretly pleased to be at the butt of a harmless joke. He probably hadn't even considered April Fool's as something to think about or notice before. He spent the next few days chuckling and shaking his head when he thought about it, and I was happy to see that he did in fact have a sense of humour, even if it was hidden behind a stern visage attempting its best Alfred Hitchcock impression.

We found a BP station that day and tried to get the lock fixed and the van's oil changed while we were at it, but the shop was experiencing some equipment issues so they turned us away.

Instead, we decided to drive to the city of Meknès, about an hour's drive west of Fes. Upon arrival, we found a place to park and immediately hired a guide, having learned our lesson from our recent antics without one.

The guide was friendly, if a bit quiet, and showed us around the old city, explaining its imperial past and showing us the Bab Mansour archway, the Place El-Hadim square, and the beautiful old mosques spread throughout the city. This time we actually got to go into a mosque and get a peek past its doors. Our guide instructed us to remove our shoes and pay homage to Mohammed in dirhams upon entering. I thought to myself that pretty much anything can be bought if you had enough money, even the entry into heaven!

The interior of the mosque was beautiful, arabesque-lined stone architecture surrounding an open floor filled with men on their knees praying. Some hard stares from those men helped to encourage the feeling that we were intruding into a world where we didn't belong, so we didn't linger for long, despite the unfamiliar beauty of the place.

The rest of the morning was spent strolling around the city, enjoying the beautiful old buildings, then we got back into the van to drive to our next stop, the Roman ruins Volubilis.

The ruins were located not too far outside the city, where we stopped again to walk around. Volubilis was an old Roman city built on top of an occupied Berber city that had existed since the 3rd century BCE. The Romans erected several of their signature arches, temples, palaces, and buildings and the city spread over 100 acres at one time. It was abandoned by the Romans in the 3rd century CE and later destroyed by an earthquake in the 18th century, finally putting an end to its inhabitation. Much of the city was carted away block by block to help build the new and expanding city of nearby Meknès.

When we visited, many of the archways and columns still stood (or had been re-built) and it was easy to imagine the city's former grandeur. The weather even helped to glorify the city as pitch-black clouds gathered on the horizon, contrasting with the still-bright sun showering its rays down upon the white ruins. The scene was otherworldly and incredible and left me with an indelible impression of the splendour of these particular ruins, especially when compared to all of the other ruins I eventually encountered on the trip.

We wandered around the ruins, studying faded tile mosaics, peering into darkened doorways, and feeling the history of the place by running our hands along the textured stone. I found myself truly impressed by the fact that this once-thriving city was constructed seemingly in the middle of nowhere!

There was a campground nearby the ruins, so we decided to stop early for the day and spend the night there. This place was very different from the last few campgrounds we'd stayed at: modern, with beautiful washrooms and a great restaurant.

We met a Canadian couple named Bob and Patricia who, like us, were leaving Morocco the next day. We spent a lovely evening together drinking wine, recounting travel stories, and discussing Morocco in general. I could tell that Uncle Hugh was itching to tell the story of our recent adventure into the Sahara and had been guiding the conversation in such a way so he could do so. Suddenly and uncharacteristically, he said, "Jim, why don't you tell the story, you tell it better than me."

"Wow!" I thought to myself, "I must be moving up his acceptance list for him to be so magnanimous."

I told the story to great fanfare from Bob and Patricia who wistfully replied that they wished they'd been there with us as well. Shortly after we packed up for the night and went to bed.

The next morning, Bob came over to the campsite looking quite shaken and upset. He explained that his engine compartment lock was also broken, even though he had wired it shut. He told us that he had wired it in a very specific way and had noticed in the morning that the wires were different. This must have happened while they were visiting us in the evening, or somehow very quietly during the night. When he opened the hood and dug around, he noticed a block of substance about 10"x6" that had been wrapped in duct tape.

He told us that he figured it must be some sort of

drugs and he was being used as a mule to bring it over the border. He expressed his fears that if someone had planted this in the vehicle, they would be coming back for it at some point, and could react dangerously if they found it gone. He became a little panicky as new thoughts washed over him: how did they know he was leaving Africa that day? Who had he told that would have sold him out? Were they watching him right now? If he replaced the block where he'd found it, what if it was found at the border? Would he go to jail and spend who knows how long in some filthy Moroccan dungeon? If he got rid of the block, what would happen to him and his wife when the owners came to retrieve it? Would they beat them? Kill them?

"Oh my god," he kept saying, "Oh my god!"

We discussed calling the police but, in the end, thought better of it. Who knew if the cops were corrupt, or even in on the whole deal? They may not believe him at all and just throw him in jail before he ever made it to the border.

In the end, he decided to bury the drugs. He'd cross the border, then take a random road out of the port as fast as and as long as he could drive, completely throwing their itinerary to the wind until they felt safe again. The sooner they could get out of Spain, he said, the safer they would feel.

I thought to myself that these poor people's trip was ruined. Even once they got out of Spain, I'm sure their paranoia would cast a gloomy veil over the rest of their vacation.

As Bob kept wringing his hands and expressing his grief over the matter, a thought suddenly occurred to me. I quickly glanced over at Uncle Hugh and could tell he was thinking the exact same thing. OUR hood had been tampered with earlier as well. We had naïvely thought that someone had been trying to steal our engine or parts of it, but what if someone had planted drugs on us? What if we were unwitting mules ourselves?

After Bob left, we rushed over to the camper and began an extremely thorough search. Uncle Hugh looked in the engine compartment, while I shimmied under the van and checked every single space that could fit something matching Bob's description. We were certainly spooked and kept lifting the hood and neurotically checking the engine compartment over and over, but luckily never found anything.

Maybe the perpetrators were scared off their mission before being able to plant the drugs on us, or maybe they were actually trying to steal engine parts, but we didn't rest easy until we had left that border far behind.

We packed up the van, took one last peek under the hood, and then left for Centa and the ferry to Spain. The trip elapsed in silence as we both brooded over our mysterious broken hood latch and Bob and Patricia's ruined trip. We arrived at the ferry port, where there were massive lineups of cars, trucks, and camper vans like ours. We got in line and then went into the office to buy tickets for the ferry. The clerk informed us that there would be a two-hour wait before we could board, so when we got back to our camper, we took out the table and chairs and started cooking some lunch.

At one point two Moroccan teenage boys came by and asked in broken English, "Give ride to Spain!"

"Not a chance!" said Uncle Hugh, shaking his head, "NO!"

"We hide! They no see! Please, PLEASE!"

Outraged, Uncle Hugh again shouted, "NO! Now go away!"

Shaking our heads at the thought of the risk involved with allowing those boys into our vehicle, we were shocked to see them approach the next camper where an American woman nodded to them, yes. She opened the camper door and the two youths quickly jumped onboard and disappeared.

"How stupid is she?!" we exclaimed. "She's going to get caught!"

We made sure to avoid her the entire way across the strait and into customs in Spain. We often wondered whether she made it through and how our friends Bob and Patricia made out.

Our travels and adventures in Africa were over. While we had a great time, with lots of interesting stories to tell, we felt much safer to be back in Europe. I was happy to finally be rid of the creepy, scruffy man who I felt had been following me around for the entire time we were in Africa, and felt a nearly overwhelming relief in the absence of his leering eyes and rude hand gestures. I just hoped that he didn't find a way to make it over the border and keep following me. I shivered despite the heat of the late afternoon.

Chapter 6

We found a nice campground not too far out of Algeciras in a place called San Roque. After setting up camp, we spent the night drinking copious amounts of wine to relieve the tension of the day. It seemed crazy that just that morning we had awoken in a campground on another continent, panicking about planted drugs.

Thanks to the wine, we slept soundly that night, then proceeded on towards Seville the next leg of our journey. Most of the way there we were treated to scenic views of the Atlantic Ocean which I hadn't ever seen before. Alongside the ocean were incredibly flat farm fields and unbroken vistas of level marshland full of feral camels foraging and roaming around. I was informed that the landscape was once all marsh, but the flat fields had been drained for agriculture.

We passed through the huge port city of Cadiz, built by the Phoenicians 3000 years ago, and the site of the launching of the famous Spanish Armada in 1588 against the British.

Just beyond Cadiz, we took a random side road towards the Atlantic and had a picnic lunch on the beach. It was a beautiful place, with huge waves crashing against the shore and a steady warm breeze blowing across the beach.

That evening we stopped in another campground, this one with very nice washrooms and showers, and even an on-site supermarket. We were both feeling a little hung over from all of the wine the night before, and Uncle Hugh wanted to get an early start to Seville the next day, so we packed it in early without searching for evening friends as we had at so many other campgrounds.

A funny thing happened early the next morning. Uncle Hugh shook me awake urgently at about 5:00 am, telling me to get dressed and that we were leaving right away.

"After breakfast," I moaned, but he was insistent. Since we had packed everything up the night before, it took no time at all before we were zooming out of the gates, with Uncle Hugh humming giddily to himself.

I studied his self-satisfied face with some groggy confusion before I realized that he hadn't paid! I opened my mouth to remind him that he had forgotten to pay for the night but then closed it suspiciously before saying anything. He had meant to leave without paying! He was giddy as a school kid and proud as hell about it.

I wondered at his motivation to screw the nice campground out of the measly few bucks they charged when he'd already spent thousands on this trip. At first, I chalked it up to the stress he had endured in Africa, but then I slowly remembered all of his other instances of stinginess; with bellboys, servers, maids, the woman whose house we had invaded to take pictures, and now campgrounds. Basically, anyone whom he deemed beneath him, he seemed willing to exploit.

The immature teenager that I was, I didn't challenge him on it, I just shrugged it off as another strange adventure with this strange man and waited for the sun to rise so I could look out the windows again.

Arriving in Seville, we took the van to the city's VW dealership to finally get the engine compartment lock repaired and get a much-needed oil change. We met a

Spanish man in the waiting room named Santiago who lived in Seville. He offered to take us for a ride to see some of the city while the work was being done on the van. We agreed and he took us through the downtown core and the Old Town, showing us some of the city's sights. He asked if we'd like to see his home and we readily agreed once more, excited to see a typical Spanish home in the city.

We pulled up to a row of Medieval-looking condos and Santiago brought us inside the one that he owned. I was surprised to see that the interior was very modern, sleek, and spacious. I suppose my undereducated mind had pictured that most Spanish people lived in hovels, but that obviously wasn't the case. I was astounded at the tasteful mixture of modern and antique furniture, appliances, and artwork that put most Canadian homes I knew to shame.

After a short tour and visit, we invited Santiago for lunch at a restaurant. He acquiesced, so I asked him to bring us to an authentic Andalusian Spanish restaurant where we could buy him lunch.

"Not TOO expensive though!" Uncle Hugh interjected.

Santiago laughed and said, "No problem, I know just the place and it will be my treat."

Uncle Hugh beamed, his rubber arm having been so easily bent, and gracefully let Santiago's offer to pay go unchallenged. Still grinning ear to ear, he clasped his hands together in delight and said how much he was looking forward to lunch as he was absolutely famished. Behind him, I simply rolled my eyes.

The Ispal Restaurante was our destination and I looked around in awe at the beautiful old brick, the lush plants, and the really cool lights hanging from the arching 20-foot ceilings as we walked through the lobby to our table.

Santiago informed us that Ispal was the original name for Seville and that it meant flatlands. This restaurant served authentic food from the region. He offered to order for us and Uncle Hugh nodded, raising his fingers to cover his mouth giddily like a Japanese schoolgirl. The pretty and friendly waitress brought over some beers, and Santiago ordered the à la carte for three.

We started with a tapa of fresh anchovies and prawns that was brought to us on a traditional wooden plate. Tapas are small traditional appetizers that actually originated in the city of Seville. They started out as small pieces of meat, fish, or bread that taverns would supply to bargoers to cover their glasses of sherry between sips so that fruit flies couldn't get into the glasses. From there, they evolved into a wide array of delicious appetizers, including the outstanding seafood tapa before us.

The main entrée was a cod and tuna dish and everything was fantastically delicious. We switched to wine and ate and drank as we chatted about Santiago's impressive and somewhat sad life. He told us that he had started in the army as a young man, then left it to become a lawyer in Madrid. He met a woman from Seville, and after they married, they moved back to her hometown. He told us tearfully that she had sadly passed away the year before from cancer.

Swigging some wine, he asked about us to change the subject. Due to my age and lack of worldly experience, I didn't have all too much to tell him; I lived in a small town in Ontario with my parents and four siblings and that was pretty much it.

Uncle Hugh informed him that he was actually my great-uncle and that he had never married. He had never gotten any support from anybody, so he had to put himself through school at the University of Toronto, where he eventually became a professor. He explained that kids never seemed too interested in what he had to say, so he quickly tired of the work and decided to change careers.

Through nothing more than eye contact and a raised eyebrow, I insinuated to Santiago that the kids were probably just tired of hearing him go on and on. Santiago grinned.

Unfazed, Uncle Hugh continued. Finished with his professor gig, he went back to school and became an architect. He then found a job at a firm in Philadelphia that was spearheading a project to transform and upgrade the entire downtown of the city into something more refreshing and modern. After many years of work as an architect, Uncle Hugh once again grew bored and decided he'd like to do something for individuals.

By this time, he had fallen in love with the States, and out of love with stolid, Victorian Canada, so he moved to Portland Oregon and went back to school to become a social worker. He loved living on the West Coast and really enjoyed his new job as a social worker. He did find it to be exhausting work though, which is why he had decided to book this trip to Europe. Of course, due to a train accident that had broken his neck years ago, he didn't feel fit to navigate himself, so he had brought his, "nephew James, here," along to help him out.

Santiago shook his head repeatedly as Uncle Hugh recounted his impressive tale, and often exclaimed, "Wow!" and "Oh my!"

We finished our meal off with Torta de Santiago, a tasty almond cake. We all laughed that we were eating a dessert that went by the same name as our host and clinked glasses to toast.

I could see Uncle Hugh surreptitiously straining to view the bill when it arrived at the table, and before

Santiago could snatch it up, it was apparent that he had caught sight of the amount. I could tell because his eyebrows almost touched his hairline as his eyes flew wide open in astonishment.

We thanked Santiago profusely for showing us around and for the lovely lunch. Shaking our hands, he offered to drive us back to the dealership, but Uncle Hugh insisted we walk back, to work off some of that fantastic meal. I honestly think he wanted to escape as soon as possible so that Santiago couldn't change his mind and request that we pony up for lunch.

We strolled over to the Alcazan, an ancient royal palace very similar to the Alhambra in Grenada, and checked out the grounds. The palace was built in the 14th century over the ruins of a much older palace, by a man named Pedro Machura, who, by Uncle Hugh's description of him, must have been a very close friend of his. The palace was built in the Mudejar style, or Muslim influenced, with scrolling arabesques and decoration. The palace had a lot of Gothic, Renaissance, and Romanesque features as well and Uncle Hugh delighted in pointing out every single feature to me, stone by stone. It was all very beautiful, with its manicured gardens, fountains, and baths. I enjoyed the scenery as Uncle Hugh's monotone washed over me.

Footsore and tired, we eventually made our way back to the dealership to pick up the van. After scanning the bill over and over again with a deep scowl, Uncle Hugh reluctantly agreed to pay for the work. I imagine he would have made the same face had he been forced to pay for that lunch.

We found a non-descript campsite not too far outside of the city, had a light supper, then turned in early for bed.

The next day we drove back into the city to visit the Cathedral of Saint Mary of the See, also known colloquially as the Seville Cathedral. The most famous tourist attraction in Seville, it is the 4th largest cathedral in the world and the largest Gothic cathedral anywhere in existence. When you enter, you are immediately awed by the 383 feet long, 249 feet wide, and 131 feet high expanse of space. There are many famous works of art inside and truly impressive examples of Gothic wood carvings. There was a huge majestic tower which we ascended via ramp instead of the usual stairs. The ramps were there because they used to have a horse carry the Queen to the top of the tower and she obviously couldn't be expected to slug her way up all of the stairs like a commoner. The top of the tower boasted a fantastic view of Seville, with all of its history, towers, and architecture.

We left Seville, heading northeast on the highway towards Córdova. Seeing a cool-looking castle in the distance, we took a side road to check it out. When we arrived, we found it to be closed for the day, but we got out of the car to check out the outside walls anyway. Seeing a likely spot where I might be able to scale the wall, I jumped up and grasped the rough stones, pulling my body up and continuing to climb my way up the side of the wall. While I was intent on storming the ramparts, Uncle Hugh was intent on repelling the attack, calling out to me in a motherly fashion, "Jim! Jim, get down! Oh my, don't climb any higher! Ohh what would your mother say if you were to fall off and die? Please get down! Oh my!"

I barely heard his screams, being so intent on climbing the wall. About halfway up, I couldn't find any more handholds, so it was time to come down. Looking down dizzyingly, I realized it would be much harder to go back down than it was to go up. I slowly made my way down, my feet slipping on the stone and my fingers taking some damage from the abrasive rock.

I lived to tell the tale and made it all the way down without any help, though I received quite the tongue-lashing when I finally did. It made me feel like I was at home again, being harangued by my parents.

Getting back into the car, we made our way into Córdova where we visited the famous mosque, which looked to me to be just another cathedral, similar to the rest we'd already seen. It was built in 785CE and has since had many additions built onto it, including an impressive minaret that was built in 958CE. It is now being used as a Roman Catholic cathedral, which in itself displays some of the back-and-forth religious history of the region.

Uncle Hugh gave me the mandatory Royal Tour and Lecture, pointing out the Moorish and Renaissance architectural features, and the historically significant minutia. I was particularly impressed with the red and white striped columns that you encountered when you entered the mosque-cathedral, but otherwise, I was beginning to feel a little over these massive Spanish churches.

Leaving Córdova, we headed for Toledo which Uncle Hugh insisted we reach that day despite the long drive. The scenery on the way started out nice, but eventually became repetitious and boring, with grove after grove of olive trees lining the highway. Eventually, the sun set and I couldn't even rely on the monotony of the olive trees to keep me entertained.

We arrived very late in Toledo, finding the campground we had chosen on the map quite easily for once. We set up beside some nice Americans, Brent and Virginia, who were from Rhode Island. We spent a pleasant evening with them, sipping on Spanish wine, and they regaled us with stories from their recent travels in Greece. They were particularly fond of the Greek Islands and insisted that if we weren't going to go anywhere else in Greece, at least make sure to see the Islands.

Uncle Hugh had been sitting on the fence on whether or not he wanted to visit any of those islands or stick to the mainland of Greece when we arrived there. The islands were reportedly beautiful, but you needed to take ferries to get to them, which took time and cost extra money. Brent and Virginia impressed him with their description of them though, and I think they were what changed his mind in the end when he decided to add them into the trip. He was nodding along thoughtfully as they described all of the beautiful sights to see, and I could see that he was impressed and that he was likely changing his mind.

They were heading to Morocco next, so we took our turn to regale them with tales of our adventures there, with many warnings about street hustlers, drug planters, painted rocks, and the importance of hired guides in the city centers.

The next day we drove into downtown Toledo and into the parking lot of yet another cathedral. The parking was free there which made Uncle Hugh happy, and there were also several El Greco paintings on display in the Cathedral which he just had to see. I tried to hide my impatience as Uncle Hugh guided me through every brushstroke in the paintings. He was a big El Greco fan and explained to me that he was a famous painter from the 16th century who had a very unique style. His paintings were vividly colourful and the people in his paintings had elongated, gaunt and tortured faces. Like most paintings from the era, there was a ton of religious significance and everyone looked miserable. Uncle Hugh explained that he wasn't a very popular painter during his time but became popular much later in the 20th century. I continued to learn about El Greco as we left the museum and walked straight to his home that had been preserved, then over to the El Greco Museum.

I tried to feign interest for Uncle Hugh's sake, but I just found the paintings quite weird and wasn't too keen on learning anything more about this guy. I was relieved when we finally left him behind and started exploring the rest of the city.

Toledo is a very ancient city, and I feel like I could have written a large book on just what Uncle Hugh imparted to me about its history as we walked around. The city is surrounded by the Tagus River and rises on all sides, with all of the roads eventually taking you to the topmost area, where a large fortress squats, overlooking the region. The fortress is an Alcazar or Moorish-style medieval castle, and this particular one was famous for being the holdout of about a thousand rebels during the Spanish Civil War. According to Uncle Hugh, their courageous resistance to the government had earned them fame and notoriety in the region and the Alcazar was adorned with many paintings, pictures, and murals denoting their glory. It seemed like the place was also a monument to the Franco dictatorship that took over Spain in the 1930s after the aforementioned rebellion.

The beauty of Toledo really struck me as we walked around the picturesque city, and I remember enjoying it despite the tedious art and history lessons that came with it.

The next morning, we packed up and headed for Madrid in central Spain, which should have only been about an hour's drive. It quickly became apparent that we were heading into a 3 million-resident metropolis as we made our way into industrial sprawl and traffic became increasingly congested. It looked like I was going to earn my keep that day as the highway quickly exploded into crisscrossing freeways, on- and off-ramps, turnpikes, and last-minute splits which created a need for quick decision-making, flawless navigation, and no small amount of legwork checking on blind spots for my stiff-necked great uncle.

Intently dividing my focus between the highway and my map, I would scurry to the back of the van checking for traffic in the left lane. "Get into the left lane, we need to turn off in less than a kilometre!" I would shout, "Go, go now!" Then I would frantically check my map for the next turn.

Sometimes we needed to make a fast-approaching exit but were completely surrounded by cars. I would run back and forth down the length of the van, frantically searching for a hole in traffic that Uncle Hugh could jam the van into.

"Slow down!" I'd shout.

"No, now speed up, speed up!"

"Do it, do it now!"

Often, he wouldn't have the nerve to blindly swerve into an open space that I assured him existed and so we missed many of our turn-offs. When this happened, I'd desperately assess the map and come up with an alternative route that would bring us where we needed to go.

Uncle Hugh was understandably very flustered by all of this and was becoming less agreeable by the minute. He would often argue with me about the route, even though I was the one with the map. Since we couldn't stop and consult it together, this led to a battle of nerves with no clear winner. In the end, we became hopelessly lost and Uncle Hugh just kept on stubbornly driving to who-knows-where.

The campground we were trying to find lay on the outskirts of Madrid according to the map, but it was becoming more and more evident that we were being funnelled into the downtown area instead. I would point out signs that said CENTRO DE LA CUIDAD, or city center, and say that we were obviously heading downtown, but Uncle Hugh would grit his teeth and just keep driving, having had enough of my input.

As we neared the tall buildings of Madrid's metropolitan center, the 6-lane freeway suddenly broke off into two directions in a massive 'Y'. In the center median of the divide were parked several police cars, probably on the lookout for speeders.

Instead of veering left or right, Uncle Hugh drove straight down the median directly toward the police cars!

I would have thought that he'd have developed some sort of distrust or apprehension about Spanish police officers after our first run-in with them, but desperation won out and he pulled right up beside them and stopped the van.

The officers, most of whom had been standing outside of their cars, looked astonished and were talking back and forth in rapid-fire Spanish. If we could have understood them, I'm sure we would have heard something to the effect of, "Who's this nutbar, what does he think he's doing?!"

Once their initial shock wore off, hands were put on holstered guns and the group deliberately walked over and surrounded the van. I'm sure if we had made any sudden movements at this time, we would have ended up riddled with bullet holes!

Uncle Hugh slowly rolled down the window as the police approached.

"Señor, qué estas haciendo?" the closest officer asked, meaning, "Sir, what are you doing?"

Uncle Hugh, nearly in tears, sputtered, "W-we're j-just Canadians. We're hopelessly lost... p-please help us, sir, we can't find our campground!"

A few seconds of grim silence went by as the officer turned to look at his buddies. His mouth quirked, and then all of them burst into laughter simultaneously.

"Sir," he said, switching to English, "this is your lucky day. We are having a nice quiet day and have little to do, so we will help you get to where you're going."

"Oh, thank you! Thank you!" Uncle Hugh exclaimed.

Then the most incredible thing happened; the officer told us to follow the police cars and they'd guide us to the campground. Two police cars, lights ablaze, pulled ahead of us, while four motorcycle police, two on each side of us, also with their flashing lights on, pulled out into traffic. The cars all slowed down to let us by and we were given a full presidential escort to our campground. The people staying in the campground must have wondered just who the important arrivals were that were given a full police escort to go camping for the night!

As we pulled up to the campground gates, the police circled us, playfully giving us salutes as they drove by, then disappeared back down the road. We were grinning ear to ear at the serendipitous change in our fortunes.

The campground was spacious and modern, and we wasted no time getting set up and hoisting up our Canadian flag. Uncle Hugh was still insisting that we immediately broadcast that we were Canadians so no one would mistake us for Americans, even though he was now an American citizen.

"Europeans just aren't too keen on Americans," he would often say while hoisting the flag, "It's all because of their domination during the war, and because of their arrogant attitudes. We're much better off pretending to be Canadians, as everyone loves Canadians."

"Well, shit, that's easy for me," I thought to myself, "I AM a Canadian."

I think we went over this conversation so many times because Uncle Hugh was trying to work through his guilt and feelings about disparaging Canada, while purposely fooling our neighbours into thinking he was Canadian.

We took a long bus ride into Madrid, then got on a subway to go downtown. Our first stop was the American Express office, which was closed when we arrived. Next was a tourist office so we could get our bearings and find some entertainment. The nearest tourist office was also closed, as was the next one. We ended up walking over two miles to find one that was open. We went in and bought a map and inquired about bullfights. There was one starting soon, but we'd have to drive there. We rushed back to the campground as fast as we could, but by the time we got back, we discovered that they had already started, so we planned to go the next day instead.

The next morning, we went to Madrid's famous art gallery, the Prado, which Uncle Hugh praised and praised before we arrived. I was actually excited about it, hearing Uncle Hugh's loquacious appreciation of the place the whole way there.

Uncle Hugh didn't want to miss a thing, so we started right inside the entryway and made our way methodically through the entire gallery. It slowly dawned on me that this place wasn't going to be quite as exciting as he had made it out to be. It seemed to me that every damn painting in the place was Madonna and Child!

Uncle Hugh informed me that before the Renaissance, the church forbade artists to paint anything but religious scenes. This gallery must have been where every single painting from that era ended up.

From the entryway, we saw a fantastic rendition of Madonna and Child. Next was Madonna and Child, then an exquisite example of Madonna and Child. "This one was painted in 1358, and this one in 1432, and this one was painted by Raffaello Sanzio, and... oh! A Luis de Morales and a Puccio Capanna, and a Fillipo Lippi!" and on and on and on it went. Uncle Hugh knew everything about everything and must have felt like it was his life's mission to cram it all into my head at once.

I was beginning to look bored and kick my feet and he became very cross with me, demanding that I, "Buck up and pay attention!"

After all, he had been kind enough to bring me along on this trip and pay for everything, the very least I could do was pay attention and enjoy this magnificent place!

Even as a sullen teenager, I knew he had a point and felt a little bad for my inattention, but I just couldn't drum up any enthusiasm for hundreds upon hundreds of dark, repetitive paintings. I tried harder, despite the trudging monotony, but after four full hours, we had only completed the first floor.

Looking at the stairs to the next level (next to an enchanting depiction of Madonna and Child) despairingly, I was shocked to hear Uncle Hugh suggest we leave for the day. Even HE had had enough for the time being.

I tried not to let the excitement show in my eyes at the prospect of leaving. Still trying to be a good nephew, I simply agreed that while the paintings and gallery were fantastic, we didn't want to overdo it and tire ourselves out. I was pretty much clicking my heels in glee behind him as we wandered back out into daylight.

Heading back to the campground, we immediately jumped into the van and drove to the arena to see the bullfight. The bullring was packed, and the crowd was very enthusiastic, full of contagious excitement. The arena was round, with high boards surrounding the dirt floor in the center. It wasn't long before the first bull, or toro, was released into the arena to the delight of the roaring crowd.

The bull was proud, strutting around the arena, snorting and looking for anyone brave enough to show their face so he could gore them with his huge horns. His shiny black coat positively gleamed in the hot Spanish sun and I found myself nearly shaking with anticipation.

Six Banderillos, a type of Matador, entered the ring to much fanfare from the crowd. The bull showed his displeasure with them by shaking his horned head, stomping his feet, and snorting loudly. He circled his opponents, visibly sizing them up before the action started.

The men all had pink capes and colourful clothes on and separated to confound the bull. They began teasing it, causing it to charge this way, then that way and the crowd roared every time the bull unsuccessfully charged. Each Banderillo had several 3-foot-long darts or lances on him called banderillas which they took turns jabbing into the bull's back after each unsuccessful charge.

The darts were designed to stick in the bull and stay there, so soon the poor creature was festooned with colourful banderillas. Pain and the smell of his blood made the bull descend into a rage and he charged and charged at his tormentors, each time unsuccessful and often getting another dart in his back for the effort.

The six Banderillos melted away and in rode two Matadors called Picadors. These men rode large, heavily-clad horses in thick quilted armour. Each carried a long lance or spear and wore a pale, brimmed, and feathered hat.

They agilely danced their well-trained horses around the enraged bull, remaining well out of reach of its horns. One of the Picadors shot in close to the bull and gave him a savage jab with the lance. As the bull's attention was fixed on the now-retreating Picador, the other one swept in and landed another blow. Again, and again, and again they jabbed.

The bull was now in a fever pitch, frothing out the mouth and blind with rage. It was time for the final or senior Matador to come in for the kill. This man was the hero of the people and the crowd showed it by becoming somehow even louder than they'd been before, cheering and chanting his name.

He pranced out into the ring, wearing a spectacular suit full of gold filigree. He elegantly waved his red cape, enticing the bull to charge straight at him. He effortlessly stepped aside as the bull rushed past him and through the cape. The crowd went absolutely wild. I half expected them to start foaming at the mouth like the injured bull.

The Matador played to the crowd, nodding graciously and bowing before brandishing his cape once more and catching the bull's attention. After several such passes, he must have decided it had gone on long enough because he unsheathed a sword and drove it down through the beast's shoulder blades as it passed for the last time.

The bull stumbled, then crashed into the dirt, letting out a piteous cry of anger and pain. Once down, the matador sidled up to the bull and pulled out a second blade, this one short and slender, which he used to finish off the bull by pushing it into its head.

The crowd clapped furiously for the Matador who made a show of bowing and prancing around the bull. During the entire spectacle, Uncle Hugh had raised his hands to his cheeks repeatedly and clapped along with the crowd. Being a fourteen-year-old, I enjoyed the show but found it quite barbaric. I couldn't help but think about the Roman gladiators and how watching a bullfight was the closest thing you could get to a modern equivalent.

The bull was dragged out of the ring and soon after a new bull was let in, just as mad as the first. In all, they killed six bulls that day, and not all of them went as smoothly as the first. One bull managed to get his horns in under one of the armoured horses and flung the horse and rider up into the air as if they were weightless.

The pink-caped Banderillos rushed into the ring to distract the bull as men came in from the other side to remove the injured horse and Picador. As the horse was lying in the ring bleeding, I noticed that there were freshly bandaged wounds beside the new ones the bull had just administered on the horse's belly. This mauling was obviously not just a random occurrence but must happen quite often.

One other injury occurred when a bull kicked out with his hind legs and caused one of the Banderillos to swing wildly with his dart, slicing the senior Matador's face and leaving a nasty bleeding gash on his cheek. The Picadors came in for the rescue and the Matador was brought behind the boards. After he regained his composure, the Matador strutted back out, bowed to the crowd, bowed to the bull, and then finished the show, driving his sword into the bull's neck. They dragged that bull off as unceremoniously as they had the rest.

On the way home, I complained that my throat was quite sore, probably from the dust and the shouting at the bull ring, but Uncle Hugh was worried. He took me to a doctor who diagnosed me with laryngitis and told me to drink lots of fluids and get ample bed rest. I spent the entire next day in bed while Uncle Hugh went to town and back to the Prado to study the next level of

Madonna and Child paintings. I imagine he was probably torn between being happy to have some time to himself and being disappointed that he wasn't furthering my education.

The nights in the camper van had been getting pretty cold, so Uncle Hugh rented out a small bungalow for the next few nights, probably in part due to his worry about my throat. I was feeling quite a bit better after a day spent in bed, but Uncle Hugh still thought we should take it easy, so we made a couple of small trips to town to visit the El Escorial palace, a massive cross called the Valley of the Fallen, and to do a little shopping at Sears.

We also visited the American Express office to post and check for mail. Uncle Hugh had left instructions to friends and family, including mine, to send any mail to the American Express office in Madrid. I was ecstatic to find that I had received a letter from home. I quickly ripped open my letter, my mother extolled how much they all missed me and loved me and hoped I was having a good time and was I getting enough to eat. And how was I getting along with Uncle Hugh? My eyes welled up with tears as I read, as it gave me an instant batch of homesickness. I reread the letter many times over the next few days as it brought me much comfort and a welcome connection to my family back in Canada. My reply letter expressed nothing but praises for the trip and of Uncle Hugh. I certainly didn't want my mother to worry or to know all the truths, including the liquor I'd been drinking. While I was absorbed by my letter, Uncle Hugh mailed all of his camera film to a processing facility with instructions to forward it to Paris. He didn't want to risk exposing the film to radiation in the airport and having it all ruined. Since I lacked the necessary funds to do the same, I was going to take my chances and bring mine with me onboard the plane.

The American Express office was oddly a very interesting place as it was the gathering point for many travelling Americans. There were dozens of people sitting and lazing around everywhere, inside and out of the office. There were many backpackers either waiting for mail or money transfers or simply looking to connect with fellow travellers. Everyone was quite talkative and you could easily walk up to anyone in the room and strike up a conversation with them, where you'd hear all about their trials, tribulations, and adventures. I figured that this is what a hostel must feel like.

We left Madrid and I navigated us out of the city heading eastwards, towards a town called Alcañiz. As the big city slowly receded in the rearview mirror, I felt a bit cheated at not having been able to explore much due to my laryngitis, but also happy to be heading back into the peace of the countryside. The lights and flash of the big city were cool and all, but the beautiful rolling hills, relative quiet, and lack of traffic in this bucolic rural area were certainly welcome.

As we neared Alcañiz, Uncle Hugh surprised me by handing me the Parador brochure and telling me we were staying in one for the night.

"This is a real deal Parador," he said, "Not like that one in Puerto Lumbreras. This one is going to live up to those ones in the brochure, believe me!"

He was right, this Parador was one of the ones we'd dreamt of; a Medieval castle retrofitted into a luxury hotel high on a hill overlooking the city. Driving right up to the massive front gate, this castle even had valet parking!

The castle was huge and had been transformed into a luxurious, but very tasteful modern building. Our room was enormous, with vaulted ceilings and a balcony with a commanding view of the countryside. The walls were naked stone, and the decorations and trappings were a charming combination of Medieval chic and modern elegance.

Uncle Hugh suggested that we get cleaned up, then put on our finest clothes and celebrate with a grand dinner. What had come over the man? I wasn't sure, but I liked it!

I asked him what we were celebrating and he responded, "Well James, you're back in good health, we've made it this far in our adventure, and I always dreamed of visiting this place! I think that warrants a celebration!"

That was good enough for me.

We always played some sort of silly game to decide who got to bathe first. This time it was guess the colour of the bathmat, and I won, so I got to hop in the tub first. I donned my see-through dress shirt, copper-coloured with blue designs, my sleeveless suit, and of course my work boots, which doubled as both hikers and dress shoes.

When Uncle Hugh was ready, we ambled down the hall, past courtyards lined with columns, trees, and fountains, making our way toward the restaurant. We arrived at a fabulous seating area with a high, arched stone ceiling and a grand stone staircase descending into the center of the room. There was a magnificently large bar to the side with beautifully carved wooden stools. Many fashionably-dressed people were already there dining, and the sounds of hushed conversation and clinking silverware filled the air. I felt like I was in an actual palace.

The maître d' seated us at a table close to the bar, but Uncle Hugh wasn't happy with the location, so he flagged the man back and asked to be moved. Smiling graciously, the man then brought us to a table under the arch, which was between the indoor seating area and the outdoor terrace. We hovered over the table with the maître 'd as Uncle Hugh hemmed and hawed over whether he was okay with this table. The man must have been wondering who these strange-looking and picky tourists were.

Uncle Hugh finally nodded and said that we'd "try it out", so we sat down. We had a very lovely dinner with white wine and a fish entrée. It was all very upscale and lush, and we felt very upper-class to be dining in such a place with such well-dressed people surrounding us.

I was just thinking to myself that I was impressed that Uncle Hugh had decided to shell out for this hotel and meal when he did something that made me grimace and squirm in my chair.

"My, we're getting quite low on condiments in the camper," he said conspiratorially, "Why, I don't think we barely have a grain of salt or a speck of pepper left."

With that, he opened his napkin on his lap and reached for the salt. Surreptitiously unscrewing the top, he dumped the entire contents into the napkin, then folded it up and tucked it away in a suit pocket. He replaced the saltshaker, then nabbed several tea and sugar packets from the holder on the table. Nodding in a self-satisfied manner, he then had the audacity to wave over the waiter, "Sir," he said imperiously, "This saltshaker is empty, could we place have it re-filled?"

The waiter acquiesced with a raised eyebrow and a knowing look. I tried my best to melt away to nothing in the chair, but I felt entirely too visible.

I could never predict what Uncle Hugh would do when it came to spending money. He would continually splurge and spend, and then suddenly balk at the smallest expenses, or would pull power moves like running out on the bill, or stealing salt as if these places owed him for having spent his money there.

Trying not to let it get to me, we spent the rest of the evening enjoying the room and getting a great sleep in big comfy beds.

The next day found us leaving Alcañiz with our condiments replenished as Uncle Hugh took advantage of the breakfast to grab even more salt, pepper, sugar, and tea. Well-provisioned, we headed off to Barcelona. The road was very windy as we made our way into the mountains and Uncle Hugh became more and more nervous as we climbed into the high passes with nary a shoulder to be seen. His body language became very jittery and I was careful not to anger or antagonize him as it became apparent that he was having a very difficult time. Moaning at every curve, he carefully guided the campervan around bends, over hills, and down switchbacks.

The colours in the rocks began to change with every passing kilometre, with reds, yellows, browns, greens, blacks, purples, and even pinks. I was spellbound by the varying hues and wanted to ask Uncle Hugh about them, but I decided not to since he was white-knuckled and focusing entirely on the road. If it had been a normal drive, I probably wouldn't have had to ask, he would have just known about them and told me why they were like that. The man was a walking database of knowledge; a Google machine forty years before Google ever existed.

We arrived at the coast of the Balearic Sea (part of the Mediterranean) with a sigh of relief, but that relief soon turned into despair as the road got somehow even worse than before. The way was dangerously tight and narrow, with sheer drop-offs hundreds of feet down to sea-sprayed rocks and no guard rails to speak of. I was very glad at this point that he had mastered the clutch and was driving relatively smoothly around all of the tight bends.

I navigated us to our campground which was called the Albatross. It was beautiful, right on the sea with lots of amenities. Uncle Hugh pried his fingers off the steering wheel and declared, "I need a drink!"

There was a small supermarket on site, with a large selection of wine and spirits. Agreeing that he did indeed need a drink, and never being one to turn one down myself, we went into the store and bought an ample amount of booze.

We had a great evening, and got quite drunk, laughing and joking about the crazy drive. "James my boy, I thought we were goners today. I was sure we were going right over that cliff! All I could think of is what your poor mother would think and how she could ever forgive me, driving you off a cliff!" He would laugh and laugh until it almost seemed like he was about to cry.

The next day we woke up a little groggy and drove into Barcelona where we found a parking lot downtown. We walked to the Cathedral Sagrada Familia, the same one we had seen but not gone to after our visit with Cousin Richard. The building was magnificent and still growing, under constant construction funded by tourist dollars and donations.

We decided to climb up to the highest spire, me scurrying up with young legs and poor hung-over Uncle Hugh huffing and puffing his 60-year-old body up the successive flights, blocking the stairs for dozens of tourists behind him. I thought the view was incredible, but all he had to say was, "We climbed up all this way just to view a smoggy city. How disgusting... what a shame, it is so polluted!" He was probably just feeling tired and cranky.

On our way back to the van, we saw a group of young people in one of the squares, lounging and listening to one of their own playing a guitar in the Spanish style. We stopped to watch and listen for a while and were amazed at witnessing this young, long-haired Spaniard singing and strumming a true Spanish guitar, making absolutely beautiful music. Even Uncle Hugh, a stout classical fan, was impressed by the man's mastery of his instrument and his awesome performance. Random little times like this stand out to me as some of the highlights of the entire European adventure.

Back on the road again, we headed to Monserrat, a Benedictine monastery and mountain retreat. Approaching it, you're left to wonder to yourself, how the hell were they ever able to build something like that so high up?

We drove on to Vic, northeast of Barcelona since Uncle Hugh had heard there was a Parador hotel there. Another one! Uncle Hugh was becoming a Parador convert. Unfortunately, it was closed when we arrived, but we managed to find an excellent hotel to make up for it. We were staying in hotels rather than camping because the temperature had taken a plunge and it was too cold to sleep in the van at night. The man may have been tight with his money, but he sure wasn't going to stay up all night, shivering.

We crossed over the Pyrenees the next day, a mountain range separating Spain from France. We climbed higher and higher as we made our way through the mountain chain, with the weather quickly deteriorating. We turned a corner into a wall of blustery snow, whipping over the windshield and making visibility a real problem. Uncle Hugh asked me to help guide him to stay on the road as he was having a hard time focusing on both the road and the way ahead.

"You're drifting to the left!"

"Now make your way to the right!"

"Do you see the big bend coming up?!"

I needn't have told him to slow down, as he was barely doing 40 kilometres an hour. We were once again partaking in a harrowing mountain drive, and you could see it in his white knuckles and in his eyes that had become the size of saucers. Cresting the peak, we finally began our descent, with the usually unreligious Uncle Hugh muttering, "Thank God!" under his breath.

The relief was short-lived, however; the snow that we had somewhat gotten used to turned to freezing rain. Uncle Hugh kept chugging along down the steep mountain roads, slip-sliding every which way in a horrendously terrifying manner. My teenage self just took it as it came, but looking back on it now, I have no idea why he didn't just pull over and wait it out a bit.

Despite all odds, we made it down safely into Andorra, a tiny independent country nestled between Spain and France. We didn't stop there, already running late, but we did note the ancient architecture and dark grey stones of the buildings there, many from the days of Charlemagne.

The capital, Andorra La Vella, was cradled in a huge valley between two mountain ranges. We again had to ascend over the next range, and fortunately, the weather cooperated with us this time and the going was much easier. Before we knew it, we were descending into France.

So far during our travels we had crossed a number of borders, including going from Europe to Africa, and never had any issues. We were always asked rudimentary questions and then waved through. This time something was very different. The French border guard eyed us suspiciously and asked us many questions about where we'd been, how long had we stayed, who had we been in contact and who was I and what relationship did I have with Hugh? We were asked to pull into the inspection area. We were met by two no-nonsense guards who asked us to exit the vehicle and go inside the building. We watched out the window as they proceeded to empty our camper, piling everything unceremoniously onto the pavement. After a thorough search they came inside and asked us multiple more questions and then simply said that we were free to leave. Uncle Hugh was very indignant on having to reload the camper and cursed them continuously until we were finished. We often questioned what that was all about and why us. We even wondered if there was a connection to our African incident with the broken hood latch and the drugs found in Bob and Patricia's camper. Or just possibly a random search, but we will never know.

Chapter 7

With no harm done we quickly put the incident behind us and carried on with our travels.

The scenery was spectacular, with huge vistas of the valleys and foothills below us, and with many deep gorges to traverse. The countryside eventually levelled out and we were now making our way through beautiful southern France, with green rolling hills, picturesque farmlands, and old stone buildings.

Driving northeast, we eventually arrived in Carcassonne, a medieval walled city and fortress situated on a hilltop overlooking the surrounding countryside. The fortress there seemed perfectly preserved and was still inhabited by some 20,000 people who all lived within its walls. We drove the paved road up to the walls and were stopped at a red light before entering the narrow, one-lane passage through the gates. Uncle Hugh informed me that before the paved road, the gate once had a drawbridge spanning a full moat that surrounded the castle walls.

I was delighted, once again mentally storming the castle walls with a besieging force whilst simultaneously playing the side of the defenders. My imagination ran wild as we entered the walled city and drove down narrow twisting cobblestone streets, past ancient houses and businesses, putting myself in the shoes of a medieval peasant, troubadour, knight, or king. If you plucked the cars off the street, it was no stretch of the imagination to picture yourself as part of a real medieval city.

Once we found parking, we strolled around the city, soaking in the colourful scenery and electric atmosphere, finding the people there to be very friendly and welcoming. We found a nice hotel with comfortable rooms where Uncle Hugh promptly went to sleep after a dull dinner, likely exhausted from his death-defying drive through the mountains. I stayed awake in bed, arms behind my head, dreaming of charging through the streets of Carcassonne on a fiery steed, in full armour and lance in hand.

The morning saw Uncle Hugh awake and in a terrible mood. He had seemingly developed laryngitis overnight and was gnashing his teeth and whining about being ill to the point where colourful Carcassonne began to turn to a sickly grey.

Under the guise of helpfulness, I offered to go find him some medicine so I could escape the 'bear with a sore tooth' bemoaning his fate so loudly. After leaving him with a nice cup of herbal tea, I went outside and took off down the cobbled streets to explore and find medicine.

I roved around a bit, finding several pharmacies, but they were all closed on Monday mornings, and wouldn't be opening until 2:00 pm. Returning to the hotel, I broke the news, but Uncle Hugh brushed it aside and said he didn't need medicine anyway. Instead, we'd go for a walk, and that would clear up anything that was bothering him. It seemed like he'd decided that he was stronger than laryngitis and wasn't going to let it stop him.

I was game, so we went back out to the streets and began strolling them for quite some time, making our way up along the walls, towers, and turrets. I was having the time of my life; this city was a boy's dream with every corner turned offering something new and exciting. Uncle Hugh shuffled along ponderously, saying nothing at all for once.

After a time, dark clouds began to roll in with a cold bleak wind that very much matched Uncle Hugh's mood. The sky suddenly turned very black and ominous, and Uncle Hugh stopped dead in his tracks and declared that we were going back to the hotel NOW. We rushed back to the hotel and arrived around dinnertime, just before the sky broke and the rain came bucketing down.

Uncle Hugh suggested we eat at the hotel again and we were served exactly the same dull meal as the night before; a chicken dish covered in stodgy sauce. Calling the waiter over, Uncle Hugh informed him that he was not at all pleased with the lousy food and lack of atmosphere in the dining room. Like it was the waiter's fault. We left, once more not leaving a tip, and I could feel the glare of the waiter burning holes into our backs on the way out.

By this point Uncle Hugh was feeling put out, really bad, just awful, fully terrible, downright nasty, vile, foul, dreadful, and horrid. I know this because he repeated it to me over and over again. He complained about everything: the room was too small, the window faced the wrong way, the lamps were too dim, the bed was too stiff, the carpet garish, the staff useless, the water pressure abysmal, the colours of the room red while he preferred green. The food stank, he wanted a new room, the city wasn't what it used to be, France was a letdown, and his company was questionable. He complained and complained until he complained himself into a somnolent stupor and eventually passed out.

Finally, some peace and quiet! I'd never known a full-grown man to be such a crybaby and was dreading the griping I'd have to endure the next day. Uncle Hugh was really trying his best to ruin what was my favourite city so far this trip.

I woke up the next morning, hearing him move around the room. Wincing, I looked up at him, fully expecting to be drowned in a renewed fit of griping, but instead, he smiled and asked if I was going to sleep in all day. What a transformation! It appeared that he was feeling fine again and was back to his glib self.

We walked back to the walls of the city again as Uncle Hugh seemed to hardly remember being there the day before. This time he lectured me the entire walk, proving he was back to normal, discussing Medieval life and warfare. I listened intently, hoping to glean more details to flesh out my colourful imaginings and fantasies.

I peered over the walls, through a gap in the crenellations, and saw scores of Spanish knights attacking the city. Stones rained down upon them, and defenders poured cauldrons of boiling oil down the machicolations and onto the hapless besiegers. The sky repeatedly darkened with thousands of arrows, falling down to thud into shields and armour to the accompaniment of anguished cries, while cannons boomed, billowing smoke over the ramparts.

Making my way down into the main courtyard, I got onto my trusty steed and retrieved my shield and lance. Calling to the guards to open the gates, I couched my lance and thundered across the drawbridge, leading my men in an epic sortie to break the siege and liberate Carcassonne from the attackers.

What a glorious time to be alive!

Uncle Hugh reminded me of the stench, poverty, deplorable living conditions, and the lack of toilet paper that came along with medieval life, but I brushed that aside, keeping my fantasies untarnished by tedious detail. I couldn't believe how lucky I was to be exploring this wondrous city.

All too soon it was time to leave though, and I watched mighty Carcassonne slowly disappear behind me as we drove towards our next destination.

As we were checking out of the hotel before we left Carcassonne, Uncle Hugh asked the staff if there were any other beautiful castles in the area. They conferred with each other in French, then let us know about an unbelievable castle in Castres, about an hour's drive away.

We arrived in Castres and drove around looking for the castle but couldn't seem to find it. Castles are usually on the highest point of an area and can generally be seen for miles, so we thought it odd that this one was being so shy. After driving around for a while, we stopped and asked some locals about the beautiful castle and where we could find it. They looked at us quizzically and laughed, saying there was no castle here, or anywhere near here. If we wanted to see a castle, we should go to Carcassonne, about an hour's drive south.

Uncle Hugh spit and spluttered, while I shook my head ruefully. The hotel staff had led us astray after too much of Uncle Hugh's miserly ways and complaining! I had to chalk it up to them, that was a good prank. Uncle Hugh wasn't feeling as generous though and started complaining about the hotel anew.

We drove on to the city of Nîmes, giving the wretched city of Montpellier a wide, wide berth. Every time we saw a sign pointing towards that fateful city, Uncle Hugh would grimace and mutter, "Never again. I will never step foot in that cursed city ever again!" He'd push down harder on the gas, driving much faster than usual in a strange attempt to get past the city, almost as if he were afraid it would lock us in a tractor beam and suck us back in for more punishment.

We arrived in Nîmes, and Uncle Hugh did his customary sighing and face-touching routine as we walked through the ancient Roman architecture that the city is known for. We bought tickets and entered the 2000-year-old Roman amphitheatre in the historic downtown. This was the world's best-preserved amphitheatre, two-tiered, and impressive in its size and condition. Uncle Hugh described how the building was designed for acoustics – the Romans, with no loudspeakers or microphones, ensured the paying customers would be able to not only see, but hear everything that happened in the center of the amphitheatre.

We also visited the Maison Carée, a white limestone Roman temple that was also 2000 years old and remarkably preserved. The city had a very different feel to it than the medieval Carcassonne.

The weather was relatively fair, so we decided to find a campsite for the night. We found one just outside of the city, but after setting it up, we quickly discovered that it was quite possibly one of the worst campgrounds in the world. The campground was run down and full of decrepit trailers that I assumed were abandoned until I saw people moving in and out of them. The people staying on the campground seemed to be living there and were very obviously quite poor, dirty and with torn and dishevelled clothing.

Hordes of kids ran around the grounds, making noise and getting into trouble. Uncle Hugh wasn't a fan of children and he watched them with leery eyes.

"Gypsies," he announced. He made it clear that this place was far below the likes of us and that we wouldn't be leaving our camper for any reason other than to use the restrooms.

We did just that, spending the night inside and talking to no one, while Uncle Hugh repeatedly pulled the curtains aside to glare out the windows.

We left the next morning in a rush; apparently another campground not worth paying for. Uncle Hugh said he wouldn't have paid five cents to spend the night at this dump, so we vacated the premises without paying, leaving the owners a little poorer than they were already.

We left Nîmes and drove the short distance to the Pont du Gard, an incredible three-levelled Roman aqueduct that still carries water to the city to this day. The ducts themselves were about 6 feet high and we were able to peer over into them and see the incredibly tight stonework that didn't allow any water to escape through the cracks. The Romans were amazing architects and their accomplishments like this Pont du Gard are astonishing even by today's standards.

We found a campground nearby that was completely the opposite of the last one we'd spent the night at. A river lined with huge oak trees ran through the campground and everything was picturesque and beautiful. I flew our Canadian flag by running a rope over the branch of an oak and sat back, blissfully enjoying the beauty of Southern France.

I suddenly got it into my head that Uncle Hugh would try to pull another fast one on the owners of this campground in the morning and leave without paying and I just couldn't handle the thought. Not in this beautiful place!

Luckily the Canadian flag did its work and a couple who spoke English wandered over and asked where in Canada we were from. Uncle Hugh instantly replied Toronto, despite all of his usual vitriol for the place.

The couple, Fred and Ria, were from Springfield, Illinois and stuck around to chat a bit. Before we knew it, we had shared dinner and wine and were getting into the whisky as the sun set. Fred was a history teacher and Ria was a social worker, which had Uncle Hugh giddy and he stepped up his boasting to be sure to impress them.

The conversation focused a lot on the political turmoil in Spain, particularly around Franco and his socialist government. Uncle Hugh was optimistic that they would soon lose their civil war, and if it wasn't for the "God-damned Germans", they wouldn't have ever come to power in the first place. He even went so far as to say that he was considering joining the ranks of the Republicans and fighting the "commies" there in Spain.

I don't know if it was the whisky talking, or if he was just trying to impress his new friends, but I couldn't even imagine him holding a gun, let alone fighting in a battle. I smiled to myself as I pictured Uncle Hugh guiding a tour of battle-hardened leftist forces on a tour through the Prado, and seeing them die off one by one from boredom.

The night was pleasant enough, but I felt out of my depth in the political conversation as I knew absolutely nothing about it. I did rest easy though, knowing that there was no way Uncle Hugh would try to flee the campground without paying just in case this couple caught wind of him doing it.

I woke up with sunlight streaming through the windows of the camper. Uncle Hugh was still sleeping, so I took a walk around the campground, meandering my way down to the river where the sun was streaming through the leaves of the big oaks.

I strolled around and reflected on the conversation from the previous evening. Adults, it seemed, were forever trying to one-up and outdo each other in conversation. I guess it was all an attempt to impress each other and if nothing else, made for interesting discussions. It still took much less to impress me. The simple fact that Fred and Ria were from Illinois, a place I hadn't even heard of up until this point, was impressive to me. Little did I realize the indelible impact that this trip was having on me and how it would shape me, and my conversations with other adults, in the future.

Making my way back to the camper, I found Uncle Hugh crawling out of bed and looking nasty with a bad hangover. He squinted, scowled, griped, and growled as he was wont to do in these situations, so I made him a cup of tea which calmed him down. I made breakfast and then packed everything up while he remained sitting and mostly silent, which I didn't mind at all.

As we left the campground, he gave me a handful of French notes and told me to go pay the owners, which I was more than happy to do.

We continued driving east into Cannes, where we left the highway for the Boulevard de la Croisette, a road sandwiched between an endless row of shops and restaurants on the north side and endless stretches of busy beaches on the south side, where the Mediterranean could be seen extended beyond the horizon.

From there we headed inland to drive through the perfume fields, which were thousands of acres of cultivated flowers, redolent of the finest perfumes, which is what they were grown for. All of these flowers would be transformed into a few gallons of perfume, which they'd then sell by the ounce. We cranked open our windows to let the intoxicating scent waft through the camper and delight our senses.

Though I was enjoying the flowers, I found myself distracted by a toothache that wouldn't seem to go away. I had hoped it would just take care of itself, but it seemed to be getting worse. I had hidden it from Uncle Hugh until this point, thinking that he might become angry or that I'd have to go home to visit and dentist and that it would ruin the trip.

Luckily, Uncle Hugh took the news with a maturity he seemed to show half of the time we spent together.

"No need to worry my boy!" he said, probably ascertaining my fears and unwillingness to be a bother, "We'll find a dentist in Nice and take care of it!"

Stopping at a gas station, Uncle Hugh chatted with the owner and asked if he could recommend a dentist in nearby Nice. The nice man dialed up his dentist straight away and Uncle Hugh had an appointment sorted out for me within the hour.

Upon arrival, we couldn't find anywhere to park. Worried that I'd miss the appointment, Uncle Hugh assured me he could find parking while I ran up to the waiting room. I was dubious as he hadn't shown much skill for parking yet and relied on me quite heavily to navigate him to parking areas and guide the camper into spots. Not having any other option though, I agreed and rushed up to find the dentist's office.

Arriving at the address, I found myself at a patisserie, or bake shop. When asked about the missing dentist, the owners shook their heads bemusedly and denied that there had ever been a dentist here. When I showed the address, they laughed and said, "No monsieur, you're at the wrong end of the boulevard!"

Many of the streets in this area would change names or numbers halfway along, and it looked like we'd found ourselves at the wrong end of the street. "Oh shit!" I thought to myself, "I'm going to be late and I have no idea where Uncle Hugh is."

Instead of looking for him, I ran down the street as fast as I could, keeping my eyes open for the dentist's office. After about 21 blocks, the street name changed and I finally found the office. Bursting into the waiting room huffing and puffing, I found that I was only a few minutes late. The dentist pleasantly took me to the chair and did an assessment, finding two problematic teeth. As he drilled and filled, I began to think about Uncle Hugh. Oh no! How was he ever going to find me?!

He had no idea where I was and I had no idea where he was. What if I never found him again? How could I survive here without him? My panicked thoughts served to distract me from the uncomfortable dental operation at least, and it was over before I knew it.

I wandered out into the waiting area and told the receptionist that I'd sit and wait for my uncle to arrive. She raised her eyebrows at me and I spluttered that she didn't need to worry and that he would pay for the work. She seemed very skeptical, and I wondered if she might possibly have caught wind of his famous stinginess. I anxiously waited for what seemed like an eternity and Uncle Hugh finally swept through the door.

The look on his face upon seeing me was heartwarming and I'm sure I mirrored a similar look on my own face. He paid the receptionist and we walked back outside while he regaled me with the tale of his side of the story.

After finally finding a parking spot, he squeezed the van in (remember, he couldn't turn his head to properly check his mirrors and blind spots) and paid a pretty hefty fee for the spot. Arriving at the "dentist's office" he too found himself in front of the bake shop. Going inside, he received the same instructions that I had. Instead of running pell-mell down the street, he went back and retrieved the van, driving it the 21 blocks to where I was. He once again couldn't find parking and circled the neighbourhood several times before finding a lot, where he had to carefully squeeze the van into a tiny spot and pay another exorbitant price to park. He then walked to the dentist and found me waiting there to his relief.

Usually, he would have been soured by such a stressful experience, but I think that he was so glad to have found me that he had remained in a good mood, which I was thankful for. We laughed as we exchanged our horror stories.

He suggested we grab a drink since he had already paid for parking, and I agreed. We had another laugh as I drooled out half of my beer since my mouth was still completely numb. We had passed a casino near the bar, and he suggested that we go pay it a visit.

I was surprised that he would be willing to gamble, but I agreed, excited to see what a casino was all about. We entered the building but were stopped by security when we went to enter the actual gambling rooms. I was too young to go in unfortunately and would have to stay in the hall. Uncle Hugh was concerned, but I assured him I'd be fine and that he should go have fun.

I thought that maybe I'd be able to sneak into the room at some point, but the security was too tight, with someone always guarding each door. Uncle Hugh was only gone for an hour or so and came back out to retrieve me, saying he'd only spent $10. When pressed, he said he'd had fun but it didn't seem like he wanted to talk about it. My imagination ran wild with what it must have been like in those rooms – fancy women in cocktail dresses with elegant cigarette holders and men in suits gambling away their fortunes. I'd just have to go back when I was older.

It began to rain, so we decided to spend the night in a hotel instead of camping. I was pleased as it was a very comfortable room, and they served a delicious French dinner on crisp white tablecloths with table service and fancy desserts.

The next morning, we left Nice and headed into the tiny country of Monaco. Finding a place to park in the city of Monte Carlo was very difficult and expensive, as the city has the densest population in the world. It was a very modern city with huge hotels and apartment buildings seemingly stacked on top of each other.

Monaco has more millionaires than Europe has Madonna and Child paintings (well, maybe not THAT many millionaires) and you could definitely tell by the expensive-looking homes, yachts, and cars.

Much of the waterfront was fenced off as they were preparing for the Grand Prix, which would take place in a couple of weeks. After watching the preparations for a while, we walked up the thousand steps to the Palace of Prince and Princess Ranier. Grace Kelly was of course the princess at the time and everyone knew her as she was a famous movie star who had quit to become a princess. It was all very beautiful and breathtaking. The amount of wealth in the palace was unimaginable and I couldn't even begin to think of what it was like to live with that kind of money.

I looked back down to the roadway and pictured myself racing through the streets in a fancy car without a care in the world. Nah. Probably wasn't going to happen.

Chapter 8

We decided to cross the border and camp in Italy for the night, so we left Monaco and crossed the Italian border into the province of Imperia, a hilly region that looked similar to where we'd just been in Monaco and France.

We stopped at the tourist station just across the border and Uncle Hugh picked up a tourist coupon booklet and some gas coupons. He really wanted to stop and see the many architectural tourist attractions that Italy had to offer and wanted to save as much money as possible.

At the register, the booklet came up to 30,000 lira. I almost jumped out of my skin and Uncle Hugh's tightwad brain nearly shut down. His hands shook and he began sweating as he counted out lira to the man behind the till. He handed over 3000 lira, but the man said, "No. 30,000 lira." He counted out more money and handed it over to the clerk, who shook his head and said, "No, that's not right."

Despite Uncle Hugh's brilliance in most subjects, math wasn't really his strong point and he hadn't figured out the exchange yet. We found out later that the exchange was about 580 lira for every American dollar, so the book was actually only about $50. This was going to take some time to get used to. The Italian banknotes were very confusing, with 1000 lira notes, 10,000, and even 100,000. It was hard to keep track of it all. Instead of stopping and thinking about it rationally though, Uncle Hugh jumped to the conclusion that the man was trying to fleece us.

"Just like in Spain," he growled, "you people are all the same, picking on innocent tourists! Do you think I was born yesterday?! You know, we're Canadians and we don't enjoy being cheated. Maybe you enjoy ripping off *Americans* and maybe they deserve it, but us *Canadians* have never hurt anyone and we therefore take offence at being treated so poorly!"

The poor bewildered clerk raised his hands to calm Uncle Hugh down. "Sir, sir. I was merely trying to tell you that you overpaid. Here is your change and the booklet. Have a nice day and enjoy your stay in Italy."

Uncle Hugh stood up straight, brusquely thanked the man, spun on his heel and left the store. I followed him, waving goodbye to the clerk, who shot me a smile and a wink.

Not done yet, Uncle Hugh got into the van and launched into a tirade. "You just can't trust these Italians; they think they can rip everyone off. Well, they won't get me goddamnit!"

I just felt embarrassed. For me, Uncle Hugh, and the poor clerk.

We drove down the Italian coastline, thoroughly enjoying the scenery. The Mediterranean and the sky vied with each other for who could be bluer and the rugged rockiness of the shore added its own drama.

We eventually spotted a campground that was right on the sea and we decided to pack it in for the night. Uncle Hugh said he was eager to get into some nice Italian wine, so he made me a deal. "James, you stay here and cook supper, and I'll go find us some good Italian wine we can share."

Sounded like a good deal to me! I made spaghetti and spiced it up with lots of garlic and oregano, which I thought would go just perfectly with the sea, the view, and the wine. We had an excellent night eating too much spaghetti and drinking too much wine. I slept like a baby that night and when I eventually woke up, it was to a beautiful sunrise over the radiant waters of the Mediterranean Sea.

We reluctantly left the campground and its incredible views only to eventually arrive in the most beautiful and picturesque little seaside village called Portofino. Bright multi-coloured houses hugged the nearly circular bay, which was filled with sailboats, fishing boats, and yachts of all sizes.

We parked and got out to explore, marching up and down steep staircases and peering down cliffs and terraced gardens to the houses directly below. Being in such a picturesque place, you know Uncle Hugh would be taking lots of pictures, complete with his ridiculous photo-taking rituals.

I would see a nice shot and take my camera out and snap a picture, but not Uncle Hugh. He would step forward with the camera held to his eye, then step back… to the left… to the right… forward again, and THEN he would start his ritual. It was hard for me to endure this over and over again and I knew my impatience showed when he would eventually snarl at me, saying I was being rude and ungrateful. I'm not sure anyone, let alone a fourteen-year-old boy, could have been patient with the man while he was taking pictures.

We found another campground nearby for the night, again right on the sea. Following procedure, I raised the Canadian flag over the camper, proclaiming to all who may be curious that we were not hated Americans, but nothing more than humble, friendly Canadians, beloved by all. It was funny though, I thought to myself, how many humble and friendly Americans we'd already met on this trip.

Before I knew it a couple from New Zealand, Victor and Donna, strolled up to the campsite. They were in their 30s and doing a European tour for a few months like we were. They were very friendly, but talked quickly and sure enjoyed the Italian wine that was brought out!

We had a wonderful night full of stories and laughter, fueled by copious amounts of wine. The next morning, we stopped and said goodbye to them, hoping that we'd meet up again at some point since we were both heading in vaguely the same direction.

The coastal road to Pisa was very windy and narrow, with lots of tight tunnels and hairpin turns. Oncoming traffic would pass by within inches of the camper and the view over the side of the cliffs that we hugged was gut-clenching. To add to our stress, there were constant turnoffs into towns and villages that didn't even appear on our maps, and the signs were confusing or non-existent.

After a few hours of driving, we'd found ourselves lost three times already, turning down roads that eventually wound up as goat paths or dead ends. The map just didn't show the forks in the road that kept popping up and I never knew whether to tell Uncle Hugh to turn right or left. He had zero patience for this and chastised me repeatedly for not doing a better job. It was unfair since I wasn't completely to blame; he'd often argue with me about the turns and take the opposite turn to the one I'd recommended and we'd end up at a dead end.

"You have to pay more attention James!" he'd complain, turning the van around and trying again.

After one particularly bad outburst where he bawled out that I was getting us nowhere, I just stopped talking altogether. I sat and stewed in my seat, looking out the window and left the old man to figure it out for himself.

He shrugged and muttered that it was fine since I couldn't seem to navigate anyways and kept up a quiet litany the whole time, which infuriated me further.

We approached a long 2-mile tunnel that was tight and pitch black. We rolled through slowly, Uncle Hugh's white knuckles on the steering wheel, trying not to bump the side walls of the tunnel. Whenever a car came by, he would wince and somehow grab the steering wheel tighter.

I developed a plan to get even with him for his behaviour; when the next car came by, I clapped my hands as loud as I possibly could in one loud CLAP. We made it past the oncoming car, but Uncle Hugh nearly lost control of the van, screeching back and forth through the tunnel. He somehow managed to miss the walls, which was good since we likely would have pinballed down the rest of the tunnel until there was nothing left of the van.

"What was that?" he screeched, "Did we pop a tire? Did something in the engine go?"

I immediately felt awful for my impulsive action. Why would I do something like that? I could have gotten us killed!

I sheepishly told him that there was nothing wrong and that it was my fault.

"Your fault?" he spluttered, "No, how could it be? There must be something wrong with the engine. Why would you say you did it?"

I meekly told him that I had clapped and that I was really sorry for having done it.

He told me that that was an awful thing to do but he was glad that I apologized for it. I think he was still reeling from the near accident and the thought that the camper might break down on these ridiculous roads. Part of his acceptance of my apology probably had a lot to do with the relief of not having to pay or deal with a broken-down van in a small village in Italy.

I stayed quiet after that, contrite and embarrassed about my childish prank, and we drove for a while in silence. Quietly, we soaked up the incredible scenery, which was a balm for our moods. Houses in every colour imaginable hugged the seaside cliffs and the Mediterranean shone in all of its glory.

In the silence, our friendship seemed to mend and we were soon pointing out beautiful sights to each other and once again enjoying the drive.

We decided to stop a bit early for the night when we encountered another beautiful-looking campground next to the highway. No sooner had we set up when Victor and Donna came strolling into our campsite like some sort of déjà vu. They pulled some lira out of their pockets, handed it to me and said, "Jimmy, why don't you go fetch us some wine?"

I ran over to the market and was feeling very grown up as I searched through and picked out four bottles of what looked like good wine. I paid for them as if I had been doing it my whole life and walked back to the campsite taller than when I had left.

We had another wonderful night, laughing and telling stories with the New Zealanders. One story that didn't come up was the misadventure we'd had that day. Instead, it got buried and never mentioned again, which I think, was best for everyone.

The next day we made our way into Pisa to see the famous leaning tower. It did lean at a strange angle, and it was a strange sight, but I was more impressed with the Cathedral behind it, which was absolutely beautiful.

Made of white marble, it had many columns and statues and I found it all very impressive. We strolled around the ground taking pictures of the tower, the Cathedral, and the other beautiful buildings. I had lots of time to explore while Uncle Hugh took photos. It was much better in a situation like this where I could move around and didn't necessarily have to wait for him.

After he was done, he suggested we climb the tower and take some photos from the top. Shrugging, I agreed and we walked over to the tower. As we approached, a man in a black curator's uniform spread his hands across the entrance and said, "Sorry gentlemen, there will be no more visitors today. We are limiting the number of visitors here and also it looks like it is going to rain soon."

Well, Uncle Hugh stared wide-eyed at the man before launching into his tirade, "We have travelled over five THOUSAND miles to see and climb the leaning tower of Pisa and now we arrive and you have the AUDACITY to tell us no?!"

"Well, I'm terribly sorry sir, but those are the rules."

"Rules, rules, rules. What rules?!" exclaimed Uncle Hugh, "We came all this way to climb the tower and so we shall! Now step aside man!"

The bewildered man looked around for support, but only saw a group of tourists crowding around, all nodding their heads that yes, they should be allowed up the tower.

The man threw his hands up in disgust and stepped away from the doorway, speaking in rapid-fire Italian. Switching to English, he gestured into the doorway and said, "By all means, help yourself in. Go ahead and climb the tower, I do not care anymore!" With that he stalked away, still muttering to himself in Italian.

Uncle Hugh explained to me as we climbed the tower stairs that after such a battle to get into the place, he would be remiss to not give me the history of the battlegrounds!

Built in 1173 and finished in 1372, this medieval tower was erected in the Romanesque style which was popular at the time. It began to lean before the construction was even complete, to the dismay of the builders.

After winning the stand-off with the curator, Uncle Hugh was in quite the mood, beaming and telling me about every brick and stone in the place. We got to the top and looked out upon the Square of Miracles – quite an impressive view. Uncle Hugh began his picture-taking preparations as the rest of the tourists began filing their way back down the stairs. After a while it began raining, just like the curator had warned, and the marble floor became treacherously slippery.

I told Uncle Hugh that we'd better get a move on, but he shot me a glare and said, "Just one more photo."

The sky had darkened an ominous black which seemed to be causing him some trouble with the settings on his camera. "Just one more my boy, I can't seem to get the aperture set correctly."

He took out his light meter, then looked into his camera, then back to the light meter, and once more back to the camera. Nodding his head once with finality he exclaimed, "Okay, I'm done!" and we headed towards the stairs, just as the rain started really coming down.

Halfway to the stairs, one of his feet went out from under him and he began to slide down the angle of the floor to the lower side of the leaning building. I thought I was going to watch the man slide right out of the tower and to his death, but he caught himself with windmilling arms and shot me an alarmed look. He went to take another step and slowly spun, sliding inexorably towards the edge. I carefully slid my way over to him and took hold of his hand. There were no railings in the building and nothing to get traction on, but I held onto his arm tightly and we edged our way towards the stairs.

Wet and dishevelled, we finally made it down the stairs, one slippery step at a time, to the bottom where a smiling curator standing under an umbrella greeted us. "I told you so Senor..." he said smugly.

Once safely out of earshot, Uncle Hugh stamped his foot and exclaimed, "Damn Italians, think they know everything!" What a sore loser.

Driving from Pisa to Florence, we took our time and stopped at a number of small towns along the way. One of those towns was Pistoia, a very old hilltop city full of colourful medieval buildings and architecture. We spent quite a lot of time walking around these towns and taking pictures, Uncle Hugh stomping around, obviously still upset about his run-in with the curator in Pisa.

Deciding on a campground for the night that we found in one of our guidebooks, we began to head there, with Uncle Hugh still in a pissy mood.

He immediately began questioning the route that I'd chosen, saying that my directions were all messed up, and began taking his own turns against my directions. Now, I'd been navigating for some time by this point and had become very adept at map reading, foreign signage, and route decisions. Uncle Hugh was obviously just being petty and argumentative again despite knowing that I spent every day telling him where to go with very few errors.

Becoming instantly lost, Uncle Hugh drove in circles for well over an hour forestalling any of my recommendations with a curt, "I KNOW where I'm going."

Eventually, he had to give up and finally demanded, "Tell me how to get the hell out of here!"

I took over navigation again and we were pulling into the campground within 10 minutes. Not willing to lose twice in one day, he said to me upon our arrival, "Now if only you had given me the right directions at the BEGINNING, we would have been here hours ago. Try to do better James!"

I felt hurt by his rudeness, but I'd been developing a thicker skin whilst travelling with him and I was growing tougher daily. I simply glared at him, while silently cultivating a plan to get even with him.

First though, we had to do our daily chores, setting up the camper and making dinner. I made spaghetti again, but this time with some fried mushrooms. That and a nice bottle of red wine did a lot to calm us down, and we ended up having quite a nice evening. Although we fought often, we usually forgot about our spats soon after and were able to travel together in harmony. I did find myself beginning to collect grudges though. There was only so much I could be chastised without any actual fault before I developed a big chip on my shoulder.

We woke up to a glorious sunny morning at the campground and it seemed that Uncle Hugh had moved on from yesterday's embarrassments and was in a great mood. Rubbing his hands together, he said, "James my boy, we are going to have a fabulous time today in Florence. You're certainly going to learn a lot!"

And learn a lot I did!

We started with the Uffizi Gallery where I was happy to see far fewer Madonna and Child paintings than in other galleries we'd visited. Instead, we strolled through the halls, viewing paintings from the Middle Ages to the Renaissance, all of the way to the Modern period. The building, constructed in 1560, had famous works from Botticelli, Leonardo, Raffaello, and Michelangelo, as well as a collection of ancient statues that once belonged to the Medici family. Uncle Hugh gave me his customary private and very detailed tour of the gallery, and I found myself actually really enjoying it. I must have been getting cultured.

The next stop was the Palazzo Vecchio, which still acts as Florence's (or Firenze as the locals called it) town hall. It was built in 1299 in the Romanesque style of architecture. A magnificent building, it dominated the town square with its crenellated roof and tall clock tower. The square itself held a copy of Michelangelo's David and multiple medieval buildings, all of which were a pleasure to look at.

We crossed the Ponte Vecchio (Old Bridge), which was an ancient two-story bridge, lined with shops and milling tourists. Tourists, from all over the world, loudly purchased the jewelry, art, and souvenirs that the vendors peddled. The bridge's upper level connected the Palazzo Vecchio with the Palazzo Pitti directly and was used by the noblewomen of the Medici family so they didn't have to comingle with the commoners, who were relegated to the lower level of the bridge. This was actually the only bridge not destroyed by fleeing Nazi troops in WWII, which I felt thankful for as I admired its robust elegance.

We made our way back over to the Cathedral of Santa Maria del Fiore, but when we arrived, we were both feeling pretty exhausted from everything we'd already seen that day. We decided to do the Cathedral the next day and instead stopped at a street-side restaurant and ordered a much-needed beer. We sat and enjoyed the beers, watching the throngs of people passing by, all enthralled with the beautiful city of Florence like we were.

On the way back to the campground, Uncle Hugh declared that we'd be enjoying a very special dinner that night, but wouldn't elaborate, smiling and pleased with his little secret.

We got back to the campground and Uncle Hugh told me to shower and put on my nice clothes. I began to suspect what he was hiding from me. While we were travelling in France, Uncle Hugh had told me several times that he would bring me to a REAL Italian restaurant, where I could experience REAL Italian food and the REAL atmosphere of a proper Italian joint. It looked like this would be the night, and I silently agreed with him, what better place to go to a nice Italian restaurant than beautiful Florence?

Once cleaned and dressed, I found Uncle Hugh in his suit, freshly shaven and reading his guidebook. He dramatically pointed to the page he was looking at and proclaimed, "James my boy, I've found the PERFECT and REAL Italian restaurant for us to go to tonight!"

We headed back into the city and I noticed that Uncle Hugh was already putting on airs. It was subtle at this point, but I'd come to know the man well and I could just tell that tonight was going to be a nightmare!

Walking through the front doors, we were greeted by the maître d', asking if he could find us a seat. Uncle Hugh ignored him at first, looking imperiously around the restaurant. He mustn't have liked what he saw, since his lip curled in disdain and his bushy eyebrows pulled down into an exaggerated frown.

"No," he replied to the man, "we would like to see a menu first." Either he wanted to make extra sure that he'd chosen the right place, or he was locked in a power struggle with the poor bemused man.

"Of course, sir, right away."

Uncle Hugh took his time, peering over the menu, obviously going over every single menu item. When he encountered something he didn't know, he would push the menu into the maître d's face, pointing to the word and demanding, "What's this?"

"Beef, sir," or, "chicken, sir," he'd reply, and Uncle Hugh's frown would deepen.

When he finally reached the bottom of the menu, he read aloud, "Mancia per il servizio 15%." Perplexed, he asked, "What does this mean?"

The server, struggling to find the right words in English, replied, "Service, sir."

"What?"

"Uhh, table service, sir," the man replied, obviously getting nervous.

"Just what, pray tell, is table service?!"

"Like a charge for the table?"

I knew he was trying to say tip or gratuity, it was pretty obvious, but Uncle Hugh bulled on, acting like he had no idea what the man was getting at.

Finally, after much back and forth, Uncle Hugh exploded at the man, "Are you telling me that we have to pay a fee for using the damn table?!"

"Ah, yes, I guess so sir."

Then the tirade started.

"I've travelled all across the world- fifty countries, five continents – and I have NEVER heard the likes of this! This is downright PREPOSTEROUS! Totally unacceptable, and I sir, will NOT stand for it!" His glare would have scared off Mussolini himself.

The poor maître d' was flabbergasted and looked like he might just start crying. He obviously didn't know what to say and stood there dumbfounded. By this time, all of the staff and patrons of the restaurant were staring and the place had gone deadly silent.

I stood there looking at my feet and thinking that all of these people staring should count themselves lucky that Grand Emperor Hugh deigned to dine amongst the common folk at this very restaurant. What an embarrassment!

A sly smile began to grow on Uncle Hugh's face and I cringed, not knowing what was coming next, but sure it wasn't going to be pleasant.

"So, you're telling me," he said pontifically with his finger held in the air, "that if we WEREN'T to eat at a table, then we wouldn't have to pay this ridiculous service charge?"

The man, thinking he was seeing a way out of this horrid situation, fell for the bait. "Of course not, senor!"

"Well then, we'll be eating THERE!" and he whipped his finger around to point at a small bar set up for the waitstaff where they would stage dishes and plates, "And we will stand!"

I groaned, and the maître d' fell backwards as if struck. "No, sir, you cannot!" he exclaimed.

Not willing to give up after going so far, Uncle Hugh told the man, loudly so the entire restaurant could hear, "Oh yes, we can, and we are going to! Come James," he said, "follow me."

His nose in the air, he marched over to the bar, with me sheepishly in tow. The maître d' scurried along, wringing his hands, "No, please sir. Sir! No, you can't eat at this bar, please sir. Pleeease. NO!"

Ignoring him, Uncle Hugh stood at the bar, proud and erect. Giving up, the man made his way to the back room and soon a waiter came out to take our order. He must have lost a quick backroom lottery as to who would come out and serve this lunatic.

We were treated like any other seated customer; issued napkins, silverware, glassware, dinnerware, and even a candle for effect.

Acting like nothing was out of the ordinary, Uncle Hugh discussed the menu options with me and settled on spaghetti and meatballs since we were there to have a REAL and AUTHENTIC Italian restaurant dinner. He ordered a bottle of red from the wine menu and made sure the waiter knew to bring us the complimentary bread.

So, spaghetti, meatballs, bread, and wine were enjoyed by two men standing in the staff area, one older, in an English brown tweed suit, and the other just a teenager, with long hair, a bright blue suit with a see-through shirt, and hiking boots. We were quite the spectacle, but Uncle Hugh did his best to ignore all of the diners staring and talking about us.

He took his time finishing the meal and savouring the wine, then asked for a dessert menu as I inwardly groaned. The dessert was delicious though and he made sure to enjoy it, spooning small pieces into his mouth and thoughtfully chewing it at the pace of an ancient tortoise.

Finally finished, he made a point to loudly call for the cheque, staring through the waiter as if he didn't exist. Of course, he didn't leave a tip after all of the trouble he'd caused. He left the restaurant the same way that he came in, nose up in the air and ass cheeks pulled tight.

Not only was Uncle Hugh not embarrassed about the whole ordeal, but he was also actually incensed that the restaurant had the audacity to assume a 15% gratuity! Who were they, trying to pull one over on him?

I found that when he got his back up like that, he left reality and entered a place where his delusions of grandeur manifested into scenes of utter buffoonery. The problem was that when he snapped out of it, he mistook his delusions for reality. It was dreadfully embarrassing to be next to the man when he was acting like that, but I had nowhere to run and hide; I was stuck with him for better or for worse.

In the end, I got to experience an authentic Italian meal that I'll never forget. I bet the owners, staff, and patrons of that restaurant never forgot the strange pair that caused such a scene to avoid paying a measly 15% tip.

We spent the next two days in the beautiful city of Florence, taking in all of its glorious sights. We visited the incredible Cathedral and climbed the 464 steps up to the Dome, where we got a tremendous view of the city. We wandered through the Baptistry and all of the other old buildings surrounding the Cathedral. We stood in awe in front of the real statue of David, completely shocked by how realistic it was and wonderful in its perfection. We also visited the Medici Chapel with its elegant stonework, the Pitti Palace with its intricate paintings and tapestries, the Boboli Gardens with its topiary and ornate fountains, and the Bargello Museum with its fantastic suits of medieval armour. We toured the Sante Croze church, which holds the tombs of Michelangelo, Galileo, and Dante, among others. We walked and visited and toured and walked until it felt like we had experienced every single thing the city had to offer.

We felt that we had seen everything we needed to and were satisfied that we'd given Florence the justice she deserved. The city itself was a history lesson in medieval marvels and Uncle Hugh had been sure to flesh out all of the details.

Finally bidding Florence farewell, we drove a short five kilometres to Fiesole, a small town perched on a hilltop overlooking the metropolis of Florence. We parked and walked up the steep road to the pinnacle to get the very best vantage point. The panoramic view of Florence and the surrounding countryside was breathtaking. Uncle Hugh took his time taking an "award-winning" photo of the city he so deeply loved, and then we walked back to the van and took a slow drive through the center of town.

When I say slow drive, I mean slow. I jokingly entered into my journal at the time that we did the ten-minute drive in a record one and a half hours.

Leaving Fiesole, we headed for San Gimignano, another Tuscan hill town south of Florence. The whole way there, I had my face pressed to the window, taking in the gorgeous green-hued countryside. We passed forests and groves of cypress trees, light-green deciduous trees, and what I called cauliflower trees; dark green trees in the shape of a cauliflower floret.

We could see the seventeen towers of San Gimignano, each a different height, well before we arrived in the walled city. Apparently, the towers belonged to medieval families vying for power and prestige, each building a tower slightly taller than the last. We climbed one of the taller towers and took in the surrounding countryside. I thought to myself at the time that this was the most beautiful place I'd been as of yet and that I could easily see myself living there.

We found a nice campground outside of a town called Siena, so we set up our campsite, raised the Canadian flag, and left to check out the town. It was bustling and we asked around to see if something was going on. It turned out that the townsfolk had gathered to practice for the Palio, an annual horserace where ten riders, each representing a contrade, or city ward, raced bareback to much fanfare.

There were seventeen contrades in total, each one sporting different colours and emblems and each vying to be part of the final ten contrades who got to participate in the race. We saw many of the representatives of certain contrades parading through the city, complete with drummers, flag twirlers, and dancers. Driving through the city was impossible as throngs of people crowded the intersections and medieval cobbled streets. The whole scene reminded me of Romeo and Juliet and the colours flown by the rival families in that story.

We somehow managed to find a table at a crowded restaurant (Uncle Hugh graciously allowed us to sit this time) and we ordered a local specialty, Fettucine Cinta Senese Ragù, a delicious pasta made with a special breed of pig unique to Siena, and a nice bottle of red.

People-watching was a favourite pastime of Uncle Hugh's and I was beginning to see why – so many colourful locals and interesting tourists from all over the world. All of the pretty girls walking by certainly kept me patient as we sat there, too.

Leaving early the next morning, we drove to Assisi, the birthplace of St. Francis. There, we visited one of the oldest Gothic cathedrals in Italy, the beautiful Basilica Papale e Sacro Convento di San Francesco d'Assisi, named after Saint Francis and built in the 13th century.

Our timing was impeccable; the town was holding its annual Calendimaggio festival that celebrated the arrival of spring. Just like in Siena, pretty much all of the citizens participated and separated themselves into different factions that each had their own colours and emblems. Large groups were parading through the streets, practicing for the main festivities that would take place the next day. Uncle Hugh purchased tickets for several of the next day's events, as it promised to be a great show.

The crowded streets were sweltering, so we decided to head back to the campground where we'd set ourselves up to change and cool down a bit in the shade. The campground owners came by to chat and suggested that we eat at a great restaurant just down the road. They said that it was a real Italian place, not touristy and that we were sure to enjoy it.

We got dressed for dinner, then strolled down the road to where the campground owners had pointed us. We arrived at what seemed to be the mouth of a rock cave with the restaurant's sign tacked to the side. Uncle Hugh immediately wanted to turn around and find somewhere more suitable, but I managed to talk him out of it. Dinner in a cave? It sounded great!

I pulled my reluctant uncle into the mouth of the cave and we were both shocked to see the interior. Inside was a huge hall with 40-foot-long communal tables replete with dozens of chairs tucked in on both sides. A giant fireplace sat in the middle, belching flames and smoke up a hidden chimney. The lighting was deliberately turned down low and the whole atmosphere had a decidedly medieval flare to it. This place was awesome!

Still trepidatious, Uncle Hugh chose a chair at an empty table and I sat across from him. Before long, people began streaming in and the tables quickly filled up; we found ourselves sitting amongst a sea of boisterous strangers. Uncle Hugh summoned the waitress over and ordered some wine. She promptly came back with a large jug filled with wine and dropped it in the middle of the table. It wasn't clear who the wine was exactly for. When Uncle Hugh flagged her down again and asked, she replied in broken English that the wine was for everybody – it was community wine.

A consternated Uncle Hugh began questioning the earnest waitress, "Well, how do you know how much we drank? How are we going to be charged for this?"

She tried her best to explain that the wine bill would be split evenly amongst all of the diners at the table at the end of the meal.

Looking down the long table and doing a quick assessment of who would be drinking, Uncle Hugh whispered to me, "Make sure you drink more than your share, I'm not paying for everyone else's wine!"

You don't have to tell a fourteen-year-old twice to drink his fair share, and I went at it with gusto. Still, I had a very hard time keeping up with Uncle Hugh, who was making damn sure that he got his money's worth too.

Pretty soon everyone at the table was laughing and joking and becoming friends. The atmosphere was reminiscent of a hall in the king's castle, with everyone festively talking at once and laughing. I was thoroughly enjoying myself.

After a few glasses of wine, Uncle Hugh beckoned the waitress over again and asked if we could order. She shook her head, saying that everyone got the same thing and that it was all served together. Bemused, Uncle Hugh kept at the wine, which may have been the only thing keeping him at this less-than-conventional restaurant.

I looked over and saw the food cooking on the big fireplace in the middle of the room, cooking lots of meats and vegetables, but they were nowhere near done. We continued drinking wine for quite some time before dinner arrived and by that time, everyone was quite drunk and extremely hungry.

Eventually, we were served a full meal including some pork and beef shish kebabs that really stood out. All in all, it was a fantastic dinner and a wonderful evening.

Although the party was still bumping, we decided to leave around midnight, stumbling and weaving our way back to the campground and into our beds. We slept like logs but woke in the morning with splitting headaches. Battling nausea, I still found myself smiling; yes, this was an epic hangover, but the memory of the fun we had the night before made it all seem worth it. Judging by Uncle

Hugh's face, I'm not sure he shared the same sentiment.

We nursed our hangovers throughout the morning, then tried to dispel them with a hearty breakfast of fried eggs and potatoes accompanied by several cups of tea. A long shower at the modern campground facilities helped me towards re-establishing myself as a human again, feeling ready to take on the day. At last, we were ready to head into town and join in the festivities.

The streets held host to continuous parades of Medieval-costumed groups, waving flags, clapping hands, and re-enacting Medieval life and music. Donkeys, horses, sheep, and chickens were everywhere and it wasn't hard for my imagination to whisk me off to an earlier time. I was especially delighted with the drumming bands who marched by and I found myself getting lost in the electric atmosphere of it all.

My favourite part of the day was the concluding event, which was a crossbow competition. The crowd wildly cheered on competitors as they shot at bullseye targets. The tense competition ended in a draw and the good-natured crowd cheered and cheered, with me and Uncle Hugh cheering along with them.

It was a very memorable day that we both enjoyed immensely, despite the rough start. When the streets began to clear out, both of us quickly made our way back to the campsite and passed right out. We were absolutely exhausted!

Chapter 9

Leaving Assisi the next morning, we made our way to Rome, stopping on the way to make a call to Uncle Hugh's friends,the Turners. Mr. Turner and Uncle Hugh had worked together in the past as architects in Philadelphia and the Turners would be hosting us for our stay in Rome. We made it to their residence without much trouble and were quickly made welcome. They had two children, Holly aged 10 and Cory age 13.

Cory and I quickly hit it off and we were soon ensconced in his room, beginning a week-long Stratego campaign. I had never played the game before and Cory very much exploited my ignorance, annihilating my legions and winning game after game.

While I was setting up a cot in Cory's room, Mrs. Turner suggested I go grab my pillow from the van. She was shocked and appalled when I told her that I didn't have one and that I'd been sleeping on a sweater stuffed with other clothes for the entire trip. No, it wasn't all too comfortable, but it was perfectly fine. Mrs. Turner didn't seem to think so, so she presented me with a pillow and said that I could keep it. Wow, what a nice woman! My nights were going to be much more comfortable, and I hadn't had to spend any of my meagre and quickly disappearing travel allowance.

That night, Cory suggested that we should go have some fun in Rome; just the two of us.

Uncle Hugh always had a plan and itinerary for what we would see when we got to a place and this plan included me – whether I was having fun on my own or not. I don't doubt that his plans included a detailed cost analysis for every penny that would be spent as well.

While I often poke fun at the miserly way he approached his spending, this trip was certainly a costly endeavour, and I don't actually have a clear grasp on his financial status at the time. Admittedly, he also had to take care of a geeky and ungrateful teenager who didn't always seem to appreciate the architecture. landscapes, art, culture, food, and the knowledge he had of all of these things. I know that adding me to his trip must have cost him a fair amount.

As with most teenagers, I had very little experience or understanding of finances, other than constantly hearing my parents declaring that they couldn't afford this or that. That ubiquitous phrase was the answer to pretty much everything we asked for at home – food, clothes, trips, or toys. Kids never seem to understand why this is until they leave home for the first time. Suddenly groceries, toothpaste, deodorant, and dish soap cost money and finances take on a whole new meaning. Before that, basic necessities simply appeared when you needed them and magically replenished themselves. Kids don't see the tired working parent behind these things, but can't really be blamed for it.

I was no exception at home, but I was a quick study under Uncle Hugh. My parents had sent me on this trip with only $200, which was expected to pay for what I needed plus film, stamps, postcards, and souvenir gifts for every family member back home. I'd already had to buy a new camera and running shoes, which had eaten into that allowance. I observed Uncle Hugh scrimping and saving pennies throughout the trip, squeezing every opportunity for a better deal or a free ride, and I followed suit as best I could, holding onto my remaining dollars with a clenched fist.

Cost aside, Uncle Hugh always had a plan for what he wanted to see, and he rarely compromised while achieving his goals during this trip. These plans and goals apparently included me as he'd adopted the concept that I was his ward and that it was his solemn duty to educate and develop this empty-headed kid until he became a fitting companion.

When Cory suggested that he take me around to show me the city, Uncle Hugh was aghast. How dare I not partake in all of what Rome had to offer without him, and potentially miss out on any number of historically and culturally significant sites and facts?

The Turners insisted that Cory knew the city like the back of his hand and that he would provide me with an excellent tour of everything Hugh had been planning. I stayed quiet during the discussion, not wanting to raise his ire and start another tirade. Eventually, Uncle Hugh relented, but not before creating a list of every site that we absolutely HAD to visit and report back to him about later. I'm sure he was thinking that two teenage boys could never visit a place like the Colosseum and absorb anything worthwhile without his constant litany of dates, construction methods, tools used, the qualities of different types of cement, the use of slavery, the history of the gladiators, the promoters, the events, the battles, the seating, the animals, the tunnels, the trapdoors, and the full history of the destruction and fall of the Roman Empire. Nevertheless, he agreed to let us go, as long we stuck to his written list.

With equal amounts of trepidation and excitement, Cory and I set out on our own tour of Rome. We left the house seeming like two young schoolkids – wait, we were just two young schoolkids. By today's standards, no sane parents would let their 13 and 14-year-old children run amok in a massive city like Rome, but it was 1972, and back then it was natural to do so.

Cory and I caught a bus outside of his home and then transferred to a subway, which brought us to the center of the city. No more shuffling along, no more stopping to rest every 100 steps, no more setting up camera angles for torturously long periods of time – we were free!

We ran through the city with the jubilation and power of youth, with no crusty adults to slow us down. We decided to hit up St. Peter's Cathedral first, as it was the largest attraction and we figured we might as well get the biggest over with first. This was the largest cathedral in the world and had a magnificent dome designed by Michelangelo when he was 72 years old. The view from the top was breathtaking, and we stood there for a while admiring the majesty of Rome below us. I never imagined a church could be so big; this one could hold thousands of people at a time for mass. I studiously read the informative placards and was sure to take everything in that I could. I knew for certain that I would be tested once I returned home. Right from where we first walked in and saw a statue of Madonna and Child, I touched everything, hoping that somehow I would be able to absorb all of the knowledge I'd need to appease Uncle Hugh through my imprint.

Next, we went to St. Angelo's Castle, where we visited the ancient dungeons, the quarters of many of the officials, and the armoury, where they displayed weapons from throughout history, from the Romans to the WWII Germans, to the modern Americans. We also got to see the Pope's escape tunnel from the Vatican to the castle in case of war or emergency which had my imagination fluttering.

Due to everything being so well-preserved, it wasn't hard for my mind to clothe us in ancient costumes, replete with shiny armour and sharp halberds, holding the enemy at bay while the Pope made his escape behind us. From there, we lived the lives of ancient Roman soldiers, fighting, campaigning, conquering, and eventually ruling the entire known world. Little did the castle caretakers know that they'd unwittingly let in two brave young Roman soldiers who could, at any moment, seize weapons off the wall and take the castle from within, declaring themselves rulers!

We eventually moved on to the Vatican, where we visited the Sistine Chapel which took Michelangelo four years to complete. It was fabulous and we spent some time looking up at it in awe. We figured he must have developed quite a sore neck after four years of painting since ours were hurting after only twenty minutes!

The Vatican's Great Hall was at least half a mile long with the walls lined by statue after statue. It was all so much more than I'd ever imagined or could even believe – simply incredible.

We made the long walk to the Monument and from there to the Roman Forum where Cory filled me in on the famous speech by Caesar (Romans, friends, and countrymen...), spoken right where we stood. I couldn't wait to tell Uncle Hugh of all I'd seen; I felt like I'd really done a good job at seeing the city and had so much fun doing it with Cory.

Once we got back home, I excitedly filled Uncle Hugh in on our day while he sat back with the downcast eyes of a teacher, ponderously nodding along and probably making mental checkmarks down the list he'd sent us with. When I was finished, he said, "That was pretty good, BUT," oh no, the dreaded "but", "not quite complete."

He then proceeded to give me detailed facts on every single thing I'd seen, making sure I hadn't been shortchanged by my dubious tour guide Cory. After over an hour of this, I finally managed to slink away and get in another game of Stratego with Cory in his room. Once again, he whomped me. Geeze, I hated losing!

The next few days, Cory and I continued our escapades around Rome, visiting old palaces called the Palentines, the Colosseum, the Victorial Monument, some old Roman baths, the Treveli Fountains, the Pantheon, and a fabulous church where the entire interior was covered in old monk's bones. There sure were a lot of dead monks in there.

We managed to break away from the ancient sights at one point to visit Luneur Park, an amusement park, where we got to go on fun rides and waited in line to go on the bumper cars twice.

We also went to see the "city beneath the city", a labyrinth of subways, and subterranean streets lined with every type of shop. There were thousands of people here rushing back and forth and a constant cacophony of noise. I'm not sure what the real attraction was here, but we couldn't get enough of it. Perhaps it was the fact that we didn't have to go anywhere or absorb any information; we were simply observers, while everyone else had somewhere to be. We would visit the Underground every chance we got, observing people scurrying by. As many adolescents do, we laughed at many of the people passing by for stupid reasons, "Look at how fat that man is!" or "Look at the dress on that old lady!"

We carried on and on, laughing uproariously and having the time of our lives. We never filled Uncle Hugh in on our daily trips to the Underground, sparing ourselves a lecture about wasting time. I did try harder and harder to impress him with the knowledge I'd pick up at the sites we saw. He seemed suitably impressed, except when it came to the bone church we'd loved so much.

"Why waste your time on something so frivolous and insignificant?" he'd mutter. I think that any trace of youth must have been blasted out of the man over a lifetime of stodgy academia.

Our days of running rampant around the city abruptly came to an end one morning, when Uncle Hugh declared that that was enough. He'd been neglecting his duties for too long and he was going to accompany me into the city to see some sites. Cory was welcome to come along of course.

"Oh, great," we responded sarcastically.

The next day, Uncle Hugh took us out into Rome, visiting many of the sites I had already visited and reported back on – apparently, not well enough!

Despite having seen the sites that week, I was actually content going back again, especially to the Colosseum. It was just such a cool place and I loved everything about it.

With Cory's guidance, I'd become quite adept at traversing the deadly streets of Rome, avoiding grifters, dodging speeding and unpredictable cars, and stepping nimbly over rough cobblestone roads. Uncle Hugh on the other hand, was having a hell of a time making his way around the city,

Crossing a busy road full of traffic to get to the Colosseum, Cory and I slithered our way across the street through cars, bikes, and pedestrians. Lacking the grace and speed of a teenager, Uncle Hugh put his foot down on the street and was instantaneously nearly clobbered by a car. Jumping back, he waited for a space in the traffic to cross through, but it never came.

Eventually, he did what he did best, putting on his best arrogant English air, raising his nose in the air and slowly walking across the street, traffic be damned. His whole demeanour shouted that he was better than these rude and uncivilized Italians. How dare they honk and yell at him? They should be ashamed!

I couldn't believe he made it across the road in one piece!

One day the Turners accompanied us, and we all took a bus to the Tivoli Gardens. It was actually our last day together as we were leaving the next day, and we all had a great time strolling around the enchanting gardens and fountains, while Uncle Hugh regaled us with architectural facts every time we turned a corner.

That night, Cory and I played Stratego for the last time and, of course, I lost, while Cory smiled at me savagely with victory. I was going to miss it here, as I'd grown accustomed to having someone my age to hang out with.

The next morning, I awoke with a terrible toothache. Prodding around my mouth with my tongue, I discovered it was the same tooth that had been allegedly fixed while we were in Nice!

Luckily, Mrs. Turner made a call to the family dentist and managed to get me in first thing in the morning. By 11 am, the tooth was fixed, we'd said our goodbyes, and we were on the road, next stop, Naples!

Well, maybe not.

We made it onto the Autostrada, and the VW wouldn't accelerate past 40km/h. Uncle Hugh figured that it was perhaps due to having left the van sitting for a week, or maybe because of the steep hills in the area, but the problem never sorted itself out, so we got off the highway and pulled into a garage to get it looked at.

It turned out that only two sparkplug wires were connected, which was the cause of our turtle-like pace on the highway. A simple and quick fix, which Uncle Hugh was happy about, but we'd wasted our whole morning and had barely made it 30 minutes from the Turners.

Instead of pressing on, Uncle Hugh decided to turn back and spend an extra night with the Turners, then head to Naples first thing the next morning.

When we arrived back at their house, Cory was happy to see us, running out to the van to meet us as we unloaded once again. Mrs. Turner on the other hand gave a strange half-smile as we clambered back into her house; I don't think she was very happy at all to see us again.

Uncle Hugh was talking about a book that he really wanted, so Cory and I offered to run into the city to find it for him; a good excuse to visit our regular haunts one last time. We took a bus to the bookstore, purchased the book, and then made a mad dash toward the underground city, where we got up to our usual shenanigans.

After supper, Cory and I played another game of Stratego and I finally won! I was so pleased with myself and he was totally frustrated, saying that I must have found a way to cheat in order to beat him. I just kept on smiling.

Chapter 10

The next morning, we actually managed to leave Rome. Watching it recede in the rear-view mirror, I contemplated how much I had enjoyed my time there. It was a life-changing city for me; at once captivating and wonderful, yet frightening and exhilarating. The sense of wild freedom I'd enjoyed there with Cory was something that stuck with me my whole life. Rome, and the entire experience of the trip with Uncle Hugh, definitely fueled an independent streak that I still carry with me to this day. Looking at my past in my own figurative rear-view mirror, I wonder what kind of man I would have been without ever experiencing this unique adventure.

We managed to get the VW back on the Autostrada, and even though the engine had been repaired, the vast majority of cars and trucks whizzed past us as Uncle Hugh putted along.

Perhaps due to not driving for the past week, Uncle Hugh was feeling a bit rusty and was quickly growing anxious and agitated on the highway, clenching the wheel until white-knuckled and grinding his teeth. I tried buttering him up a bit, in the hope that it would cause his foot to grow a little heavier on the gas pedal, "Uncle Hugh, you've got that clutch working now, so smooth! You've really become an expert at driving in Europe."

He thanked me, taking my praise as a given, but nevertheless, we didn't end up going any faster. I slumped in my seat and sighed as a 120-year-old woman peering myopically over the rim of her steering wheel zoomed past our van, causing us to choke on her dust. It was going to be a long day.

We finally entered the outskirts of the Naples suburbs and Uncle Hugh commented on the terrible smog enshrouding the city. "You can't even see the outline of Mount Vesuvius!" he exclaimed.

European smog was turning into one of his favourite subjects. "Every city we visit on this continent is covered in smog. Not like back home on the West Coast. We don't get any smog there, just beautiful mountain air, kissed by the sea. You can always see the mountains... it's really one of the most beautiful places on earth."

He couldn't help but include my home in the discussion. "Not like southern Ontario. It's so plain and... blah. Smog everywhere too. If you had a mountain or two in that flat, boring landscape, you certainly wouldn't be able to see it through the smog! Nothing but urban sprawl and ugliness there, if you ask me."

I hadn't asked him. In fact, I was getting more and more offended with each vitriolic remark he made about my home. It frustrated me and took a lot of the pleasure out of the sites that we were seeing at the time. I felt that Uncle Hugh was good at creating smog in my head which put me in a bad mood and didn't allow me to see things clearly.

We eventually pulled off the highway and stopped at a gas station to fill up and make some lunch. We ate and carefully went over the route we were going to take to the campground we had chosen the night before.

We made it there without any issues and I got things set up, hoisting the Canadian flag while muttering to myself about Uncle Hugh's hypocritical thoughts about Canada.

We decided to take a stroll around the campground to check it out but were left pretty underwhelmed with the place. It was very unappealing – sloppy campsites, short, stunted trees, trash and dirt everywhere; the entire place was extremely run down.

Uncle Hugh pointed all of this out to me as if he were lecturing me at a museum, "Look at that building! Shabby and dirty. And those latrines! The paint is peeling and it looks like they might just fall over at any minute."

I suggested that we leave the campground and go visit a nearby beach on the Mediterranean.

"Good idea, my boy," he said, and we drove down to the beach.

Unfortunately, the beach wasn't all that nice either, full of junk and debris. Uncle Hugh added it to the growing list of issues he had with Naples.

We stopped at the supermarket on the way back to the campground and purchased some olives, cheese, bread, some sort of canned meat product like Spam, and of course, some red wine to wash it all down.

When we arrived back at the campground, someone had set up a camper beside ours, so we went over and met the owners, who happened to be American. They had rented the camper in Rome and were starting their big Italian tour.

We had a pleasant evening hanging out with them, drinking wine and regaling them with stories. They laughed and applauded our daring as we told them of our African adventures. They broke out a bottle of whisky to share and I took my first sip of the stuff. I can't say that I was a big fan, so I went back to the sweet red wine. That would all eventually change though. I now count it as my favourite drink!

The next day, we said our goodbyes to the Americans, then headed to Ercolano, or Herculaneum as Uncle Hugh called it. It was an ancient town situated at the base of Mount Vesuvius and, like Pompeii, was destroyed by the eruption in 79CE. Unlike Pompeii, which was blanketed in ash, Herculaneum was covered in mud. Over time, a new city was built on top of the dried mud, making it difficult for archaeologists to excavate the old town.

Where they could, they did some excavations, and the buildings they unearthed are incredible. Once cleaned of the mud, the buildings were pristinely preserved both inside and out. Wooden beams were easily visible, as was furniture, like tables, chairs, and even a crib.

I found it all so fascinating and was completely enthralled with what we were seeing. Uncle Hugh was happy to see my interest, so he launched into a detailed lecture, which I soaked up eagerly. "Just wait until you see Pompeii Jimmy!" he crowed.

We made our way to Pompeii and I could immediately see that he wasn't wrong; to this day, it was the most incredible thing I'd ever seen.

We walked for hours, taking in the details of every house, government building, and chariot rut. Uncle Hugh became giddy with my enthusiasm for the place, even going so far as to pick up his pace while we moved through the streets. He pointed out sight after sight, and I eagerly absorbed the information, almost disbelieving that a place could be so utterly cool.

Despite the kilometres and kilometres we'd walked, we still hadn't seen the entire site when it was time to go. We were both reluctant to leave, but our schedule dictated that we simply had to go.

We got back to the van and drove down the peninsula to Sorrento and found a spot to stop for the night on the outskirts called the International Campground. It was a beautiful, well-maintained campground with a great view of the sea. With its lush vegetation, clean modern bathrooms, and a restaurant with a patio overlooking the Mediterranean, it was quite the contrast from the dump we'd stayed in the night before.

After setting up camp, we got washed up and headed over to the restaurant for some dinner. After all of the walking we'd done that day, we were both feeling pretty footsore and exhausted, not to mention starving.

We sat on the outdoor patio and ordered a couple of beers, which we quietly enjoyed while looking out on the sea. We must have made a bit of a peculiar sight; not just that evening on the patio, but everywhere we travelled – a greying scholarly-looking man, with a young, long-haired teen. We certainly weren't your typical travellers. Up to this point, the vast majority of other travellers we'd seen were either retired couples, or whole families, who could easily be pointed out by their clothing, or by the way they gawped at the local sights. Most travellers were better dressed than us (you can only do so much for your appearance when you're living in a van!) and could be seen with some type of luggage or local shopping bags.

I think we made quite the odd couple, but I sometimes wonder if that allowed us to meet so many people on our trip. We sparked a lot of curiosity, which caused people to approach us to chat. I wonder if they'd be so interested in approaching a couple talking softly to each other, or a boisterous family?

Our appearance obviously sparked the interest of a group of English speakers who were sharing the patio with us, and one of them came over to invite us to sit with them at their table. I tensed; Uncle Hugh generally wasn't all that good at dealing with invitations like this and he began displaying his usual body language and facial expressions that would send any sane person running. Surprisingly, he pulled it together at the last minute and declared in his best snobby English voice, "Why, that would be wonderful. Thank you, my good man."

He must have been feeling lonely or bored that night!

I was happy to have a break from the tired, if comfortable, silence that had been the evening so far, and we settled ourselves in amongst the two British couples.

Immediately, I could see that these people were hilarious. The one I remember most, Adrian, was from Liverpool and was perhaps the funniest person I'd ever met. He immediately had us in stitches with his stories, rattling off jokes and anecdotes non-stop. As the alcohol kept flowing, his jokes just got funnier, and he had us all roaring with laughter.

Adrian's wife Susan was the only one at the table who didn't seem too keen on hearing all of Adrian's stories and jokes, particularly as the night went on and the jokes got more and more vulgar. She sat alone in a huff, staring daggers at her husband and eventually told him right out to stop.

"This child is only fourteen years old!" she told him, "You need to check your mouth!"

"You should have seen the things I was saying and doing when I was fourteen, not to mention what I heard and saw!" he replied jovially.

This started a fight that quickly cut through the mood at the table. Before long, it got bad enough that the evening halted abruptly, and everyone parted ways.

Uncle Hugh surprised me the next day when he brought up the event and took Susan's side on the matter. He'd been laughing just as hard at everyone else the night before, but now he declared that Adrian's vulgar jokes were worth nothing more than a passing amusement.

"Adrian is an example of the lower-class Jimmy my boy, street-level and crude and certainly not worth our time," he lectured.

I stayed silent, shrugging it off, but thinking to myself, "Jeeze. Adrian wasn't crude; he was a master storyteller who held us all enthralled the entire night. He was a comedic genius!"

I thought Uncle Hugh was a straight-up snob and no better than Adrian... or anyone else for that matter. I added it to the quiet list of resentments I'd made about the man and turned my mind toward the day ahead.

Uncle Hugh went over to the park office and arranged for us to join an organized tour of nearby Capri. The beautiful island of Capri is known for its fantastic scenery, excellent restaurants, posh shops, fancy yachts, and the rich and famous who frequent the place. Everyone who goes wants to see who's there and also to be seen there themselves.

It was quite the journey. First, a car picked us up at the camp office and drove us to a bus station, where we boarded a bus that took us to the Senate Harbour, where we boarded a ferry, which took us to the island, where we boarded yet another bus which took us up through the mountains to the town of Anacapri.

The road to town was very windy and the bus driver refused to slow down around the tight switchbacks up the mountain. Uncle Hugh clenched the seat and screamed along with the women on the bus every time the driver swung us around another bend, seemingly hanging over nothing but air every time he did so. I found it all to be very exciting, but beside me, Uncle Hugh was scared to death and had lost all of the colour in his face.

Upon arrival, Uncle Hugh slowly regained his composure as we wandered around town, soaking in the beautiful buildings and picture-perfect setting. We enjoyed the gorgeous views of the Villa San Michele before taking a chairlift up the final ascent of the mountain, to the very top of Capri. Despite the lift moving extremely slowly, the experience of being in that little chair, hanging free in the mountain air with the entire island below us was nothing short of incredible.

Once we got to the top, we walked around, enjoying the sights, until we were quite tired and thirsty. We approached an outdoor café and Uncle Hugh stopped to review the menu at the entrance. He recoiled from the piece of paper, visibly aghast at the exorbitant prices, and suggested that we go find someplace else to try.

After stopping at a few more bars, restaurants, and cafés, we came to the realization that they were all the same – ridiculously overpriced.

"Highway robbery!" he declared, ignoring the fact that we were in a very touristy place known for its high rollers.

Just then, he spotted a Coke machine peeking out from a nearby alcove. He rushed over and bought two Cokes from it.

Feeling mischievous, he suggested that I quickly go sit down in a chair at one of the expensive cafés we'd passed so he could take my picture. "No one will ever know that we didn't actually eat or drink there," he whispered conspiratorially, "You can show everyone how we hob-nobbed with the rich and famous!"

He instructed me to sit and wait until he was ready to take a picture, and under no circumstances to drink my Coke until he was ready. He hurried the best he could, but even moving fast, Uncle Hugh was the slowest photographer I'd ever seen.

Finally, he called, "Okay James, pretend as if you're casually sitting there like you belong!"

I noticed the waiter making his way towards me, so I posed and mentally urged him to take the photo quickly. Once he snapped the photo, I jumped out of the seat and scurried back outside the fence before the waiter could reach me and kick me out. The look on his face said, "Scram! Get out of here you riff-raff; who do you think you are?!"

It was getting late, so we reversed the route we had taken in, enjoying the breathtaking beauty of the town and the blue, blue sea behind it. Uncle Hugh wore a permanent smug smirk after his little trick at the café. I think he was delighted with himself.

The next day, we left Sorrento and drove along the Amalfi Coast, which boasted more incredible views. There was nothing but steep cliffs and sparkling cerulean sea around us and we felt like we just had to stop and take it in. We found a place to park at a beach and waded into the water feeling blissed out and relaxed.

Getting back into the van, we made our way to Salerno, a seaside city built right into the rock cliffs with spectacular ancient architecture and even more spectacular views. Despite the beauty of the place, Uncle Hugh didn't want to tarry long. He was anxious to make up the lost time we'd spent in Rome and eager to make it across Italy so we could make the ferry to Greece on time.

We regretfully passed through Salerno and got back on the Autostrada, blazing our way across southern Italy to Bari, and then to Brindisi, where we'd catch the ferry to the next country on our list.

Once at the port, Uncle Hugh checked us in before driving the van onto the ferry. Feeling generous, he declared that we'd splurge and get ourselves a berth for the day-and-a-half trip across the Adriatic Sea.

"What else would we have done?" I asked myself, "Sleep on the deck?!"

The boat was huge and beautiful, and I quickly took my leave from Uncle Hugh to explore it from end to end. Eventually, we reconnected and lounged back in deck chairs, reflecting on our Italian adventures. Italy was just so beautiful and magical, and I'd had such a fun time in Rome with Cory. I'd absolutely fallen in love with the country and promised to make my way back there as soon as I could.

We met some fellow Canadians in one of the lounge areas on the boat, Rick and Brenda, who were from Nova Scotia. They were doing a two-week trip through Italy and Greece for their 25th wedding anniversary. They said the trip had been a whirlwind so far, as they were trying to fit as much as they could inside the short time frame they'd allotted themselves.

Being very nice and talkative, they helped to pass the time as we cruised across the azure waters. They were in awe of the adventures we'd had up to that point, which Uncle Hugh and I delighted in recounting to them, often butting into each other's stories to add details or make corrections.

As the Greek coastline rolled by, I soaked in the sun and fresh sea air, feeling like a rich person on a Mediterranean cruise, and not some kid whose great uncle had loaded onto a ferry for a night.

Chapter 11

We stopped at the island of Corfu to let off some passengers, then were quickly brought across the strait, through the Ionian islands, to Patras on the Greek mainland.

There was a campground a few kilometres away from the ferry docks, so we made our way there and set up camp, raising our Canadian flag. The campground was small, but very nice, overlooking the sea.

Our fluttering maple leaf flag soon brought over two curious boys who began bombarding us with questions in broken English, "Who are you? Is he your father? Where are you from? What are you doing here? Where are you going?" The questions went on and on.

Though I was enjoying the company of kids closer to my age, Uncle Hugh was quickly losing his patience with the interrogation. "Why don't you kids move on?" he suggested.

Whether due to misunderstanding him or perhaps simply ignoring him, the two boys remained where they were and continued hammering us with questions.

I could see his ire growing; his brows tightened, his shoulders rose, and his face turned down into a grimace. He was obviously getting ready to shout at them to go away.

"Want a Coke?" I offered.

Uncle Hugh became apoplectic, but the boys' eyes grew large and they both nodded. "Right-o," said one of them, which I assumed meant "yes".

Uncle Hugh shot me a glare, but otherwise kept his temper tantrum to himself and went and made himself busy preparing supper. The boys sat down with me and comfortably cracked open their Cokes as if we were all old friends. Their names were Yiannes and Yiroges, which Uncle Hugh told me later meant John and George in Greek. They were hard not to like, and even Uncle Hugh began warming up to them eventually. He began asking a barrage of questions himself, "Where do you live? Where are your parents? Where can we get gas and groceries?"

The boys told us they'd come along with us the next day and show us everything we needed, maybe for another pair of Cokes?

I was surprised when Uncle Hugh agreed, telling them we'd see them tomorrow in what was obviously a hint to skedaddle. They took the hint this time and took off, but were true to their word and were waiting for us at the picnic table first thing in the morning.

They jumped into the camper van, grinning ear to ear and quickly led us to the closest gas station, where we filled up. They then guided us to the local grocery store, and we grabbed some supplies. Uncle Hugh surprised me by suggesting I buy them something small for helping us out. I bought a couple of little bags of candy and hid them in my pockets for the time being.

Patras was located on the Peloponnesian Peninsula, which was connected to the rest of Greece by a narrow isthmus. Uncle Hugh was planning on visiting Delphi across the channel and didn't want to drive the entire way around to get there so he asked the boys if there was a ferry that could take us across. "Right-o!" they said in unison.

Bringing us to the ferry dock, it was time to say goodbye. We both thanked them for the help and I pulled out the candy to give them. The look of awe and gratitude on their faces was heartwarming. It was like I'd given them a bag of cash! They yelped in triumph and stood there waving goodbye the entire time it took us to get onto the ferry.

As we ferried across the channel, I slowly came to the realization that we'd taken the boys many kilometres from their home and had simply left them at the ferry dock with no way to get back. They would have had to walk for hours or hitch a ride with a stranger to get back to their parents. I worried and stewed over this the entire ferry ride. Why wouldn't Uncle Hugh have considered this? How could an adult just leave a pair of children somewhere after driving them across the countryside?

Maybe it was because he'd never had kids and didn't really know how to deal with them, but the fact that he did it really bothered me. I sure hope those boys made it back home safely.

After an hour and a half, we made it across the channel and drove into the ancient city of Delphi. Founded in 1450 BCE, Delphi was once considered the center of the world. The city looked like it could still be out of that era, with simple white buildings boasting red clay tile roofs and lots of ruins.

We walked through the ruins of the Temple of Apollo (known as the navel of the world), nestled in the dry olive tree-studded hills, with its outdoor amphitheatre, Treasury, Stadium, and topless columns. We went inside the museum, where we strolled around, stopping at every single item on display. I thought that we may have to stay overnight, the way Uncle Hugh oohed and ahhed, took painstaking photos, and lectured me at length about every single thing we saw there. Eventually, we made it back outside with barely enough daylight left to find ourselves a campground for the night.

Luckily, there was one nearby, a beautiful little campsite perched on a cliff overlooking the sea. "I hope no one plans on doing any sleepwalking here!" I thought to myself.

The next day we spent the morning touring Delphi, then began the long drive to Athens. We made it most of the way without incident and stopped at a campground in the late afternoon about 11 kilometres outside of the city. After setting up camp, brewing some tea, and enjoying a nice meal of creamed peas on toast, we figured we still had enough time to go into Athens and take a look around.

We decided to take the public bus into town rather than attempt driving and parking, which was an interesting experience as it was pretty chaotic – heavily crowded with locals who eyed us suspiciously.

After we'd strolled around for a while, we asked for directions to the American Express office. We'd had all of our mail forwarded there and were anxious to see if anything was waiting for us. We also had mail and postcards that we needed to send out.

American Express offices acted as a rallying point for Americans abroad and were consistently bustling with Americans sending or receiving money transfers and mail as well as getting tourist information from the front desk workers.

Upon entering the building, you first had to make your way around the rows and stacks of luggage on the floor. I stopped at a set of conspicuous luggage and read the labels as Uncle Hugh stood in line, memorizing them for something to do. Once we were done with our mail, we decided to sit down at one of the tables in the corner and have a Coke before heading back out.

An American family sat down next to us and struck up a conversation. They asked where we were from and Uncle Hugh told them Portland, Oregon, seeing that it was safe to say he was from America to fellow Americans. What a turncoat. He introduced me as his Canadian great-nephew.

Before the Americans could respond with their own names and origins, I decided to take a chance and blurted out, "Let me guess. Are you Judy Brennan from Newark, New Jersey?"

Her mouth dropped open, as did her husband's and children's.

"Yes, I am," she replied, consternated, "Have we met before?"

Uncle Hugh looked at me like I had two heads with a face that said, "What the hell?!"

Taking the ruse a little further, I went on to say, "Ah yes, so you live at 345 Hayden Street?"

"Why yes, we do! How in the world do you know that?!"

Smiling, I replied, "Maybe I'm a psychic! Should I tell you your phone number?"

I wasn't actually sure if I'd be able to recall it properly, but didn't have to. Judy was beside herself that they could travel all the way to Athens Greece and meet a little Canadian kid they'd never seen before who knew everything about them.

She kept repeating, "I can't believe this! I simply can't believe this! How? Please tell me how, please!"

I finally relented and confessed that I'd read their luggage tags while waiting in line.

The entire family roared with laughter and Judy looked very relieved that it was something as simple as that.

"Good one!" she exclaimed, "You really got me good! I can't wait to tell everyone back home about this!"

Proud of myself for my hijinks, we left the office, Uncle Hugh patting me on the back and saying, "Good one James, you really put one over them!"

We retraced our steps and were successful in finding the correct bus to take us back to the campground. The next morning, Uncle Hugh was up bright and early, ready to get back to town to visit the Parthenon. Just like a fat kid in a candy store, he was giddy with anticipation, champing at the bit to see the magnificent temple, which was built on the Acropolis, overlooking the city.

We spent many hours soaking in the site, strolling around and eventually sitting on the steps, admiring all of the ancient buildings and doing some people-watching. It was a very hot and sunny day, so we eventually went in search of some shade and beverages down the long stairway back into town. We eventually found a modest outdoor restaurant and took a seat in the shade, enjoying a drink and watching the crowds shuffle by.

Getting hungry, we ordered some souvlaki that came with a horiatiki salad and a big bowl of tzatziki, along with some tasty Greek wine. It was a fabulous meal and the atmosphere of the street around us was awesome. Sitting there, drinking foreign wine and eating foreign food in this big ancient city should have been alien to me, but by this time, I'd become a veteran traveller and took it all in like I was born to it.

After dinner, we roamed the streets, taking in the sights, and eventually came across a tourist booth. Uncle Hugh saw something that interested him there and came back holding two tickets. Apparently, they were doing a sound and light show in the skies over the Acropolis that night. It was called "Son et Lumiere", which was French? Uncle Hugh thought this was amusing, since we were in Greece. I guess it sounded better in French?

We found our way to the outdoor seating area and sat back to enjoy the show. Music boomed out of the impressive amplifier system and lights played out of the most advanced mechanical lighting system I'd ever seen. We sat transfixed as the music roared and the lights played across the sky above us. What a show!

Tired, we made our way back to our camper via the same crowded bus we'd taken the day before and were fast asleep in a matter of minutes.

Wanting to experience the Greek Islands, Uncle Hugh went to the camp office the next morning and inquired about transportation to the island of Mykonos. The man working there told him that there was a daily boat that left at 2:00 pm. We drove to the nearby port city of Piraeus and parked the camper, paying for several days. Packing up some essentials in backpacks, we headed over to the ticket office.

"No boats today!" the man there yelled, "Come back tomorrow!"

This unexpected turn of events obviously didn't sit well with Uncle Hugh. We drove back to Athens in stony silence, the pall of Uncle Hugh's displeasure spreading to a 100-foot radius around us and affecting anyone who came close. Anyone would have been angry and disappointed at something like this, but Uncle Hugh was exceptionally good at holding onto his anger and making everyone else suffer as if it were their fault.

We went back to the American Express office to pick up some forgotten traveller's cheques, then brusquely walked around the city in an effort to cool down his hot head. I'm not sure it worked, but we managed to get a spot in the campground again for the night, Uncle Hugh being sure to let the man at the office know that he had grievously let us down.

The next day, we made our way back to the port and were successful in booking passage on a ship called OIA. Being in a much less generous mood, Uncle Hugh booked us as third class, which meant that we couldn't enjoy the lounge, sit down in the deck chairs, or even visit the restaurant. It was up to us to find ourselves a ledge or box on the deck to sit on for the journey. To be fair, Uncle Hugh was under the impression that it was only a two-hour trip, which would have made our uncomfortable situation bearable, but in reality, the boat ride was five hours long.

The journey was much harder on the 60-year-old Uncle Hugh than it was on me, and I could see the stubbornness of sticking to his decision warring with the desire to improve our situation on his face. Most of the other third-class passengers were young people in their early 20s and they crowded around the boxes we'd eventually found to sit on.

The boat was relatively small, and spray from the wavy sea regularly came over the railing to splash us. The seas weren't rough exactly, but you could feel the boat pitch over every single wave. I thought it was quite exhilarating, but Uncle Hugh didn't seem to agree.

Eventually, a young man broke out a guitar and began entertaining the group of passengers around us, playing Greek songs that everyone seemed to know. Soon, everyone was clapping and singing along and the whole situation took on a real Woodstock atmosphere, only at sea!

Sitting nearby was a beautiful young blond woman from Toronto. She struck up a conversation when she heard us speaking English, and I ended up chatting with her for the entire journey. Her name was Jane and she had just finished college and taken this trip to Greece on her own as a reward. I was very much wishing I was a little bit older so I could make a better impression, but it was obvious she was talking to me like I was her little brother. Still, I was happy to be chatting with her either way, and the friendly conversation helped the time pass quickly.

Despite my earlier misgivings about being booked as third-class passengers, it actually turned out to be quite a lovely experience – a beautiful girl to talk to, fun music and camaraderie, and the beautiful fresh sea air. I'm not sure Uncle Hugh enjoyed it quite as much as I did.

As we approached our destination, Uncle Hugh prepped and grilled me about what we'd find in Mykonos. He'd thoroughly researched the historic, cultural, and recreational significance of every place we visited, and this was no exception.

He told me that he didn't want to stay in a modern hotel while on the island, but rather somewhere more special and fitting. He'd heard that you could rent a room from the locals for much cheaper, staying in their home and experiencing the local flavour.

As our ship jockeyed for position with a large cruise ship and two other vessels around the same size as ours, carrying about two hundred passengers each, we settled up to a long pier. We could see a group of what we believed to be locals, many of them holding signs, at the end of the pier. Uncle Hugh thought that they must be locals trying to entice tourists to stay at their homes. We noticed several tourists engaging the locals with signs and then leaving with them.

Uncle Hugh began to grow anxious as we finally docked and the first and second-class passengers slowly made their way off the boat and onto the pier.

Impatience poured off the man as we watched the crowd of locals with signs dwindle as our upper-class shipmates left the pier with them. When we finally got to disembark the ship, shuffling along the gangplank with the last thirty or forty straggling passengers, Uncle Hugh bemoaned the fact that we had surely missed out on the opportunity to stay in a local home.

I fought to hold my tongue. Reminding him that his miserly ways had put us in this situation in the first place didn't seem wise. Instead, I volunteered to run ahead and try to secure a place to stay.

Uncle Hugh agreed, so I nimbly slipped through the passengers in front of us, causing a stir of muttered complaints. I spotted a nice-looking lady with a sign held up, saying "Room for Rent", so I approached her and asked if the room happened to be in her home. She nodded and replied that, yes, it was in her own home, so I asked her to please wait for my uncle to arrive.

I stood my ground as the other passengers made to approach the woman, trying to look important and giving a fierce scowl to anyone who came too close. When Uncle Hugh finally arrived, I called out to him, exclaiming that I had secured us a room.

Instead of looking happy, he walked up grimacing, rudely scanning the woman from head to toe as if she had a disease. I looked at the woman again but found nothing unsavory to see, except maybe for the fact that she was dressed in regular modern clothes as opposed to the more traditional garb many of the other locals had been wearing. I figured he must have been frowning that way because she didn't meet his view of what a quaint Greek peasant should look like and must have been thinking that she was going to lead us to a modern apartment building or something.

The woman bade us to follow her and led us through the narrow cobblestone streets, hemmed in by gleaming white-washed buildings. It seemed like pretty much everything in this place was painted white – white walls, white roofs, white window frames. Despite its monochromatic simplicity, I found it to be incredibly striking and beautiful.

Arriving at the woman's home, she led us around the whitewashed wall to the back and showed us our room. Smiling, she wished us a pleasant stay in Mykonos and reminded us to just ask if we needed any assistance.

The room was relatively modern and didn't look too different than anything else we'd stayed in thus far. One sheepish look at Uncle Hugh, and I knew what was coming. As soon as the woman left, he blew up, "THIS IS NOT WHAT I WANTED! Not at all! Why did you have to pick THAT woman?! You knew what I wanted, but you failed to do your job properly. You clod, you silly boy, you are not worthy of accompanying me on MY trip! I should have just gone and done it myself. I supposed it's MY fault for delegating important jobs to a CHILD that can't follow simple instructions."

I did feel bad about the whole thing, but, like most teenagers, I soon shrugged it off. I was getting used to his tirades and knew that we probably wouldn't have gotten any place to stay at all if we'd done it at his pace.

He eventually cooled down as we unpacked, though he still took the time to remind me every few minutes of his extreme displeasure and disappointment in me. I bet that he had read an older book or pamphlet on this practice of locals bringing tourists into their homes but with the boom of tourism in Greece at that time and the huge amount of travellers looking for authentic experiences, most locals did the same thing as the woman we'd found had done: buy an extra house, or build an extra room or two to accommodate tourists for extra cash. I'd guess that there were very few sign-holding locals on that pier that were offering what Uncle Hugh had imagined.

It was what it was though, so we got cleaned up and then walked the cobbled streets, taking in the sights and sounds of the place, joining the many other tourists milling around the popular sites and shops.

With the cerulean sea in view and the deep blue sky overhead contrasting with the shining white buildings, I was left awestruck by the beauty of the place. We found an open-air restaurant in the square overlooking the traditional Greek windmills around the old harbour and had a wonderful meal with some Greek wine to accompany it. We stayed until evening, watching the sunset and having a very pleasant evening, despite the way the afternoon had started.

The next day, we went for another stroll around town and ran into the gorgeous young woman from the boat named Jane, who struck up a conversation. We excitedly talked about how beautiful the place was and asked her what her plans were while here? She asked if we were interested in visiting a beach she'd heard of with huge waves, located across the island. She was planning on taking the bus there tomorrow and would love it if we'd come along.

Uncle Hugh hemmed and hawed, but eventually declined, saying that sitting in the hot sun and sand just wasn't for him. Seeing my crestfallen face, he followed by suggesting that I go with her alone and that they'd have more fun without him. She seemed receptive to the idea, and I certainly wasn't going to pass it up. A day on the beach with a hot 18-year-old? Count me in!

I suspected that he might want a little time alone himself, after the "disaster" of our arrival on the island, and truth be told, I wouldn't mind some time apart from him as well, hot girl or no.

Jane said she was going shopping and then would pick me up at 1:00 the next day. Excited thoughts about going to the beach with her consumed my thoughts for the rest of the day.

Uncle Hugh and I spent the rest of the afternoon wandering the narrow streets and twisting alleyways. Some climbed, twisting and turning, up the rocky landscape, packed with elegant white homes, shops, and restaurants. Many streets either circled or dead-ended at the harbour, presenting an artist's masterpiece of glistening sea, blue sky, and dramatic white buildings. The centerpiece was an old windmill that balanced the entire scene with its focal beauty.

We spotted an outdoor restaurant sitting directly on the beach below the windmill, and we made our way towards it, deciding to have dinner there. The restaurant and its food were beautiful, and we enjoyed a cold local beer as we sat and watched the throngs of tourists happily stroll down the streets and the beach. We ordered some freshly caught fish and a bottle of delicious Greek white and ate, enjoying the warm breeze off the Aegean Sea and watching the sunset. It was another pleasant night and Uncle Hugh seemed to have forgiven me for ruining his entire trip by picking the wrong lodging.

True to her word, Jane arrived at 1:00 to pick me up and we made our way to a bus stop, where we caught a local bus heading towards our destination. The ride took about 20 minutes, and I sat beside Jane feeling nervous and a bit strange. I found myself talking a mile a minute despite my brain screaming at me to shut up. To my chagrin, I talked her ear off the entire ride, not even knowing what I was talking about, but unable to stop. I wasn't too impressed with myself as we reached our stop. "Very suave Jimmy," I thought to myself.

Making the short walk from the bus stop, we arrived at the beach and were immediately in awe. The crystal white sand was being pounded by surf; massive waves crashing and then rolling up the shoreline before receding.

We ran down the beach and splashed into the foamy water, jumping into the waves, swimming, and dancing in the surf for hours. We laughed and joked and sprayed each other with water, moving about trying to find the biggest waves to launch ourselves into. We were having an amazing time and the whole experience felt surreal and magical.

Jane suggested that it may be time to get back to the beach to lie down and work on our tans. I was already red as a beet from being out in the sun for 2 hours, but thinking about the bikini she was wearing, I said, "Sure, Jane. Whatever you want is okay with me!"

Jane set her towel out, lay face down on it, and undid the back ties of her bikini in an attempt to get rid of the tan line. I surreptitiously watched out of the corner of my eye, pretending not to notice. "This is pretty cool," I thought to myself.

Not being much of a sunbather, I simply sat on my towel watching all of the activity on the beach. I'm not sure how much time passed as I sat with my thoughts, but then something happened that shocked me to the core.

Jane stood up and dropped her bikini to the beach. My jaw dropped as I stared at her perfect breasts, smooth skin, and little patch of fur. I may have even gulped.

"Come on James!" she said, running towards the water, "Come and make love to me in the surf!"

Was this happening? Could it possibly be happening?! This is exactly what I had been dreaming about all night after receiving her invitation.

"What are you waiting for?" she called.

I snapped out of my haze, standing up and fumbling with my shorts. I turned ten shades of red as she turned around and looked at me quizzically, noticing the... situation in my shorts.

Jane smiled and said, "Come on in, let's go for another swim."

I was glad she was walking in front of me while I waddled back to the water, hunched over and embarrassed, trying to hide my discomfort.

Luckily, Jane's friendly demeanour quickly made me forget about my embarrassment, and we spent the rest of the afternoon having a lovely time.

We chatted like old friends the entire way back to where we were staying, feeling much more comfortable than on the way out. Uncle Hugh met us at the door and asked Jane if she'd like to join us for dinner. I was very pleased when she agreed, just asking for enough time to go get cleaned up and put something nice on. Secretly, I wished Uncle Hugh would just invite her along for the rest of the Euro trip, fantasizing about romantic rendezvous on beaches across the continent. Well, that was unlikely, but at least we'd get to spend the evening together.

We ate at the harbour-front restaurant again and it was one of the most pleasant dinners we'd ever had, jane's charm working wonders on Uncle Hugh. He stayed friendly and jovial all night, telling stories and laughing at his own jokes. We ate and drank and talked and laughed and I never wanted the night to end.

Unfortunately, the dinner eventually wound down and Jane said she was getting tired and it was time for her to go. We hugged tightly, saying our goodbyes and I watched her walk away.

Uncle Hugh and I wandered the streets for a while in silence, both lost in our own thoughts. We began to notice more and more sailors on the streets, all decked out in their smart white uniforms. The sailors were all speaking English as well. As we rounded a corner, we were astonished to see two American battleships anchored in the harbour. There was a steady stream of sailors hurrying down the pier and into the town, talking raucously in small groups.

Before long, we could hardly traverse the streets, so crowded were they with American servicemen. Everywhere we looked, sailors were running around, laughing, joking, singing. Military police patrolled the streets, keeping an eye out for fights or unruly sailors and the tourists all stopped and gawked. It was like something out of a movie!

Uncle Hugh and I walked around, watching their antics for a full hour before we began to get tired. I stopped at a shop on the way home and purchased two beach bags for my sisters as souvenirs, then we made our way back to our totally unacceptable lodging for the night.

Waking early the next day, we chartered a boat to the island of Delos, an abandoned island once home to 30,000 Greeks. The boat held about 20 passengers and rose and fell over the waves with the poise of a bucking bull.

As we approached the island, we could see that it was mostly treeless, and those trees that still clung to the thin soil were stunted and windswept. Sunbaked white ruins dotted the rocky hills, and piles of rocks forming the shapes of foundations were a testament to how many used to live on the island.

Disembarking, we immediately made our way up a huge hill to get a better look at the island. The boat captain had warned that we only had 2 hours to spend on the island, so Uncle Hugh hustled faster than I'd seen him move in some time. The view was magnificent and well worth the effort of climbing the hill. Not wanting to dawdle, Uncle Hugh snapped a few photos quite hastily. My jaw dropped for the second time in two days; that was very unlike him!

Scrambling back down the hill, we explored as much as we could in the time allotted to us, seeing the terrace of lions, a row of weathered lion statues proudly poking out of the tall grass, as well as some arches, columns, and headless statues.

Riding the bucking bull back to Mykonos, we found ourselves a nice outdoor café to have lunch in and sat people-watching for a short time, entertained by all of the tourists bustling around buying baubles and knickknacks to bring home.

We quickly packed and barely made it to the 4:30 ferry back to Athens where we were reacquainted with the VW camper that we'd left at the campsite.

We decided to take a bit of a break the next day and get some chores done. We washed the camper, creating mud underneath it from several different countries, and Uncle Hugh said he needed to visit a bank.

Finding the bank closed when we got to town, we decided to go for a stroll instead. Oddly, we found that nearly everything was closed. We searched for an explanation but couldn't find any. With nothing to do, we thought it might be nice to go see a movie.

Finding one that Uncle Hugh thought he'd like, we made our way to the theatre and found that it was closed too – and for two months! Why advertise movies if your theatre is closed?

We strolled disconsolately around town and eventually stumbled on a small theatre that actually happened to be open. They were even showing a movie in English. The movie was restricted and the man in the ticket booth looked me up and down several times before finally smiling and handing the tickets over and saying, "Enjoy the movie." He seemed to be looking right at me when he said it.

The movie was okay, but was chock full of violence, killing, and nudity. Uncle Hugh wasn't very impressed, and he told me that he regretted bringing me in to see it. I, on the other hand, thought that it had everything that I liked in a movie: violence, killing, and especially nudity!

It certainly wasn't something that I was used to seeing back home on the CBC. Well, there *was* lots of violence on Hockey Night in Canada, and lots of killing on old Westerns, but it wasn't quite the same. There certainly was never any nudity, which was quite new to me, and I thought it was great. I did, however, feel a little uncomfortable having to sit next to Uncle Hugh while I watched it, though I think he felt the same way. After voicing his displeasure at the movie, he was rather quiet on the way back to camp.

Chapter 12

We left Athens the next day and travelled to Epidaurus where the best-preserved ancient Greek theatre in the whole country can be found. Even though it was built in the 4th century BCE, the acoustics in the theatre are still perfect. It was a lot of fun to test it out when we visited. Standing in the center of the lower platform, you could whisper and the people in the upper platforms could hear you clearly. Clap your hands, and it sounded like thunder. We took turns testing it out with the other tourists and laughed, praising the ancient engineering that went into the lovely amphitheater. It must have been an incredible thing to see when it was built nearly 2500 years ago.

We toured the connected museum, as well as the gymnasium and some other buildings and ruins until we were satisfied that we'd seen it all.

From there we drove towards Tolon, a seaside town southwest of Athens. There were numerous signs for campgrounds near the town, which presented a new problem. Up until then, we were often lucky just to find one single campground, but now we were presented with an abundance of them. Which one to pick?

Uncle Hugh was hell-bent on choosing the best one the region had to offer, so we drove up and down, scouting the camps from the shoulders of the road. He made observations about each one, visibly making mental notes in a growing inner database of campgrounds. "Oh, that one doesn't have many trees... hmmm, oh that one looks far too hilly, oh no, that one is unkempt and overgrown, and so on.

He just couldn't decide, so we made a list of the top three as the sun began making its descent behind the hills. We drove into all three, putting around the camps while peering out the windows.

An hour and a half later, with the sun completely down, he finally decided on the camp we'd stay in for the night. He immediately began second-guessing himself as we set up camp, wringing his hands and bemoaning the fact that he'd obviously made the wrong choice. I gave very little input during this whole ordeal, as I was still feeling a bit sensitive about Mykonos and didn't want him to blame me for the final choice after all of his vacillating.

We hoisted the flag and explored the campground a bit, which was beautiful, before taking an evening swim in the Argolic Gulf.

Uncle Hugh thought that since we'd put so much effort into choosing this campground, maybe we should stay for an extra day or two. Accordingly, we drove into town and grabbed some groceries and a few nice bottles of Greek wine.

Back at the camp, our flag brought over some visitors – a family of six from Buffalo, New York. Fred and Carol Mueller were touring Greece with their four children William, Frederick, Joanne, and Christopher, before taking a ship to Israel.

They were a nice bunch, and I was happy to hang out with the kids, who ranged from 8 to 15.

They came over the next day and hung out, the kids running around the campground and beach while the adults stayed near the site. We had dinner together and everyone laughed and clapped at all our adventurous tales. They thought it was just marvellous that we'd taken this trip together and were astounded at everything we'd seen so far. The kids thought it was incredible that Uncle Hugh treated me as an adult, and I drank wine ostentatiously while Uncle Hugh called out, "James, tell them about our adventure in the Sahara!" or some of the other stories we'd accumulated.

The parents shushed the children a lot, nagging them not to butt in and to be quiet. It reminded me of life at home with my own parents and made me reflect on how comfortable I'd become in this new life I found myself in. I did miss home, but I'd gained so much independence on this trip that it felt strange to think about going back. While Uncle Hugh could certainly be a challenge, I was getting used to him and he wasn't as tough as he let on. Plus, he treated me like my own man much more than my parents ever had, even if he did lapse every now and then. I realized that he was a lifetime bachelor, stuck in his ways and definitely not used to a smart-aleck teen. Spending time with this family got me feeling introspective about home and about how lucky I was to be experiencing so much of the world. Most of the adults I knew back home had never dreamed of seeing so much!

We ended up staying at the campground for another whole day, with Uncle Hugh proudly boasting about his excellent choice in campgrounds. He seemed to forget all about his handwringing the first night. We spent the days lounging around and swimming in the sea. It was like a mini-vacation on our vacation. All that driving and moving around did get tiring, so it was nice to relax for a little while, especially somewhere so beautiful.

The next morning, we bade farewell to the Muellers and drove to the ruins of an ancient acropolis in Tiryns.

Although the site was popular and was linked to Homer's Iliad and Odyssey, we both found it quite boring as it was nothing but a pile of ruins. We walked around for a while, but even Uncle Hugh couldn't pretend it was all that great, so we got back into the van and moved on.

We made the short drive to Nafplio, a small city with a huge castle perched high on a mountain slope. We parked the van at the bottom and got out, seeing a sign that said that there were 895 steps up to the castle. I couldn't wait to run up to the top.

I tried to wait for Uncle Hugh, but he stopped every twenty steps to catch his breath. It seemed this was torture for both of us – me, because I couldn't go up fast enough, and him because he had to go up at all. I eventually ran out of patience and left him far behind as I scurried up the stairs to the top. I'd already explored nearly half of the castle by the time he made it to the top, huffing and puffing. When I found him, he was sitting on a parapet, sweating his ass off and mopping his forehead with a handkerchief.

"Oh, there you are Jimmy!" he exclaimed when he spotted me, "I was so worried about you; I thought I'd lost you! You shouldn't go running off like that, leaving an old man to potentially have a heart attack on these steps. Then what would you have done? Here, all alone, no one to look after you... what would have become of you?"

"Oh, I'd just carry on the trip by myself. I can probably drive the camper better than you anyways, and I have the itinerary, so I'd be okay." I thought to myself, holding the words in before they spilled out.

The castle was very cool, and we took our time exploring it as Uncle Hugh wanted time to get his energy back for the long climb down.

From Nafplio, we headed to Mycenae, perhaps the most important site in all of Greece according to

Professor Hugh. He had stuffed me full of information and grilled me on it for several of the days leading up to this so I could fully appreciate what we'd see.

Mycenae was built between 1350 and 1200 BCE and was one of the greatest cities of the Mycenean civilization, renowned for its architecture and for its technical and artistic achievements. It was the mythical city of Agamemnon, from where the King led his troops against Troy, eventually using the Trojan Horse to help sack it.

I was enamoured with the place as soon as we entered, first encountering the massive lion gate, built of enormous stones. I thought to myself about what an achievement it must have been to manoeuvre those stones into place without the aid of modern machinery.

We ourselves left no stone unturned as we made our way through the historical site, visiting the beehive tombs, cisterns, temples, and various ruins. Once through with the city, we entered the museum and gazed in wonder at all of the treasures it held. From exquisite pottery, to items made of pure gold, to statues, tools, weapons, and armour, the museum had it all!

There was so much to see that we came back the next day, exploring the palace where we got to see the traditionally dressed guards on duty, wearing white skirts and stockings. At one point, they began a highly stylized high-step march back and forth in front of the gates. The palace gardens were magnificent and the shady areas we found to sit down and relax in were a breath of fresh, cooling air after the hot Greek sunshine we'd been exposed to so much.

Despite the site being engaging and amazing, even to my 14-year-old self, Uncle Hugh's obligatory and continuous commentary on everything we stopped to look at buzzed monotonously in my ear. I knew he meant well and was attempting to educate me, but I found the constant litany irritating. What kid my age wanted to be regularly lectured and chastised when not paying enough attention? I thought this was supposed to be a break from school! At least in school, you had recess to give you a bit of a break.

If I let my eyes wander, my shoulders sag, let out a sigh, or showed anything but absolute attentiveness, I was quickly reprimanded by a man who seemed to think I was personally attacking him and his intellect through inattention. I'm honestly surprised that he didn't have written exams waiting for me back in the van, replete with the requisite 2B pencil.

Of course, according to him, I was being unfair and ungrateful. Looking back as an adult now, I'm sure it was somewhere in the middle. Having no kids himself, Uncle Hugh didn't understand why a young teenager would have a hard time focusing on ancient history for 10 hours at a time.

Having spent two days enjoying Mycenae, it was time to move on. We drove a short way to Thebes, just north of Athens and found a beautiful campsite there. Adjacent to the sea, the campground was full of amazing trees and had a real wilderness feel to it. The only negative was a railway line that ran right alongside the campground, and the constant sound of trains blowing by interfering with the otherwise idyllic natural location.

Setting up camp as usual, with the Canadian flag raised proudly, we caught the attention of four young long-haired Canadians who were all in their twenties. Stopping by our campsite to chat, they quickly ran up against the stern wall Uncle Hugh put up with his body language and clipped one-word answers. Sure enough, their quick wit and friendly demeanour eventually broke through, and he reluctantly gave up his spikiness.

Two of the young men left and quickly came back with a bottle of ouzo and we all settled in for a night of fun. Before I knew it, Uncle Hugh had somehow transformed into a young college beatnik, travelling around Europe on a shoestring. I was delighted, as I'd never seen this side of him, even if his jokes were a little corny. Well, they were really corny, but he was still being funny.

The guys didn't seem to mind, they laughed along at the jokes, shared the ouzo, and included us as if we were part of their group. I'd never tried ouzo before, and I quickly became a fan of the strong, licorice-flavoured spirit. It wasn't long before we were all feeling its effects, laughing our heads off and loosening up.

The guys began telling their story as the sun went down behind the trees. Merv, Bob, and Howard were all from Toronto, while Randy was from Calgary. They'd all gone to college together and had decided to do a Euro-trip before starting their careers. Merv and Bob had plans of hitchhiking to Istanbul, while Howard and Randy had their sights on Athens.

In a shocking turn of events, Uncle Hugh stood up and suggested Merv and Bob come with us to Istanbul, since that was where we were headed next. Flabbergasted at his rare generosity, I looked from the guys to Uncle Hugh and back again with wide eyes.

"Sure," they replied in unison, "Thanks a lot, we'd love to!"

We went on to have a great night, evidenced by the small pile of ouzo bottles we had to clean up in the morning.

With pounding heads and tight eyes, we packed up camp, said our goodbyes to Howard and Randy, loaded up Merv and Bob's gear, and hit the road.

It was a lot of fun having some other passengers to chat with, and their presence kept Uncle Hugh in his youthful and exuberant mood. The kilometres flew by as we laughed and told stories on our way to Thessaloniki up the coast and into the north of Greece. There, we went shopping to replenish our stores and to re-stock the important stuff like wine. Uncle Hugh seemed much less miserly when in the company of our new friends. I thought to myself that this was how we should always travel!

Driving on, the fertile farms surrounding the city eventually turned into hard, barren land that seemed almost primeval. The buildings dotting the landscape and the people we encountered in the area seemed to echo that feeling.

The long, monotonous drive was wearing on Uncle Hugh, so he let one of the guys drive for a spell, which I'd never seen him do before. We eventually found a likely State Ruin Campground and turned in to set up camp for the night. The campground was huge, with three separate restaurants and even a big wooden map so you could navigate your way around the place.

The guys set up their tiny tent beside our camper, and then we reconvened to decide which restaurant to go to for supper. Despite Uncle Hugh always being so picky about such things, he let Merv and Bob decide, waving his hand and saying, "Sure, good choice," when they came to a decision.

Man, I wish it had been that easy for me. I began wishing these guys would stay with us for the entirety of our trip.

We had a great dinner and some exceptionally good wine, though we took it a little easy since we could all still feel the effects of the ouzo from the night before. We got back to our camp after dinner and were all sawing logs before we knew it.

The next morning, we got up extra early in order to make it to the Turkish border before the crowds started. Upon arrival, there was barely a lineup and we were standing in the customs booth in short order.

Uncle Hugh and I went first; the customs agent hardly checked our paperwork before he stamped us through. Bob went next and was let in with no trouble. When it was Merv's turn, the agent spent a long time checking his passport, and then denied him entry. Merv protested, but the border guard didn't speak English. When Merv refused to leave, he sent for someone to come and help and pointed to a bench where Merv could wait. We all waited for over an hour until a friendly-looking woman came out and began speaking to Merv in English. She explained that Merv had a stamp in his passport showing that he'd rented a car and explained that the border guard wanted to know where the car was.

He explained that his party had split up and that his friends had taken the car to Athens. Her friendliness slowly vanished as she told him that this wasn't an acceptable explanation. The burly, militaristic guard showed up again and shook his head ominously when she explained the situation to him. She asked over and over where the rental car was, despite his answer always being the same.

Suddenly she pointed at us where we were sitting and demanded, "Who are you? What is your connection to this man? What are your plans in Turkey? Where is this man's rental car? Why is he with you?"

Uncle Hugh quickly realized that we could be embroiled in something serious here and made what was probably a tough, but in the end, safe decision. "We don't really know these men. We are simply tourists and picked them up at a campground when they asked for a ride. We have no involvement with them and are not part of any schemes or illegal activity."

Apologizing to the two men, Uncle Hugh asked them to please go get their gear from the camper van and go their own way. After a quick goodbye, we abandoned our stricken friends at the Turkish border.

Without the modern-day luxuries of cell phones and social media, not being able to contact their friends in Athens while in a foreign country must have been frustrating and devastating for them. I guess they must have found a ride heading back toward Athens where they could hopefully reconnect with their friends and continue their trip. I often think about them and always feel bad that we were forced to leave them stranded.

Not knowing what to expect when we crossed into Turkey, we were both very eager to see what lay ahead.

The barren countryside of Greece continued on into Turkey, so our first impression wasn't too exciting. There were a lot of people on the road who we had to squeeze the van by that were either walking or being pulled in carts by oxen or donkeys.

We found a BP (British Petroleum) campground just outside of Istanbul. As we drove around the grounds, looking for our site, we were surprised to see our friends Victor and Donna from New Zealand whom we'd met in Portofino, Italy. We had a fun night catching up on travel tales while enjoying some Turkish raki, a clear liquor similar to ouzo with a nasty punch.

The next day, the four of us piled into the camper van and drove into downtown Istanbul. My first impression upon entering the city was that it was a bewildering mix of ancient and modern. In the same view, you could see brand new cars and laden carts pulled by donkeys, contemporary tall office buildings and ancient medieval architecture that was still in use. It was the same with the people, some in business suits and others in traditional garb.

We parked the van and found a tourist booth where we picked up some brochures and a map to help us get around. Our first stop was the Hagia Sophia, a famous blue-domed mosque that was originally a Byzantine church. Since the mosque doubles as a museum, we were able to enter and were astounded at the dizzyingly high ceilings and massive columns. The colours, art, and mosaics all added to its immense beauty.

After spending some time in the mosque, we left and Victor asked around for a decent restaurant in the area. We were pointed towards one and were soon sitting down to shish kebabs, fries, and a round of beers.

We spent the time after lunch strolling the streets and alleyways, enjoying the hustle and bustle of the city, along with all of its unique sights, smells, and sounds. Everything seemed very different here than in Greece, including the people and the way they dressed.

In yet another surprising turn of events, Uncle Hugh suggested that we splurge on supper. "How about the Hilton?" he asked.

Everyone agreed, so we made our way to the Hilton restaurant and sat down. Upon receiving the menu, I was very excited to see hamburgers, so I ordered one with a Coke.

Uncle Hugh was not impressed, "Who in their right mind would order a hamburger when there are so many nice meals on the menu? And at $1.00?! My word, that is outrageous for a hamburger!"

Luckily, we had company, and he wouldn't get away with castigating and glowering at me all night for my choice. With Donna and Victor looking on, he was reduced to simply shaking his head and exclaiming, "Teenagers!"

Everyone laughed about it except for me, but I got my hamburger in the end, and it was absolutely delicious. I felt like I was back in Canada again; this was the ultimate comfort food.

Over the next few days, we routinely left the van at the campground and took a bus, called the Dolmus, into town. We visited many sites, including the Blue Mosque, the Palace, and a few museums. Turkey was a nearly overwhelming smorgasbord of sights and sounds; it was all so strange and wonderful.

One day, we took a Dolmus to the docks, where we took another Dolmus taxi to a second set of docks, where we had to climb over four boats to reach the one we'd hired previously at a tourist kiosk.

We got on the boat and motored out into the Bosporus Strait, stopping at several towns and villages on the water, where we'd stroll and check out the wharves and beaches. At one point, we came across a man who was cooking fresh herring that he'd just caught and he welcomed us to sit and share his meal. Wow, were those fish ever good!

We continued on into the Black Sea and were amazed to see several huge crowded beaches there, with hundreds of people wading out and swimming in the sea. We stopped at one of the beaches, grabbed a Coke and sat down to people-watch for a while.

On our way back, we made a few stops on the Asian side of Turkey which I found impressive. In one day, I'd been to Istanbul, the Black Sea, and Asia!

The day after that, we took a water ferry across the Bosporus Strait back to the Asian side of Turkey. The countryside was a bucolic mix of farm fields and rolling hills and I found it quite beautiful, especially with the water of the Strait lapping against the shore.

It was time to leave Istanbul, so we packed up the van and drove to the ancient city of Troy which can be found near Hisarlik, southwest of Istanbul. We found another BP campground, which was reliably clean and orderly, and stayed there for two days while we explored the ruins and museums in the area. One day, we encountered a caravan of Romanlar (Gypsies) resplendent in a multitude of colours, with equally colourful horse-drawn wagons adorned with bells. Watching them felt like a vision from the past when compared to the modern buildings and cars in the area. I felt like they could have walked straight out of the ancient mosaics we'd been looking at all day.

After seeing Troy, we drove to a ferry and re-crossed the Bosporus, making our way back to the Greek border. As we crossed through, I kept my eyes open for Merv and Bob, knowing that there was very little chance I'd see them, but hopeful all the same. Their memory still ate at my conscience.

After a quiet night spent at a non-descript campground, we made our way up to Yugoslavia, my first communist country.

Chapter 13

Trepidatious about entering a Communist stronghold and being apprehended at the border, I was mildly surprised at how easy it was to cross. After a few brief questions, we were let through with no issues. I wasn't sure whether to be relieved or disappointed at the lack of adventure.

We stopped for the night at a campground in the city of Skopje on the border of modern-day North Macedonia and Kosovo. We went downtown to grab some dinner, and afterwards took a stroll through the surprisingly modern city and discovered there were thousands of people, mostly teenagers, doing the same thing. I was a little shocked at how sharply dressed everyone was; very modern and far nicer clothes than anyone I knew wore.

The stores were also all very modern, with goods that would be found in any of the major cities we'd passed through so far on our trip. Uncle Hugh had told me this city was built 4000 years ago, so I was not expecting such modernity. Apparently, a massive earthquake had destroyed much of the city in the 60s and 80% of it had to be rebuilt. We moved through the well-lit streets along with the throng of people, who were all conversing casually and laughing, and it all felt very surreal for some reason.

The next day, we packed up and moved on to Titograd, what is now known as Podgorica in the modern-day country of Montenegro. The way there was through mountainous terrain and the road twisted and turned quite dangerously. The road had very little in the way of shoulders and looking over the edge from the passenger seat window, I could see that it dropped off hundreds and even thousands of feet in some places. With the steep and curvy roads along with the lack of guard rails, Uncle Hugh was white-knuckled on the wheel.

The crosses didn't help. I had never witnessed this before, but along the side of the road were dozens of markers and crosses, some with flowers and pictures of lost loved ones. It seemed that many people had accidentally driven over the edge to their deaths. As we drove on, the crosses multiplied until they were at nearly every tight turn in the road. Some corners had several different crosses and tributes to the dead, some with grim reminders of humanity like shoes and other clothing hung on the crosses. It was sobering to watch so many of them go by, and neither of us could help but imagine what it would be like to skid over the edge and plunge to our fiery deaths.

It got to the point where I was no longer focusing at all on the incredible scenery around me, instead just counting crosses and hoping that no one would have to erect one for us. Uncle Hugh was obviously feeling the same way and was driving so slowly that he created a more dangerous situation since so many cars attempted to pass us. The blind corners didn't stop them from racing past us in the oncoming traffic lane and he gasped every time a car or transport truck did it, putting our lives and theirs in danger. They would lie on their horns as they did so, waving their fists as Uncle Hugh kept crawling along, sweat beading on his forehead and white knuckles glued to the wheel. For once, I didn't blame him; this was the scariest road we'd been on yet!

Finally arriving in Titograd, Uncle Hugh declared that he was NOT amused by that drive, and I had better find us a campground stat. It was time to have my wits together and not waste any time or send him down any wrong turns while getting there. It was time for precise map reading and clear and concise directions.

I harrumphed to myself. By this point, I'd become more than adept at using the map to navigate and the majority of wrong turns and wasted time could be laid at his feet from when he was being particularly mule-headed. Still, I gave clear and concise directions to El Capitan, the Grand Poohbah of the VW van explorers, and got us safely and quickly to a suitable campground.

Driving through the campground, I pointed out a couple that we'd met while camping near Madrid in Spain, Wendy and Dan. "Just what I need," he growled, "company, tonight of all nights!"

Despite his grumbling, he changed his mind after setting up camp and a soothing cup of Earl Grey tea. "Maybe we should go take a stroll and see how those Americans are doing," he suggested.

Upon arriving at their campsite, Wendy and Dan warmly invited us over for supper. Never being one to miss out on a free meal, Uncle Hugh acquiesced and sent me running back to our campsite to grab a bottle of wine. We had a tasty dinner, meat patties washed down with plenty of wine, and a fantastic night ensued. I really liked Wendy and Dan and it was fun reliving everything that had happened to us since last seeing each other.

After such a stressful day, Uncle Hugh overindulged in the wine and ended up getting quite drunk. I eventually had to carry him home and help him get to bed.

Leaving Titograd the next morning without checking out the city, we headed north towards the Adriatic Sea. Around noon, we encountered a sign that pretty much had Uncle Hugh's name written all over it: FREE CAMPING →.

No matter that it was only noon, no matter that we'd planned on camping at another destination altogether, no matter that we were supposed to be sticking to our itinerary, Uncle Hugh wasn't going to pass the chance for a free night of camping. Tires squealed as he cranked the wheel to send us off the highway and down the dirt road that the arrow pointed towards. Soon, we were driving over dunes, following tracks in the sand that led us down towards a massive beach. There were about 8 campers stretched along the beach – trailers, vans, and tents of all sorts.

There were lots of people milling about, so we pulled up to someone and Uncle Hugh leaned out of the window asking, "Hello, can we camp here? Is it free?"

"Right, you are!" the apparently British man responded, "Set up anywhere you'd like!"

We found a spot to park the van, and since there were no trees to hoist our Canadian flag, I hung it on the side of the van. We strolled back to where all of the people were hanging out and noticed that they were all quite young. Now, when I say young, I mean younger than Uncle Hugh, but a fair bit older than myself. Most were probably in their 20s or 30s. They were all very friendly and welcomed us as if we were long-lost friends.

Before we knew it, we were laughing and joking over beers with Americans, Australians, Brits, and one Canadian couple. We all went for a swim and after a while, a couple of people said they were going into town for some supplies, and asked if we wanted to come along. I quickly said yes, but Uncle Hugh shook his head no, and I felt myself deflating.

"Well, why don't you go along with them my boy, it will be fun for you."

Great news! Without hesitating, I jumped into their van, but Uncle Hugh came running over. "Wait, wait!" he said, and gave me a list of supplies we needed and some Yugoslavian money.

When we reached town, the guys wanted to grab a beer, so we found an outdoor restaurant and ordered a round. We sat around sipping our beers and laughing just like a bunch of pals; I was already having so much fun and feeling very adult-like. After a couple beers, we got the supplies we needed, then headed back to the beach.

That night, I made spaghetti for supper, with fried mushrooms and plenty of garlic and oregano, which we washed down with some red wine. Afterwards, someone lit up a bonfire and all of the campers gathered around it. Everyone was sitting around the fire, laughing and joking as if we'd all known each other for years. All of these folks were free-spirited, just living life carefree, and I felt like I was spending time with the hippies I'd seen on TV. I was having a blast!

The next few days were much the same, swimming, strolling, drinking, bonfires, and good times. I borrowed a mask and snorkel and swam for hours and hours one day. When I came back to shore, my back had the worst sunburn on it and it hurt for days. Still, I was having the time of my life, and Uncle Hugh must have been enjoying himself too because he made no move to leave despite our itinerary.

One morning, I realized that I'd lost my high school ring somewhere in the surf and sand. It must have slipped off my finger while I was swimming. I looked for hours but to no avail. That night, I drank more than my fair share, drowning my teenage sorrows and was reprimanded by Uncle Hugh in the morning for my excesses, despite me so recently carrying him home after his bad day. Sorry Uncle Hugh, but it probably won't be the last time.

We had such a glorious time on the beach that we never wanted to leave. Still, we had to continue the trip and one morning Uncle Hugh reluctantly said that we'd better get back on the road. So, with lots of hugs and kisses, we said goodbye to our new friends, sad to be leaving them and unaware that we'd end up running into several of them in the future.

We headed towards Dubrovnik and then to Split in modern-day Croatia and were impressed by the beautiful scenery along the coastline. The two stunning medieval cities were built with fortifications to the sea and terraced streets that ran up the mountainside. We took our time touring through the towns, mostly because the steep streets were taxing on Uncle Hugh. He struggled up the slopes, huffing and puffing, but stubbornly pushing on as he wanted to see it all and didn't want to miss anything.

After Split, the going became quite monotonous, with boring scrubland and poor towns and villages. Everything, including the people, seemed poor and ragged. People's clothes were dirty and torn and most didn't have vehicles so they either walked down the road or rode in carts pulled by mules or horses. It was quite a contrast to the people we'd seen in Skopje, who were all well-fed and well-dressed. These people were a sad sight to see.

Chapter 14

We passed through the border of Italy without issue and drove straight to Venice, where we found a nice little campground on the mainland. We spent the next three days in Venice and the best word I could come up with to describe it was magical. It is simply the most fabulous place you could imagine. The best way to explore it is on foot, and with 400 bridges, you can access every corner of the city. Getting somewhere more quickly than by walking was easily accomplished by taking Vaporettos, or water buses, which we did quite often as well.

A more famous option for getting around was via gondola, where a man in a striped shirt would pole you around in a traditional long boat, but after approaching at least ten of them, Uncle Hugh deemed it far too expensive, despite wanting to experience it. We stuck to the Vaporettos and watched the more spendthrift tourists floating around the canals in gondolas.

Whilst milling about in St. Mark's Square one afternoon, eyes roving over the multitude of statues and architectural whimsies, we were surprised to run into some of our friends from the Yugoslavian beach party, Leanne and Glen.

We talked for a while in the square, then decided to stick together and explore the city as a team for the day. I was glad for the extra company, as Uncle Hugh was always a little lighter and more jovial when we were spending time with other people. He was also hesitant to delve into his long-winded lectures when other people were around, which was a refreshing change of pace.

We waited in line to get into St. Mark's Basilica and then made our way in to take a look around. The place was absolutely beautiful with jaw-dropping art, architecture, and furnishings everywhere. We worked our way through the halls and eventually ended up on the Doge's private balcony, overlooking the square where we had just been. As we stood there, enjoying the view, a woman's voice drifted up to us, spoken in what was obviously a New York accent. The woman was saying to her companion that yes, Venice was quite beautiful, but she believed that the Italians had built it all simply to rival Disneyland in America. I'm sure she could hear our laughter drifting down from the balcony, as we were all in stitches over what she'd said. We laughed about it for days and days after that!

That evening, we sat down for dinner on an outdoor patio and had ravioli, fish, and squid, with large amounts of wine, and then had gelato for dessert. It was nice to share the meal with our friends as there was much more conversation than when Uncle Hugh and I had dinner alone.

We left no stone unturned in Venice, visiting every attraction the city had to offer, including every single canal, building, and bridge, not to mention the Gallerie dell'Accademia, where we reviewed every painting, artifact, and sculpture in superfluous detail. Despite Uncle Hugh's monotonous descriptions, I still found it wonderful and to this day, can't praise Venice and its beautiful glories enough.

Characteristically, Uncle Hugh wasn't quite as lavish with his praise. Despite very much enjoying what the city had to offer, he had a fair amount to add to his list of European disappointments. The canals were disgusting, full of brown water that was obviously polluted, there was a constant haze over the city, probably from industry located way too close to the city he happened to be visiting, and the whole city was sinking, rendering many ground floors unusable as they were inundated with water. The affrontery of this historically significant city sinking seemed to really eat at him. He did love Venice, but he figured there was a whole lot more they should be doing to preserve it to his specifications.

We reluctantly said goodbye to Venice after too short of a time there and headed for a whole new country: Austria. It was pouring rain that day, causing the traffic to be terrible, which made for a stressful and exhausting drive. Uncle Hugh requested that I find an alternate route that avoided the busy major highways, so I quickly penned a new one onto the map, directing him onto less busy roads that made the drive slightly easier.

Due to the low cloud cover, we didn't even notice the mountains until we were suddenly climbing them. The roads here were less stressful than on other mountain passes and we quickly made our way into Austria with no issues. We got to the city of Lienz, where we drove around, stopping at hotels and private homes offering rooms, eyeing each up and reading the guidebook reviews if there were any. As per usual, the offerings didn't meet Uncle Hugh's exacting standards, but we finally found one that he approved of, after turning down a dozen, and we got to have a nice dry night in a comfortable room rather than a loud night in the van with rain beating on the roof. The room came with those thick European duvets I loved so much, and I happily cuddled up into them, falling asleep at once.

We continued to travel for the next few days, crossing the mountains and driving around hairpin turns and steep inclines; one was on a whopping 14% grade. We drove over the Grossglockner Pass at 8000 feet, where we stopped and visited the impressive Franz Josef and Edelweiss-Spitze glaciers.

Coming out of the glaciers, we managed to find ourselves on a very expensive toll road that wasn't listed on the map. Somehow it was my fault for letting it happen, even though there weren't any alternate roads to take and Uncle Hugh had seen the signage on the way into it. I don't know. Maybe we should have ditched the VW and hiked our way around it, or found a likely elephant or pack mule to take us to the other side?

The road took us across the border with Germany, then back into Austria several times on beautiful, but challenging mountain roads that tested Uncle Hugh's driving and clutch work. He would hardly be himself if he wasn't stressed out in these situations but he had progressed since we started the trip, and managed to plod along, successfully making it to the city of Salzburg without burning out the clutch.

Uncle Hugh found us a "campground" on the outskirts of the city that was attached to a schoolyard and seemed suspiciously not like a campground at all. You never knew with Uncle Hugh, who took every opportunity to save a buck or two, whether by stealing salt, pepper, sugar, napkins, or even whole ketchup or mustard bottles from restaurants, sneaking out of campgrounds before first light without paying, or putting us in steerage on boat journeys.

He would often surprise me with what he'd sometimes dole out for though and this was the case in Salzburg, where he purchased two very expensive tickets to the Minarette Opera. He splurged on very good seats and the opera was actually amazing. We were so close that the minarettes seemed to come alive, and the singing and dancing were fantastic.

We just spent just one night in Salzburg, then continued on our way, spending the next few days driving through Bavaria in Germany. Considering Uncle Hugh's interest in architecture, we had to stop at some of the castles built by the Mad King Ludwig II.

Ludwig was obsessed with castles and built one after another in the region which resulted in Bavaria being known to have some of the most magnificent castles in all of Europe.

Neuschwanstein Castle had to be the most impressive, as it sits on top of a mountain, resplendent in its pale white and grey glory, overlooking the entire countryside. It was actually the inspiration for the Magic Kingdom castle in Disneyworld. I'm sure that the woman from New York that we overheard in Venice would just be disgusted that Germany would try and copy America's Disney castle!

Ludwig's Herrenchiemsee Castle was another impressive example. Built on an island, this castle was meant to rival Versailles, and shares many similarities to the French palace.

Ludwig's obsession with building castles and his eccentric attitude proved to be financially disastrous for the region and the populace eventually had enough. One day he was found drowned by his servants, floating facedown in the lake of his latest castle.

Once Uncle Hugh eventually tired of these architectural wonders, so we made our way across the bottom of Germany and into the tiny country of Liechtenstein, which we crossed in barely half an hour.

That brought us back into Switzerland, but from the east rather than the north.

Driving through more pouring rain, which was interrupted by countless long, long tunnels through the mountains, we finally made it to Zurich and found a campground close to town.

Uncle Hugh happened to have some old friends in Zurich, so we took a bus from the campground into town, then jumped onto a streetcar for the last leg of our little journey. Well, we thought it was the last leg, but we happened to take the streetcar the wrong way. Realizing our error, we got off, but couldn't for the life of us figure out how to get back on the car heading the other way. Eventually, we gave up and just walked, our jackets soaking through with rain and our shoes squelching with every step.

We walked for kilometres before eventually stumbling across the street that they lived on, and then finally finding their house. Looking back on these moments, I'm once again astounded at how much easier things would have been with the modern convenience of a smartphone!

Nora and Jon were lovely people and made us feel instantly welcome in their home, giving us towels to dry ourselves off. They had adopted two Tibetan children about six years before. Their son Zerdan was ten and their daughter Kasa was eight years old. I went off with the children and they showed me their rooms, then brought me outside to play some soccer in the yard as the rain had finally let up.

Nora and Jon brought us out for dinner that night for a hearty meal consisting of leeks, potatoes, and chunks of sausage in a warm casserole. It was accompanied by some delicious German white wine.

Our hosts thought it was funny that I automatically offered my glass to be filled, exclaiming that I must be turning into a European.

We spent the night back at the campground, then made our way back to their house in the morning, this time taking the camper van to avoid any public transportation mishaps. Their natural-born son Daniel, who was in his mid-twenties was home for the day, and he was very interested to hear our stories, while the younger children were excited to climb around the camper van.

We had a delicious lunch of roast beef, French fries, and spinach, then said our goodbyes after lunch, driving down into the valley town of Lauterbrunnen. The town was on the flat bottom of a steep-cliffed valley, nestled between massive mountain ranges. The verdant slopes were dotted with dairy cows and small log buildings, and the houses in town had steeply sloped roofs. The place reminded me of the children's book Heidi, and I half-expected her to pop out at any moment.

We found a campground and set up camp, quickly attracting the notice of a couple from Boston with whom we spent a very pleasant evening, swapping stories over glasses of delicious red wine.

The next day, we drove to the end of the valley to visit the glacier at Grindelwald, which was a beautiful pale azure. On the way back to the campground, I noticed two girls hitchhiking and impulsively called out for Uncle Hugh to stop and pick them up. I was surprised when he followed suit and braked hard, lurching off the road and pulling up beside them. I rolled the window down and asked if they wanted a ride in my most debonair voice.

Smiling, the two cute teens, Ava and Presley, agreed and jumped into the camper and instantly we all started chatting like we were long-lost friends. The girls were from the UK, hitchhiking their way across Europe. It came up in conversation that one of them had actually lived in Javea, Spain for a while, the same place where Uncle Hugh's cousin Richard lived. She hadn't met him, but it seemed like such a small world when you randomly met someone in a far-off place who shared a connection with you, however small.

Uncle Hugh, having warmed up to them after discovering their connection to his cousin, asked where they were heading to and where they'd be spending the night. They replied that they only free-camped when they got to their destinations for the night since they were travelling on a shoestring and had very little money.

Uncle Hugh shocked me by offering to let them pitch their tents on our campsite and telling them they should join us for dinner. I was giddy with excitement at the thought of sharing our campsite with two cute girls for the night!

They asked to stop at a store to buy some wine to help pitch in, and I offered to make supper, probably trying to impress them by seeming older than I actually was. While they went off for a hot shower in the camp restrooms, I whipped up some fried potatoes with cabbage, corn, and beef. The meal went over well, and we had a great night with the girls doing the majority of the talking.

They told us all about their travels up to that point, including several stories of scary rides they'd had, which they laughed about as they told us. Apparently, there was no shortage of creepy older men who wouldn't hesitate to pick up a couple of young girls, and sometimes they'd have to resort to extreme measures to get away. Still, most of the rides were from tourists like us whom they'd also shared meals with, and they had plenty of fun stories about all of the people they'd met.

I loved listening to them tell their stories all night, intently watching their pretty faces as they snorted and laughed at what they'd been through. Of course, every good thing had to come to an end, and this was no different. We eventually said goodnight and all turned in (me very reluctantly).

I stayed up half the night wondering if I could sneak out of the camper without waking Uncle Hugh and go climb in between the two girls in their tent but eventually drifted off to sleep.

I got up early in the morning, only to find that the girls and their tent were gone. Had they really been here, or was it all just a pleasant dream?

Uncle Hugh had little to say about it, other than that he'd had a pleasant evening and that he was happy that I wasn't a female.

We decided to spend the day hiking in the mountains, so we filled our backpacks with food and drinks and walked to the funicular, a cable railway that would take us up the slope to the town of Mürren, perched on the precipice above us. From there, we found the trailhead and hiked through beautiful meadows with waist-high wildflowers, eventually reaching rock outcrops that we had to scramble up. Continuing our way up and up and up, we got to a point where we could look in any direction for miles and it felt like we were the only ones on the planet. It was a gorgeous day, beautifully warm, with the sun shining down gently over the snowcapped peaks. What a wonderful experience – the view, the fresh mountain air, and the feeling of complete freedom. I felt totally elated.

The next day, we left Lauterbrunnen and continued our drive through the mountains, driving through valleys and up over crazy Alpine peaks. Uncle Hugh maneuvered the van through the various twists, turns, switchbacks, and severe gradients with a renewed confidence, though he eventually came to be frustrated that he couldn't see any of the scenery as he had to focus solely on the road ahead of him. I understood his frustration, as I was able to watch the scenery unfold and was consistently flabbergasted by the beauty of it all.

He confided that the steep drop-offs and dangerous turns reminded him of the dramatic train derailment that had broken his neck. For the first time, he related the entire tale to me.

He had taken the train from Philadelphia to Oregon and had paid extra for a sleeper car since he doubted he'd be able to get any sleep sitting up in a chair for the entire journey. One night, while he was fast asleep in the car, the train rounded a bend in the mountains, encountering an avalanche of snow that completely covered the tracks. The engineer was unable to stop in time and the train plowed into the deep snow, causing it to derail. The engine and cars went over the side of the bank and plummeted down the 1000-foot decline. Being in the middle, his sleeper car travelled down the slope nearly upright, but when it crashed into ground at the bottom of the slope, a half-asleep Uncle Hugh was thrown forward, smashing into the far wall, and hitting his head so hard that he blacked out.

He woke up later to the sounds of screaming and crying and crawled his way out of the train car in daze. Through the swirling stars before his eyes, he could see people climbing out of smashed up train cars; those who were mostly uninjured helping the less fortunate back up the steep bank and away from the train. The scene was confusing, with dozens of people screaming into the dark for lost loved ones.

Not wanting to remain with the carnage on the valley floor, Uncle Hugh began to make his way up the bank with a crowd of others. He was still in a complete daze, couldn't see straight, and was having a hard time processing what was happening.

He joined the others at the top of the bank, where they sat down on the tracks and waited hours for rescuers to show up. When they eventually arrived, paramedics took Uncle Hugh and many others to the nearest hospital.

Still complaining of vision problems, lack of focus, and an incredibly sore head and neck, he was diagnosed with a severely broken neck. The doctor was astounded when he heard that Uncle Hugh had made the climb back up to the tracks on his own. The doctor told him that he should have never moved at all, and the fact that he did could have easily severed his spinal cord, killing or paralyzing him instantly.

The recovery was going to be awful, but Uncle Hugh counted himself lucky to be alive. Eleven people had died in the crash, and many of the survivors had even worse injuries.

The doctors installed a plaster cast on him from directly under his chin to his waist and he stayed immobile like that for six miserable months. The worst thing about it, he said, was the itchiness. Often, he would ask people around him, including my mother, a teen at the time, to shove sharp sticks down under the cast to scratch the incessant itches. After the cast was finally removed, his spinal disks had fused, causing his head and neck to jut forward, and his back to arch, giving him the appearance of a slight hunchback. The disks in his neck were also fused, meaning that he'd never be able to turn his head from side to side again and that was the reason he'd needed to bring me along on this adventure in the first place.

It was quite the story and, hearing it in full, it had me feel a little more forgiving towards the guy, who was at once a mentor, parental figure, friend, teacher, travel partner, and sometime-nemesis to me.

Chapter 15

Finally coming down off the mountain roads, Uncle Hugh decided that he wanted to spend the night with the Frei family, back in Versoix, Switzerland. Instead of taking a break after a strenuous drive like we normally would, he had us drive and drive until we finally reached the village, which was sandwiched between Lake Geneva and the French border. It felt like a lifetime ago that we'd been here, but everything looked the same.

I was anxious to see the girls again, who I'd had such a lovely time with, but was disappointed to learn that Ann was in England and Barbara was at a friend's. The Freis planned on leaving to join Ann in England for an extended vacation in the next few days.

They did happen to have some friends staying with them when we arrived, a family from Montreal who were old friends of Mrs. Frei. They had two kids, Jany who was 14 and Steven who was 11. Despite living in the French province of Quebec, they were actually from an English neighbourhood and spoke very little French.

In an effort to bring the kids up to speed, Mrs. Frei decided that all conversations in the house for the four-week duration of their visit would be held in French. She said that total immersion was the best way to learn any language.

They were on the last week of their visit, and after three and a half weeks of communicating only in French, the kids had caught on astoundingly well and could converse quite fluently, carrying on normal conversations with ease. Our visit threw a bit of a wrench into the works, as neither of us spoke any French, so we forced everyone to switch back to English to accommodate us.

Barbara arrived home from her visit at her friend's place and suddenly the world, and my visit at the Freis', seemed brighter for her being there.

Mrs. Frei pulled out the raclette cooker and we had a fantastic and hearty dinner of fried potatoes and melted cheese. Everyone at the dinner table was anxious to hear about our travels, so we regaled them with our stories throughout supper and into the night. Since they were full hosting another family, Uncle Hugh and I spent the night sleeping in the camper van in the driveway.

The next morning, Barbara led me and the other two kids to Lake Geneva for a swim. Not wanting to miss an opportunity to show off in front of Barbara, I was the first in, cannonballing into the freezing cold water and trying to act nonchalant when I surfaced, even though I wanted to gasp and shiver and carry on. My fellow Canadians let down me and their whole country by refusing to enter the water due to it being "way too cold".

No matter. Barbara, who had now been nicknamed Ba Ba, jumped in, and we had a great time frolicking in the water, and an even better time having a rollicking towel fight once we were out.

Back at the Freis' that afternoon, we watched French movies with English subtitles and wiled away the hours playing endless rounds of Crazy 8s.

The next morning, the four of us were given permission to take the ferry into Lake Geneva, so we walked out to the pier and booked a five-hour trip that would bring us the length of the entire lake, with a stop at Chateau Chillon, a castle poking right out into the lake.

We spent the entire ferry ride in stitches, with Ba Ba talking rapidly in English, then switching seamlessly to French, then to Italian, then to German, all without missing a beat. We laughed uproariously and were a general menace on the boat, as only unsupervised young teenagers could be. The other bored and irritated-looking passengers on the ferry must have been wondering who owned this gaggle of misbehaving children and why we were doing touristy things!

The Chateau Chillon was a very cool spot, and I loved exploring it with the freedom of a young and a cute girl my age at my side, rather than with a well-meaning, but boring, stolid, slow-moving, and garrulous great uncle. We ran and climbed and crawled and shimmied into every nook and cranny of the castle, enjoying the dungeons most of all, where we took turns playing at captor and prisoner.

Instead of taking the slow ferry back, we returned to the Freis' by train. Navigating a series of connections and transfers, I felt like such a mature adult; almost as if I'd been naturally doing this kind of thing for my entire life.

After dinner, the four of us spent the evening in Ba Ba's room, sitting on the floor and listening to the album Jesus Christ Superstar! on her record player. The album was played repeatedly and eventually, we were all dancing like maniacs and bellowing the lyrics at the top of our lungs. We were having a blast!

Luckily the Freis' house was large and built solidly enough that no adults came upstairs to shut it all down or tell us to be quiet. That wouldn't have been the case in my house back home... that is if I were allowed to have a record player in my room, or even friends over in the first place. This trip was introducing me to freedoms I'd never even imagined before leaving for it.

We did have one visitor eventually make their way up to the room when Uncle Hugh poked his head in and said that it was late and time to get out to the camper to get some sleep. The magical evening was abruptly cut short, and I lay down in my sleeping bag, humming songs from Jesus Christ Superstar! with visions of a Ba Ba dancing around in my head.

The next morning, I woke up to find Uncle Hugh preparing the van to leave. He told me he was heading into Geneva to do some shopping and shooed me out into the house without even asking me if I wanted to come. He knew where I wanted to be, and I'm sure he would value some alone time himself.

Mrs. Frei's Canadian friends were leaving that day, so she piled us all into a car and drove to Geneva to do a little shopping and run some errands before dropping them off at the airport.

We ended up close by to the office where Mr. Frei worked and Ba Ba thought it would be a great idea to go surprise him at work. Mrs. Frei sent us along, saying she would drop everyone else off at the airport, and then come back to the office to pick us up.

After a tour of the office which wasn't quite so fun as I thought it would be, Mrs. Frei came back to pick us up and we went out for lunch for hot dogs. The hot dogs reminded me of home, but also had me pensively considering how different my life here was from back home, and how different home, and I, would be when I returned. We spent the rest of the afternoon clothes shopping for Ba Ba, which wasn't all too much fun, considering how many times an indecisive teenage girl had to try on different combinations of outfits before deciding on any. Despite the boredom I felt sitting on benches, waiting for her to decide, I couldn't think of anywhere else I would rather be. I was smitten.

On our return home, Uncle Hugh announced that he wanted to bring us all out for a nice supper at a nearby fancy restaurant. My eyebrows tried to climb all of the way up my forehead at the announcement. I wondered what he had encountered in town that had put him in such a good, generous mood. Maybe it was my absence for the day?

Supper was delicious. I had a marvellous fish dish with frites and lots of white wine to wash it down. I sat on the same side of the table as Ba Ba and we chatted privately the entire time, not even hearing what the adults had to say. We finished dinner and went outside to wait for Mr. Frei to pull the car around. It had started raining while we were eating dinner, but despite that, Ba Ba asked me if I wanted to walk home instead of getting into the car.

Of course! I hardly noticed the rain as we slowly meandered our way back home, chatting animatedly the entire time.

The next morning was a sad day for me, as the Freis were leaving for a vacation to England and it would be the last day Ba Ba and I could hang out. As we were saying our goodbyes, Mrs. Frei asked if it was possible to potentially meet up again in England if our schedule permitted it. Uncle Hugh wasn't sure it would work with our timing, but a beacon of hope began blazing in my head.

"We'll see you there," I said confidently as Ba Ba got into the car to leave. I was the navigator, wasn't I? I would get us to their place in time, even if it killed me.

On the road again, we made the short drive into France, assuming our roles as driver/educator and navigator/student. I think we had both thoroughly enjoyed our little break apart from each other and soon slipped back into our normal routine, but feeling a little lighter and refreshed.

Uncle Hugh began his lecturing as soon as we crossed the border into France. We were heading to Ronchamp where a Roman Catholic chapel had been built by Le Corbusier in 1955. The chapel was regarded as one of the most important European buildings of the century, as its revolutionary design was instrumental in completely altering the modernistic style of architecture at the time. Although it was much smaller than I envisioned, it was actually sort of cool and was certainly different from all of the architectural styles I'd seen in religious buildings up to that point. The smooth white walls and strange sloping peak of the chapel reminded me of a boat like Noah's Ark.

We couldn't find a campground anywhere nearby that evening, so we ended up finding a random country lane, driving a way down it, and finding a secluded spot in a farmer's field, hidden by a clump of trees.

Camping like this was a lot of fun, at least until it came time to "use the facilities", or lack thereof. We spent the night unmolested and didn't even need to sneak away without paying. Uncle Hugh made sure I looked outside every fifteen minutes or so to make sure the farmer wasn't coming to kick us out. As we made our way towards Fontainebleau, the French countryside was incredible, the tree-lined roads passing through rolling hills dotted with barns and farmhouses all in the local building style. At one point, we saw a rustic sign pointing the way to a local castle and we pulled off to check it out, straying from our itinerary in an unplanned lark.

This Chateau was somewhat more humble than others we had visited, but it still had a full moat and a drawbridge, which was enough for me. The same family had been living there since the 1700s and now allowed the public to visit for a small price to help pay for upkeep. I enjoyed every castle we visited, and this one won extra points for its moat and drawbridge. There was something very romantic about castles and I imagined myself living in one like the family at the one we were visiting. Maybe one day I would! [Author's Note: shockingly, I'm still not living in a castle.]

Chapter 16

We made it most of the way to Fontainebleau but couldn't find a campground anywhere. I suggested staying in a field again, but Uncle Hugh was nervous about it, considering our proximity to Paris. We spotted a parked police car and Uncle Hugh sent me over to ask them for directions to a place we could camp. The officer simply said, "Follow me, sir." and we had another police escort directly to a campground.

That evening, Uncle Hugh began a long lecture on Napoleon Bonaparte. His history, his rise to power, his exploits, the French Revolution, constant wars with everyone, his successes, his failures, and his fanaticism for glory, power, and personal gain. He told me about how Napoleon was finally beaten and imprisoned, but that his right-hand man, Marshall Ney, led loyal troops to free him and how he once again battled all of the surrounding countries. They eventually had to band together to defeat him a second time.

Uncle Hugh informed me that Marshall Ney was my great, great, great, great, great, great grandfather, which really got my attention and instantly made me hear the just-given lecture in a different light. My active imagination spent the night dreaming up scenes of Napoleonic battles with me leading troops to free the great king.

The next day was spent touring Fontainebleau, and everything there spoke to me with a certain intensity now that I knew there was a family connection. I stood in the square, envisioning Napoleon standing on the horseshow staircase, bidding farewell to his loyal followers before being sent away to the island of Elba, never to return.

The palace itself was fabulous; opulently furnished and beautifully decorated. Throughout the entire tour, I walked beside an imagined Napoleon, discussing battle plans and celebrating sure victory.

We strolled through Napoleon's gardens, which were extensive and perfectly manicured in the French fashion. We found a swing in a small corner of the gardens and stopped there to enjoy a lunch that we'd packed, which consisted of baguette, cheese, and saucisson. It was a special lunch, swinging in the shade of a weeping willow, surrounded by the heady scent of roses of many colours.

We were reluctant to leave the palace, but we had to make our way to nearby Paris before it got dark. Still, Uncle Hugh said it was an absolute necessity to make a quick stop at the cathedral in Châtres just outside the city. He said that it was the most beautiful of the Gothic cathedrals still remaining, and I couldn't help but agree when we arrived, despite being underwhelmed by his description. Built in the 13th century, the cathedral was mainly done in the Gothic style, but also displayed architectural styles such as Romanesque, French Gothic, and High Gothic. I enjoyed visiting the cathedral, especially when we went inside and saw the sun coming through the impressive stained-glass windows, but I was experiencing some lecture fatigue and was starting to ignore everything that Professor Hugh said, interesting or not.

Not able to make it into Paris before dark, we stopped in Versailles instead and found a campground for the night. The site was only okay, but we did enjoy a really nice meal of pasta with onions, tomatoes, and mushrooms, joined by a nice bottle of French red and some millefeuille for dessert. We'd stopped at a patisserie on the way in and the millefeuille looked so good, we had to get it.

The next morning, we made our way into Paris, promising to come back to Versailles sometime later. We found a campground, le Bois de Boulogne, which is located right on the Seine River and is only about 15 minutes from downtown. The campground was crowded, with the campsites cheek by jowl and everything feeling run down. The camp store and washroom facilities had constant lineups which was frustrating. Once you finally got into the washroom, you couldn't wait to get back out again, since they were rarely cleaned. We hoped that its proximity to downtown would be worth it.

We took a subway into the center of town rather than driving and walked the streets, admiring all of the beauty while threading our way through the thousands of people doing the same. We wandered over to the Eiffel Tower, ready to walk right up it, only to find a milling line of hundreds of people waiting to get in.

Queuing and lining up certainly cannot be listed as Uncle Hugh's strengths. He'd walk up to a long line with a slightly confused grimace on his face, seemingly expecting everyone in line to recognize him and whisk him to the front of the line. When this inevitably didn't happen, he would stand, staring at the line disapprovingly for long minutes, before eventually sighing and shuffling his way to the back, deigning to join the commoners, but still giving off the impression that he was better than this... and them.

We finally got in and took the lift to the first level, which housed a small restaurant. Though we were both starving by that point, Uncle Hugh decided that the restaurant would be too overpriced due to where it was and that we'd have to wait to eat. Poking around the level and looking longingly at the restaurant while our stomachs rumbled in distress, we returned to the lift and took it up to the second level. We exited, only to find ourselves at the back of another long line with an indeterminable waiting time.

Uncle Hugh was becoming noticeably impatient and exasperated, to the point where I noticed people whispering about us. He began pacing back and forth in the small space, grumbling under his breath, and throwing up his hands. I winced, as I saw the whispered conversations about us spreading down the line, with several people surreptitiously staring at us. I expected him to start shouting at any moment, "This is unacceptable! You can't do this to me, I'M AN AMERICAN CITIZEN!!!!"

Luckily, the line reached the lift that would take us to the top before he actually exploded. As we approached the lift, several people moved out of our way to let us on before them. Uncle Hugh strode past them with his nose in the air, accepting the commoners' deference to his higher learning and debonair appearance. I slunk in behind him, seeing instead the looks shooting our way that silently said that we must stink terribly. In truth, they probably just didn't want to get on a tight lift with a maniac.

The view from the top was incredible, but it quickly became apparent that Uncle Hugh was going to take his time to enjoy it. He had spent hours getting up to this point, so he was going to take full advantage. Out came his camera case and he began setting up shots in his meticulous and vexatious manner. He took picture after picture, seemingly taking one for every degree of the 360° view. Of course, every photo was preceded by light meter readings, aperture adjustments, focusing, and refocusing, not to mention loudly bullying people to get out of his way and much flapping of hands.

I had completed my tour of the top of the tower and had taken a heap of pictures in less than ten minutes, and found myself standing next to Uncle Hugh while he fussed over his camera, feeling embarrassment and boredom grow to an unmanageable amount.

Just before I flung myself off the top of the tower, a group of French girls in matching school uniforms with white shirts and little skirts spilled out of the lift doors. Saved from a young and tragic death due to boredom, I nonchalantly left Uncle Hugh's side and began following them around. This was way more interesting than aperture adjustments and the new view I was seeing was easily as beautiful as the view from the tower.

Time was suddenly passing effortlessly as I casually followed the group of girls around, trying to look suave and maybe get noticed. I was shocked when Uncle Hugh's voice suddenly broke through the buzz of the crowd, "Well James, have you seen enough of the sights of Paris? I have. Despite the ridiculous wait, I thought it was just wonderful. Did you?"

Taking one last longing look at the short skirts, I turned and replied, "Yes, everything I can see from here is spectacular!"

Back on the ground, we spent an achingly long time taking pictures of the Eifel Tower from the bottom, then made our way to the grounds of the Louvre to get a look at the grand museum we'd be visiting on the morrow. "Oh goody," I thought to myself, "another art museum. Hopefully, they have a rendition of Madonna and Child somewhere in there."

We left for the campground, stopping on the way to pick up a bottle of wine and some groceries and supplies. While eating an early supper at the campsite, hemmed in by loud families on all sides, Uncle Hugh announced that he had a surprise for me. He insisted we get showered and put on our nicest clothes for where we were going that evening, staying completely silent on where exactly that might be. No matter how much I pestered him to do so, he refused to offer even a hint!

I did everything he bade me to do, anxiously intrigued as to what we were going to go do. All spiffed up, we took the subway to the center of town again, then walked to the Theatre Folies Bergère, where we approached the front desk to buy tickets for the show.

Hemming and hawing over which tickets to purchase, Uncle Hugh eventually decided on reasonably good tickets on the second level, in the front row. He was worried that since the second level was much cheaper, we wouldn't get a good view, but his fretting was in vain. The front row seats afforded us a fantastic and unobstructed view of the stage and Uncle Hugh was giddy with delight.

I still had no idea what we were there to see, gamely following along to see Uncle Hugh's big surprise. I figured it was likely something boring that he wanted to expose me to; maybe opera or some sort of ballet.

Turns out, I was wrong. Oh, so wrong.

I knew I was in for something special as soon as the music started. Before I knew it, dozens of near-naked women appeared on stage, breasts bare, hips gyrating and shaking, bodies moving in ways I hadn't ever seen before. Oh my.

I'm not sure if I'd ever seen an adult woman's naked breasts in person before, but during this show, I got to see more than I could ever hope for, and then some! It was almost too much for a 14-year-old to handle. I couldn't believe how beautiful each woman was, in all of their naked glory and I couldn't believe I was there to see it. Quite a surprise indeed.

At one point the women all gathered on a metal structure which was raised upward so that they were all dancing mere feet away from where I sat in the second level. I'm sure I just sat there, dumbstruck with my mouth hanging open, while Uncle Hugh, eyes bright, rubbed his hands together as he cooed and almost hummed with glee.

I honestly can't even remember what the show was called, or what it was supposed to be about, just the pure excitement of it all and the vision of those women seared into my brain. I wrote that it was the best day of my life in my journal that night.

After the show, as we were strolling out of the theatre, Uncle Hugh asked me what I thought of the show.

"It was okay," I replied, trying not to let on how flabbergasted I was at the nudity.

"Only okay?" he replied.

"Well... I thought it was really good." I kept downplaying the experience, even though I was trembling with the need to somehow immediately tell all of my buddies back home all about it.

Uncle Hugh just gave me a knowing smirk and kept on walking. It was a gorgeous summer night, made all the more beautiful since we were experiencing it on the charming streets of Paris.

As we approached the subway to make our way back to the campground, Uncle Hugh suddenly stopped and said, "Let's make this amazing night continue. No need to go home just yet."

Heartily agreeing with him, I turned around and followed him to an outdoor restaurant, where we sat down and had a nightcap in the form of a few local liqueurs.

The rich alcohol warmed my belly as we sat there quietly enjoying our drinks and watching the people go by. Our excitement at the show and the liqueurs combined to create a wonderful glow and we sat there, feeling more amicable towards each other than ever before.

It was a truly magical evening, left somehow more sacred by the fact that we never talked about it again.

As promised, we returned to the Louvre the next day, spending the entire day in the famous museum. I was still riding high from the night before, so I suffered through it all without whining or complaining, despite its tediousness. And boy, was it ever tedious.

We stopped and admired every picture, treasure, statue, and artifact in the damn place, with Uncle Hugh giving a near-constant monotonous lecture on the artist, time period, significance, and any other applicable fact. I enviously watched tour groups nearby who were given a concise explanation of each piece and then moved on. I, on the other hand, sat and listened to the finer points of each piece while tour group after tour group came and went. I was learning details I'm sure no one else but Uncle Hugh knew or cared about in the whole world.

There were certainly magnificent things to see, and I genuinely did appreciate the place, but Uncle Hugh had a way of stripping the joy and wonder away from things with his educational sermons. It all felt like a detention at school while your friends played outside. It was a detention-study period; no breaks, no distractions, no discussion, just pure edification delivered without feeling, or inflection, or emotion. Just naked facts, which certainly weren't as titillating as naked women!

The only breaks in the constant litany were when he noticed I was going slack-faced or staring at something he wasn't talking about. Then came the "Are you listening?!",and the "Do you not even care?" and worst of all, the "Don't be a disappointment to me!"

We left in the evening, the janitorial staff shooing us out as they locked the doors. As we walked out into the warm Paris evening, Uncle Hugh declared, "Well, there's one floor complete. We'll have to come back another day to do the second floor!"

I strongly resisted the urge to dramatically smack my head and curse aloud.

The next few days were spent enjoying what Paris had to offer; the incredible Notre Dame Cathedral, St. Chapelle with its floor-to-ceiling stained-glass windows, the Arc de Triumph, the grand Champs-Élysées with all of its shops and stores, and of course, more time spent at the Louvre. It was all stunning and I quickly came to realize that Paris was indeed one of the great cities and a superb place to visit. I'll never forget that magical place.

All good things come to an end though, and before I knew it, we had to leave to complete the next leg of our journey. We drove back to Versailles, which is barely seven miles outside of Paris, but the traffic rivalled Toronto's stretch of the 401 highway in congestion and its crawling pace. After an achingly long trip for such a short distance, we finally arrived in Versailles and stopped to see the Palace.

The Palace of Versailles is almost beyond words in its beauty and enormity. Inside, the furnishings and décor were mind-bogglingly luxurious and over the top. When you consider how these nobles were living compared to the average commoner, it was no wonder the last time Louis and Marie left the palace, their heads were to be separated from their bodies.

We marched through room after room, shaking our heads at the extravagance of it all until we arrived at the

Royal Quarters, which were beyond anything we'd seen yet. I was shocked to learn that the barrier installed to keep tourists out of the King and Queen's bedroom was not a modern addition. Apparently, people used to come into the palace daily and wait outside of the Royal bedroom to see the King and Queen wake up and get out of bed. I figured it was a good way to keep track of your King's regularity, by watching him use the chamber pot upon awakening. Crazy.

Outside was just as lavish, with meticulously tended flower gardens, ornate fountains, fanciful topiary, and strategically placed wooded areas. The entire grounds were simply stunning.

We took a tour through the Petits Apparts, which were not very petit, but certainly smaller than the nearby Palace. Marie Antoinette's play farm, a full-size working farm with sparkling clean animals tethered for tourists to gawk at was like something out of a movie. I could hardly believe my eyes, but there it all was, right in front of me. There was no denying the excessive splendour and grandeur of it all.

We found a campground nearby the Palace and camped for the night before returning to the Palace once more, just to make sure we hadn't dreamt the entire thing up. It was still there, and just as bewildering in its resplendence. We spent the morning strolling around the grounds, once more admiring everything it had to offer, then reluctantly pried ourselves away, getting on the road again to head north out of Paris.

The drive out of Paris was extremely difficult, and it took every iota of skill I'd picked up as a navigator to direct Uncle Hugh into the proper lanes, the right exits off the highways, and to find the right roads to take. We certainly had our spats that day, as he would constantly question my directions and disagree with my decisions, nagging me constantly. He would often take a different route than the one I suggested, instantly get lost, then turn and blame the entire thing on me.

We eventually got out of the massive metropolis and finally stopped about 75 kilometres north of Paris in a town called Beauvais. Beauvais was home to an architectural wonder, its cathedral, whose construction started in the year 1225 and is still not finished! Two collapses didn't help, and when it was close to completion in the 1940s, bombs dropped during WWII set the finish date back by who knows how long. The excuse they gave concerning why it wasn't finished was a lack of money, but I wonder if it was maybe being built by the same people who built bridges in Ontario. Many workers start their careers as apprentices on a certain bridge and retire from their careers before it's finished.

The building itself was unimaginably tall and massive; truly something to see. Inside was a complex astronomical clock that was very cool and showed not just time, but also the planet's view to the sun, and the view of the stars in the night sky.

We found a campground quite early in the afternoon where we had a quick and early dinner. We wanted to get a really good rest before the next day when we'd attempt to drive to Calais and leave France for England.

On the way to the coast the next day, we stopped in Amiens as there was yet another beautiful and significant cathedral to see there. Unfortunately, it was a Sunday and that meant that there was a service going on in the cathedral when we arrived, so we didn't stay long. We would have been welcome to join, but of course, an intellectual of Uncle Hugh's calibre wanted nothing to do with it. A man of history and science didn't believe in old stories!

While he had no religious fervour to speak of, the man did enjoy the architecture and artwork the Catholics provided for him; he just couldn't get enough of it. To be honest, after seeing hundreds, maybe thousands, of Madonna and Child paintings everywhere we stopped in Europe, I was feeling a bit of a disconnect with Christianity myself.

Chapter 17

We made it to Calais in time and drove the camper onto a huge hovercraft ferry. It was so cool driving across the English Channel on a bed of air... and all within 30 minutes! Immigration was a breeze and the customs agents barely even bothered looking at our passports. Customs had taken on a bit of a nerve-wracking quality after our experience at the Greek/Turkish border with Merv and Bob, but we never had any issues, wherever we went.

There was a substantial duty-free shop there and Uncle Hugh took full advantage, buying the absolute maximum amount of goods he was allowed to. He and the cashier did the math at the checkout as a line grew behind him, removing items one by one until he had the exact amount he could buy without paying any extra taxes.

We found a campground not too far from where we arrived and got set up for the evening. The site next to us was jam-packed with three families all travelling together. The three couples were from Chicago and had eight kids between them. They invited us over to their campfire after supper and we passed around a bottle of sherry as we swapped travel tales. Soon it was just us doing the talking, regaling the crowd with stories to much clapping and oohs and aahs. The sherry may have helped embellish our stories a little bit, but the couples all seemed to appreciate them, especially when I told the harrowing tale of Montpellier and the clutch. Uncle Hugh wasn't too happy that I brought up that story, but laughed along grimly when the story reached its climax. The looks he shot across the fire told me I'd be hearing about it later though.

I woke up the next morning with the sudden realization that I was actually in England. That, and a bit of a hangover from all the sherry. England was the birthplace of my mother's parents, my grandparents, and also my father's more distant ancestors. I couldn't help but feel that it was a bit of a homecoming for me and I was very excited to get out and explore the country. The fact that everyone spoke English helped to make the place seem much less foreign.

We hadn't experienced any major issues when it came to language and communication on our trip, but it did feel comforting to know that wherever we went, everyone would be able to speak English with us. It didn't take me long to learn though that, despite everyone speaking English, I wasn't always going to be able to understand the accent! I often found myself saying, "Pardon? What was that? Could you repeat that?"

We said goodbye to our friends from Chicago and departed for Canterbury, where we stopped to visit, you guessed it, another cathedral. Touring the huge cathedral, Uncle Hugh told me the story of King Henry II and how he had a disagreement with Thomas Beckett, the Archbishop of Canterbury. He had his knights kill the archbishop, who was eventually awarded sainthood. We saw the graves of both the king and the archbishop at the cathedral, as well as the graves of the black knight and Henry's wife.

We left the church and found ourselves driving down a very narrow lane bordered by tall hedges. Things were going great until we met up with a car approaching head-on, with no space to pass us by. The other driver signalled that it was our responsibility to back up out of his way, which I'm sure he instantly regretted. He probably still remembers the time he was stuck behind a camper van attempting to reverse for over 30 tortuously long minutes.

Uncle Hugh was notoriously bad at reversing, and in this situation, he needed me to climb to the back window to shout out directions. This proved to be very difficult for me, since when I called "left" it was the driver's right, and to aim the back of the vehicle left, you'd had to turn the steering wheel right. This breakdown in communication coupled with my confusion, Uncle Hugh's poor driving skills, and his unwillingness to listen to directions led us directly into the hedgerow on the left side. The other driver had to reverse in order to let us pull forward to correct ourselves. Uncle Hugh then immediately backed into the hedgerow on the right.

We repeated this ludicrous dance for way too long of a time, reversing, crunching into the hedgerow, pulling forward, reversing, crunching into the hedgerow on the other side. By the time we finally got to a spot where the other driver could get by, he'd cracked his teeth and pulled out the entirety of his hair, surely leaving the scene irreparably emotionally damaged. Uncle Hugh wasn't much better off, while I was stuck somewhere in between laughing manically and sobbing.

We finally arrived in Rye, a town that many of our ancestors hailed from. There was still one relation living there, my grandfather and Uncle Hugh's cousin Christine, who was the sister of Cousin Richard whom we'd visited in Spain. We walked the beautiful cobblestone roads until we found a payphone, which Uncle Hugh used to call Christine, who ended up inviting us over for supper the next day.

After checking out all of the cool old buildings, streets, and alleyways, Uncle Hugh spotted a pub on the corner called the Golden Unicorn. He suggested we go in and experience a real English pub. I agreed though I wasn't quite sure what a "real" English pub was, having been too young to visit the pubs and bars in Canada.

We entered and Uncle Hugh let out a great sigh, saying he desperately needed a drink after the harrowing drive down that narrow lane. We descended into the dark, low-ceilinged room where we saw several men sitting at tables, with more standing and milling around the bar. Glasses hung over the bar and behind it, there was a large display of liquor bottles underneath a big central mirror. Neon lights and humorous signs served as décor and a haze of smoke swirled towards the ceiling. I'd never seen anything like this before and thought it was all very cool. Most of the places I'd drank at up to this point on the trip had been at hotel bars or on patios outside.

As soon as we entered, a hush fell over the crowd, and everyone stopped to look at us. I felt pretty uncomfortable under their scrutiny, wondering if it was my age that was causing an issue. I hadn't thought to ask if England had a minimum drinking age like Canada did. Unfazed, Uncle Hugh continued making his way in, then said in his most snobbish English accent, "Good day, gentlemen. As you were," as if he was a commanding officer walking in on his troops enjoying some downtime.

Surprisingly, the men responded with a few nods, some raised pints, and then went back to their conversations. The bartender motioned for us to take a seat, then said, "What can I get yous?"

Uncle Hugh casually raised two fingers and, keeping up the accent, said, "Two pints, good sir."

He could sure put it on when he wanted to. Now that he was in England, he was no longer the proud American or the sneaky Canadian; he was back home, a true English lad having a pint at his local pub.

Some of the men at the bar were curious about us and approached our table, asking where we were from, where we'd been, and where we were going. Soon, our table turned into the centre of attention and we were quickly adopted into the group. We were swapping stories as pints were downed and soon, we had half the bar laughing uproariously. Many of the men took a shine to me, especially when they learned I was only 14 years old. Before I knew it, I had several pints in front of me that were paid for by the locals and people were slapping my back as I told stories.

Eventually Uncle Hugh insisted to the men that we had to leave, and after much hand shaking and back slapping, we managed to make our exit, stumbling out of the pub and making our way to a nearby campground.

We woke the next morning with splitting headaches and Uncle Hugh was very slow in getting moving. After a shower, a strong cup of Earl Grey tea, and some breakfast we felt a little more human again and were able to get going. We drove around the countryside, visiting many of the small villages around Rye. We stopped at a small church and Uncle Hugh led me to a cemetery where several of my ancestors were buried.

It was interesting to see where my ancestors came from and to discover my roots by visiting this place. It was so different from my home in Southern Ontario, but still, it had the feeling of home and familiarity to it. I left the cemetery feeling contemplative and a little more mature.

We drove back to town and found Cousin Christine's place, a neat little cottage home. Christine, a very friendly older woman, and her husband greeted us warmly at the door. They were simply agog at meeting us and couldn't do enough to make sure we were comfortable. We had some tea while they bombarded us with questions, and then, before we knew it, it was supper time.

Supper turned out to be a large salad full of many things, including fruit. Now, everyone who knows me, knows that I can't stand fruit in salad. Why would you go about ruining a good salad by adding fruit to it? Not that I don't like fruit, because I do but it doesn't belong in a salad. I figured it must be a defect running through my family, as Uncle Hugh always put fruit in our salads, despite my complaints. I would pick around each piece every time, eventually throwing out what was left in my bowl. Uncle Hugh would then take the opportunity to scold me for my pickiness, each and every time.

When Uncle Hugh saw Christine's salad, he laughed like a little girl, holding his hand up to cover his mouth, and then sent a wink my way. He watched me, grinning smugly, as I was forced to eat the entire bowl, fruit and all, as I didn't want to offend our kind hosts. I slowly ate the salad without a word of complaint, silently plotting my revenge on him.

Christine asked if I wanted any more salad, then tried to insist when I refused. "A young man your age always eats like a horse!" she said, but I insisted that I'd filled up on tea and cookies and couldn't fit in another bite.

After supper, we sat around the table telling stories over small cups of sherry that Uncle Hugh and I sipped gingerly at. We were still feeling the effects of the night before and couldn't stomach too much of the stuff.

We slept in our camper in the driveway that night and Christine made us a fabulous breakfast of eggs and kippers, with no fruity salads in sight. We said our goodbyes, and after some big hugs all around, we were back on the road.

We weren't on the road for long that day, as our destination, Little Common, was a mere 18 kilometres away. This was where the Freis were vacationing for the month, and boy were they vacationing in style – a Tudor-style mansion with a swimming pool, tennis courts, extensive gardens, and most shockingly, servants.

I had a joyous reunion with Ann and Ba Ba and they took me for a whirlwind tour of the mansion and its grounds. After lunch, we all went to the beach in nearby Cooden. The water was too cold to play in, but we still had a great time on the beach, running up and down and chatting the entire time, catching each other up on what had happened since we'd last all been together.

Leaving the beach, we drove to their friend's place, which was even more impressive than the mansion they had rented out for the month. It was like a palace, and the servants there served us tea, fancy cakes, and rolls. The girls and I played a couple of rounds of tennis, and I was extremely amused when a servant approached me on the tennis court saying, "A refreshment sir? Perhaps a cold lemonade?"

"Wow," I thought to myself, "this is how rich people live." A beautiful house, beautiful girls, and being waited on hand and foot? I could get used to this.

The girls asked if I wanted to go to the beach again the next morning, just the three of us. I was wondering how we'd get there when the time arrived, but one of the girls simply picked up the phone, dialed one number, and then said into the receiver, "We'd like to go to the beach. Pick us up at 8:00, please."

The chauffeur arrived promptly, and we piled into the back of the limo with our beach gear, only to be beset by a thick fog. Not able to see anything past the windows, we sat in the driveway, waiting for the fog to clear, laughing and chatting effortlessly in the back seat. Once the fog lifted, we were driven to the beach and we got out of the car with instructions for the chauffeur to pick us up again at 2:00. Was I living the life, or what? It was like I was in a movie or something.

The next few days were much the same, with games of tennis, badminton, ping pong, being waited on, being driven to the beach, long walks, and all in the company of two beautiful girls I was completely smitten with. I think I could have stayed there forever in spite of missing my family and feeling a touch of homesickness. My friends and family seemed very far away and in a different world, and I felt like a very different person now. I was having a magical time in this place and I didn't want it to end.

The end did come though, and sooner than I wanted it to. Soon enough, we were once again saying goodbye to the Freis and driving away on narrow British roads with heavy hearts.

The first stop after our visit was at Hever Castle, one of Henry the VIII's castles, and where Anne Boleyn lived. There was a long line to get in and for once, Uncle Hugh's patience lasted for the entire queue. Amazingly, the castle was still occupied by the Astor family, which was interesting since the whole place took on the feel of a lived-in house rather than a museum. With the antique furnishings everywhere, it was easy to imagine running into Henry the VIII in one of the hallways.

Of course, Uncle Hugh would be remiss if he didn't give me a verbal dissertation on the entire life and exploits of Henry VIII. Quite the character King Henry was, and Uncle Hugh's lecture served to make the tour feel even more realistic, as my imagination filled in the gaps of time. I visualized King Henry walking in our footsteps, chasing women around the castle, and ordering everyone around.

We left the castle and drove to the village of Abinger Hammer outside of Dorking, where we were to visit Uncle Hugh's friends, the Brownfields. Bevil Brownfield was a retired engineer, and his wife Janet was a retired nurse. They were very friendly and we spent a few days there, reminiscing about old times and drinking sherry while we watched Uncle Hugh's slides.

Janet had a 1965 convertible Aston Martin sports car, and she took me with her when she went shopping. I'd never been in a sports car before, or a convertible, and it was so exciting racing through the countryside with her. It felt freeing to be a passenger in a vehicle that wasn't ponderously skulking its way across Europe. What a life I was living – mansions, servants, sports cars!

While there, we also visited the Royal Pavilion in Brighton, which looked like an Indian palace. This Taj Mahal-looking structure was about an hour's drive away and was quite impressive. We also drove around checking out the many grand homes and mansions in the area.

Bevil and Janet fed us very well and made kippers for breakfast, something I'd grown to love after trying it for the first time at Cousin Christina's place.

It was time to go again, so we said farewell and drove up to Surbiton, a neighbourhood in the Southwest corner of London. We were there to visit the Archies, more of Uncle Hugh's friends. John Archie was a fellow architect and the home that he'd built showed it, being ultra-modern and all white. I'd never seen anything like this back home, where all of the walls and furnishings were colourful. This stark whiteness was a real contrast to what I was used to. It was quite impressive and certainly before its time. We had a great visit, drinking cider while John and Uncle Hugh reminisced about old times.

The next morning, Uncle Hugh and I went into downtown London and visited the National Gallery and the British Museum. I was very much getting used to museums at this point and found many fascinating items and exhibits, even if I had to endure hours of Uncle Hugh's lectures and pop quizzes. We were fortunate enough to be at the museum when the mummified Egyptian king Tutankhamun was being exhibited in England for the first time. Uncle Hugh was so excited, he didn't even seem to mind the long line leading up to the sarcophagus. He was so giddy that he kept breaking out in giggles, reminding me of his behaviour at the Follie Bergere show. Tutankhamun was cool and all, but he didn't quite add up to the same excitement I got from naked dancing women, that's for sure. Still, the exhibit was truly amazing, and we were unprepared for high quality and the sheer number of items on display.

At that point, we'd only ever heard of Tutankhamun's treasures on the news, as the internet didn't exist yet, and television wasn't that sophisticated. We took our time and thoroughly enjoyed every item on display.

The next day, we toured London on a double-decker bus which was a lot of fun. Sitting on the top floor, we got to see lots of the sights London has on offer. We got off and dropped into Madam Tussaud's wax museum, which was a nice change of pace from all of the history stuff. The wax figures looked so incredibly real and I wanted desperately to stand in one of the exhibits, stock still, and see if anyone noticed that I was a real person.

We got back on the bus and got off again at the Tower of London, which I was very excited to see, but the line-up there was insane, and Uncle Hugh said he had no stomach for it. For once, I was suggesting that we go into a museum, but he said, "No way!"

One day we drove to Enfield where Uncle Hugh and my grandfather had lived as boys. We visited the school they'd gone to and the house they'd lived in fifty years before. We tried knocking on the door to the house and the people who answered turned out to be very friendly. They brought us inside for a little tour and even showed us the bedrooms that used to belong to Uncle Hugh and my grandfather. Uncle was not impressed by how the room had changed, as there were rock posters plastered over all of the walls. He glared around the room and grumbled under his breath. Later on, he told me that he was disgusted with how they'd let the room go and that he and it were defamed, as if he still occupied it.

He sure was a funny bloke, as the English would say.

Despite his rude looks and grumbling, the nice woman had us sit down for tea and chatted as if we were long-lost relatives. We stopped at another family home nearby and the owners acted in the exact same way, kindly giving us a tour of their home. These English people sure seemed nice and accommodating. It was great to get to see the places where my relatives came from, and it helped me understand Uncle Hugh a tiny bit better.

Another night, Uncle Hugh took the Archies and me to a restaurant called the Horseshoe. Our waiter for the night was a Portuguese guy who I thought was hilarious. He would stand behind Uncle Hugh, mimicking his strange mannerisms and snobbery for my benefit. I got several dirty looks from Uncle Hugh that night as I continually burst out laughing while seemingly looking at him. He couldn't turn his neck to look behind him, so the waiter was safe from being discovered. When he'd finally spin his chair around to see if something was happening behind him, the waiter had inevitably replaced his goofy impressions with a serious and professional expression. "May I help you sir, is something the matter?" Uncle Hugh must have thought I'd lost my marbles.

"Why don't you take it easy on the wine tonight, Jimmy boy?"

Jimmy boy meant that I was quickly edging out of Uncle Hugh's good books and that I'd better be careful. I responded by snorting and choking on my wine, much to Uncle Hugh's chagrin, as the waiter waggled his eyebrows at me ponderously behind him.

Despite the hijinks, the supper was delicious, and soon everyone was back in good spirits, laughing and joking and telling stories.

One morning, Uncle Hugh declared that he needed to go to Air Canada in order to arrange a flight home, as his airline wouldn't fly in or out of Germany. He also needed to get to an American Express for mail, traveller's cheques, and who knows what.

John said no problem and offered to spend the day with me. He took me to a private club where we swam in pools, or baths as they called them there. The whole place was made out to look like an ancient Roman bath and was really cool, though the men there, and it was all men, were very snobbish and made me feel uncomfortable.

He then drove us out to Leith Hill, where we made the two and a half mile hike up the highest, and very steep, hill in Southern England. We climbed the tower on the top of the hill and had a great lunch of sandwiches, buns, and wine that he'd packed. We ate and drank while admiring the view of the surrounding countryside in amiable silence.

On our way down it started to rain and then to pour. We both got absolutely soaked to the bone and laughed and laughed about it when we finally made it to his car. I had a very nice day with John and really enjoyed his company. It always seemed so surreal, but at the same time, so natural to be doing all of the things I was doing. Meeting so many people, visiting so many places, and doing it as if I'd been doing it my entire life. I seemed to adapt readily to these new situations, which would prove to be a great asset later on in life.

Uncle Hugh's departure that day to figure out a way home had me feeling a bit pensive. This was the first big sign that this wonderous trip was soon coming to an end.

We continued our quest to explore London for the next few days, going to two theatres, one the New Theatre, where we saw a hilarious production of London Assurance, and the Dairy Lane Theatre, where we saw an incredible performance of Gone with the Wind. There were cannons firing with smoke and real horses on stage and I was blown away. That show is something I'll never forget.

We managed to make it to the Tower of London when the lines were much shorter, and also visited Westminster Abbey and the Parliament Buildings where we sat through a debate about Ireland in the House of Commons, and then another in the House of Lords. Afterwards, Uncle Hugh purchased a special pass that allowed us to eat at the Parliament restaurant. The special pass puffed up his ego and made him feel extra important. He put on his best aristocratic accent when we sat down for lunch, ordering the waitstaff around like he belonged and ate there on the regular.

One of the days we ate burgers and chips at a Wimpy's and another day we went for an all-you-can-eat lunch at a Lyons. Of course, Uncle Hugh sternly told me to be sure to eat my fill so he could get his money's worth out of the place. I took his admonishment seriously and chowed down until I was nearly sick. Between the two of us, I bet they lost money on our visit that day, especially since Uncle Hugh took advantage of the condiments and loaded up his pockets with salt, pepper, tea bags, and sugar.

After almost a week of visiting the Archies, we said our goodbyes and drove the camper van through the heart of London, which was a torturous journey that frayed both of our nerves. Between the busy traffic, endless lights, one-way streets, narrow lanes, not to mention driving on the "wrong side of the road" as Uncle Hugh put it (he may have been born in the UK, but he truly was an American at heart now and thought everything American was superior), it was a wonder we ever made it through the heart of the city.

In fact, it took all of my skill and energy as a navigator to get us through the gauntlet of London without getting into an accident. I ran back and forth and side to side in the camper, shouting out instructions to Uncle Hugh, who, thoroughly frazzled, yelled obscenities back at me, as if I were to blame for all of the congestion and craziness.

As the crow flies, we weren't actually going that far, as we were on our way to visit more yet more of his friends in the north of London. This friend, George, was not as well off as many of the other friends and relatives we'd visited so far, but he was just as accommodating.

When we finally arrived at his place, a row house in a busy neighbourhood, he was waiting to greet us outside. I thought Uncle Hugh was going to dive out of the van and start kissing the sidewalk like a shipwrecked soul who finally washed up on a beach.

George and his wife shared their small home with three of their kids who were in their twenties, and two of George's sisters, which made for quite the crazy household. Despite the chaos of having so many people in a small space, I found everything to be very interesting and a lot of fun. They made us feel at home and broke out the sherry to help us sooth our nerves after the drive. Then came some whisky, and then some wine.

We had a great evening; everyone telling funny stories and clapping and laughing as if we were all the best of mates. We stayed up late into the night and by the time it was time for bed, we were all drunk as a skunk. We ended up having to sleep in the camper while it was parked on the street as there wasn't any room in the house for us and because they didn't have a driveway. Normally Uncle Hugh wouldn't have been very pleased with this set-up, but since he was so inebriated, he shuffled off to bed without complaint. I think he really needed a night like this after our hectic day.

We slept in late the next day, waking up with dry mouths and aching heads. We said our goodbyes to George and his family, then drove an hour north to Cambridge where we toured the King's College Chapel.

From there we found a really cool campsite nearby that was located on an island in the middle of a river. After setting up camp, we took a stroll down the bank of the river through willows, oak, and beech trees, watching the swans swimming around without a care in the world. The walk did much to clear our heads, which had still been quite foggy with our hangovers.

When we returned to the campsite, Uncle Hugh stopped in at the office as he wanted to exchange some money and purchase a few sundry items. When he approached the man working in the office he was met with a mystified headshake. "We can't do any of that here."

When Uncle Hugh demanded that it be so, the man shook his head again and replied, "Sir, this is an office, not a fucking hotel. I'm sorry, but I just can't help you."

Not one to be rebuffed, Uncle Hugh gave the man a hard time for an embarrassing number of minutes.

"I have never been so insulted in my whole LIFE!" he harangued the man, who stood there stoically, "We certainly won't be coming back here ever again, you can be sure of THAT!"

The look on the man's face said, "Of course, you big man-baby, you're travelling from away, and this is a campground... obviously you won't be coming back."

Stomping out of the office, Uncle Hugh kept up his hissy fit, swearing that he'd be leaving this dump (which had so recently been a beautiful spot – just gorgeous) without paying in the morning. Once he calmed down, he thought better of it and ended up begrudgingly paying the man when the time came to do so. He knew that the campground had our license plate and descriptions and that we would likely be caught if he were to try to run out on this one. Wisely, I kept my mouth shut through the entire ordeal.

Departing the "wretched dung pile" of a campground, we drove north of Nottingham to the Sherwood Forest, where we got to see the Major Oak, colloquially known as the Robin Hood Tree. The massive, spreading oak is hollow and over 500 years old. It is said that the infamous Robin Hood hid in the tree from the Sheriff's men at one point. Although the tree and its ties to folklore were very interesting, Sherwood Forest was, well, a forest, and so wasn't all too fascinating.

We couldn't find a campground anywhere nearby for the night, so we once again found a copse of trees in a farmer's field and set up camp behind it. There was no flag-raising or noise-making when we did this and Uncle Hugh set me up on sentry duty like the last time. "Keep your eyes peeled, James! We don't want to be caught unawares."

We were in Code Yellow mode, ready for a quick getaway if need be. Luckily, we weren't discovered and were able to depart by 7:00 am after a quick breakfast. We were heading for Doncaster that day, but made a last-minute visit to Roche Abbey on the way. This was one of the monasteries that Henry the VIII had destroyed when he became enraged at the fact that the Catholic Church wouldn't let him divorce his wife. He had the old monasteries torn down and instituted his own church, the Anglican Church, with him as its leader. There wasn't actually much there to see, but Uncle Hugh was sure to bore me with a long version of the story that included a superfluous number of dates and names.

Chapter 18

Back on the road, we eventually arrived in Doncaster, and made our way right to the hospital there, which was once run by Uncle Hugh's parents, or my great-grandparents. They were Master and Matron of the hospital and my grandfather and Uncle Hugh had spent 8 years of their childhood there. It was Uncle Hugh's first 8 years, as he was actually born in the hospital.

Upon arrival, Uncle Hugh presented himself to the head nurse, explaining who we were with his usual pompous air. He always wanted to be seen as a gentleman, a real person of stature, and someone to be respected. I found that most people could see right through the façade.

Despite that, the head nurse was very nice and graciously offered to personally give us a tour of the hospital, which had been overhauled and modernized since he'd last seen it. I thought to myself that it was unlikely he'd actually remember much of it, but according to him, he remembered every room, nook, and cranny in the place; –even those parts that seemed suspiciously new. Despite my misgivings, he did seem touched by the experience, and he reminisced about happy times when his family was all still together there.

The head nurse mentioned that there had recently been an old photo published in the local newspaper that showed the hospital as it was back then, with all of the staff present. She commenced to dig through stacks of newspapers and magazines in the common room, muttering to herself that it must be there somewhere. Eventually, she found the paper and brought it over to us.

Uncle Hugh was flabbergasted. It was a photo from over 50 years before, with him and his brother sitting down in front of the staff, which included his parents, who were still Master and Matron of the hospital at the time. He asked if he could keep the paper and the nurse agreed enthusiastically, very pleased that she had been able to find a deep connection for these two strange visitors.

After thanking the nurse profusely, we drove to the newspaper office. Uncle Hugh brought the paper to the front desk and asked anxiously where they had gotten the photo and why they had decided to publish it. They explained that the owner of the photo, a former nurse who was now an elderly woman, had submitted it, so they decided to publish it as a historical item. They kindly gave us the name of the woman and her address, so we decided to go pay her a visit.

A bespeckled, gray-haired, and stooped woman answered the door, shawl on her shoulders, and cane in hand, asking, "Hello, what could I do for you?"

Uncle Hugh showed her the paper and explained that his parents used to run the hospital and that he was one of the boys in the photo. His face lit up as recognition dawned on hers. "Boy?" she exclaimed.

His exuberant expression dimmed. "No, not Boy," he said, "I'm Hugh."

Boy was how my grandfather, Uncle Hugh's brother, was known back then. Now it was the woman's turn for her face to fall. "Oh."

It turns out that my grandfather was a cheerful boy and full of life, everyone's favourite, while Uncle

Hugh was reserved and pouty, always hanging on to his mother's sleeve.

Still, she was excited about our arrival and invited us in for tea. We had a very pleasant chat, as she reminisced about her tenure at the hospital with lots of unheard stories about my great-grandparents. There were also lots of references to Boy, much to Uncle Hugh's chagrin. "Oh, Boy was so much fun. Oh, he was SO cute! Oh, he was such a nice young man."

Eventually, Uncle Hugh's pride was hurt to the point where he interrupted, exclaiming, "Do you even remember me at all?!"

"Oh yes," she said, "I do remember you, Hugh. You were always crying and calling for your mommy. I remember the time when the War was finally over, the first one, and everyone at the hospital was preparing for a big celebration. Your mother was very busy, having everyone cooking and baking cakes and sweets. See, the hospital was very full of young men returning from France and she wanted to make sure that there was food for all of them. She was pretty much run off her feet. She went to go grab something in the pantry and found you there on the floor, surrounded by half-eaten cakes and pastries with icing all over your face. Half a dozen or more cakes lay strewn around with only one bite out of each. You started bawling, but not quite as loud as when your father came in and tanned your hide!

"We didn't think you'd ever stop," she continued, "Then they sat you in a highchair in the middle of the dining room while everyone else ate and you were forbidden from eating any sweets. You had to suffer in silence too. Your dad threatened to beat you silly if you so much as whimpered. Oh, that was something!"

The shame of that day must have returned because Uncle Hugh's face was deep red and he looked like he was about to cry. I tried to steer the conversation away by asking about the soldiers and what it was like working during the war.

After we left, Uncle Hugh was very quiet and sad, and I felt sorry for him. "Why don't we go out for supper and have some spaghetti?" His favourite.

That did it. He smiled and said, "Good idea."

This was shocking, as usually his bad moods lasted for hours if not days.

We drove from the woman's house to the North York Moors where we found a campground and got set up. The campground happened to have a restaurant there and they even had spaghetti on the menu. The noodles in the spaghetti were abnormally long, at least 2 feet each, and we had a good laugh at that. We ate in companionable silence, enjoying our pasta and a good bottle of red wine.

The next day, we took a drive through the rolling hills of the North York Moors. It was a very desolate place, with no trees or anything to look at; just rolling, barren landscape. This wasn't too exciting for a 14-year-old and I must have let my impatience show. He decided to use my displeasure to take a dig at me. "It really reminds me of Ontario," he said. "Nothing at all to see, just a rolling blank canvas."

He knew this would bother me and it did. Why pick on me, or Ontario?

He'd been speaking a lot about wanting to see Whitby Abbey, one of the best-preserved abbeys that Henry VIII had demolished. Even though it was well out of our way, he thought it would be worth the trip. I didn't have any say in the matter, so we drove the long way to the abbey and up to the front gates. There was a gate attendant waiting there who politely said, "That will be 50 pence to enter, sir, for parking."

Well, this was too much for Uncle Hugh and he blew a gasket. "What?! I drove 50 miles out of my way to come here and now you want me to pay 50 pence for parking?! I don't think so!"

He backed up the camper and performed an awkward 5-point turn, then pulled onto the shoulder of the road leading up to the abbey. We exited the camper and Uncle Hugh took a number of painstaking pictures from the side of the road. "We may as well get some pictures to say we were here," he grumbled. "The nerve of these people trying to charge ME 50 pence. I'm not going to be taken advantage of!"

This strange man would spare no expense for certain things he wanted to do, but would balk at petty expenses like parking, camping, tolls, tips, condiments, or any other mundane item.

We left the abbey and the bemused gate attendant and drove to Scarborough in silence. On the way there, it began to pour, which lasted for quite some time. We drove in circles around town until the rain let up, and then got out to visit the Scarborough Castle and to walk along the quay, where dozens of people suddenly sprouted up now that it wasn't raining. Uncle Hugh used the time to give me a long dissertation on the history of Scarborough, focusing on Viking raids and its occupation.

Leaving town, we found a campground a few miles away in the suburb of Scalby. The campground was relatively non-descript, but it had nice showers, which were much welcomed.

The seam in my pants had opened up and needed mending, which I showed Uncle Hugh. He said, " So mend them," to which I replied, "How?" He chuckled and promptly brought out needle and thread, showing me how to thread the needle. And then proceeded to make the first few stitches and then handed the needle over to me. As I struggled to stitch up my pants, he very seriously expressed that, "You can't go through life depending on others. You need to learn to do things for yourself Jimmy my boy." I took this to heart and have done my own mending ever since.

The next day we headed to York and toured the York Minster Cathedral there, with its famous Five Sisters stained-glass windows. We walked the castle walls and saw some Roman ruins while Uncle Hugh droned on about the history of York. It was actually a very exciting and rich history, full of Romans, Vikings, Scots, rebels, and civil wars, but his monotonous delivery tended to detract from the actual interesting information.

The clutch in the camper was beginning to slip again, so we drove to Skipton to see if we could get it repaired. We were told they'd be able to take it in the next day, so we drove to Malham, a huge natural 260-foot-high limestone wall that formed a semi-circle. It was formed 12,000 years ago by an ancient waterfall and made an impressive sight. We took the stairs to the top, where the remains of a riverbed, basically a limestone pavement trail, stretched for miles. We walked a few miles down the river trail, but Uncle Hugh eventually began flagging and said we'd have to turn back as he didn't think he could do the entire thing.

The van was held up at the mechanic's for most of the next day, so we wandered through Skipton on foot, strolling around and admiring the picture-perfect little British town. It had a 900-year-old castle there, which I really enjoyed since castles were probably my favourite thing to see and explore. I had a blast running around on the ramparts and exploring its nooks and crannies.

Leaving the campground the next morning with a brand-new clutch, Uncle Hugh declared that we'd be taking all English lanes today. He must have gotten his nerve up since our last experience. He said that he really enjoyed them, despite constantly worrying that he might have to reverse for several miles. We visited Malham Tarn near the limestone cliffs, a glacial lake surrounded by rolling green hills studded with grazing cattle. We then made stops at Kendal and Windemere Lake but gave up exploring after dealing with unrelenting rain.

We drove through Patterdale in the English highlands, and followed signs to a campground while rain pattered a hectic drum beat on top of the camper. The campground was located in the notch of a deep valley. The valley was beautiful, studded with big rocks and climbing and rolling up into the highlands. The camp itself though was a stain on this beautiful picture. Muddy, disorganized, and unkempt, this was a very poor example of an English campground. Between the incessant rain and the unpleasant digs, Uncle Hugh was quickly becoming surly, particularly when he saw how much he had to pay to stay there.

We set up in the rain, then retreated inside the camper. What do you do at a campground in the rain? The same thing everyone does, drink and play cards. Cards are always more fun with a few drinks, and soon Uncle Hugh was cheerful again, laughing and smiling ruefully if I won a hand. Uncle Hugh always loved a good drink and a game of cards.

The following morning, the rain had finally let up, so we strapped on our hiking boots, and backpacks loaded with raincoats, fruit, bread, cheese, and some bottles of pop, and proceeded to climb Helvellyn, a 3100-foot mountain rising over the valley.

The beginning of the climb was quite steep and Uncle Hugh immediately began to flag. In one spot, you literally had to scramble up a rock face, being careful where to place your hands and feet to pull yourself up. I shot up the rock face and stood at the top, waiting for Uncle Hugh to slowly and carefully make his way up to meet me. By the time he got to the top, he was already out of gas, but I was raring to go.

It wasn't that Uncle Hugh was all that old, though he seemed nearly ancient to me at the time, but his bent and fused spine and the lack of mobility in his torso, made climbing rather strenuous for him. I tried to be patient, but the plodding pace was beginning to wear on my energetic teenage self. I told him that I was going to go ahead and that I'd wait for him further up. He didn't look too pleased but said nothing to stop me, so I ran up ahead, quickly eating up the steep slope.

I would stop and wait for him every once in a while, watching to see him plod up to a certain point, then I would charge ahead again. Climbing one small ridge, I popped over the edge, and to my delight, found myself in the midst of about 30 schoolgirls around my age. They were there for a hike with several of their school masters. Being young girls, they immediately surrounded me and inundated me with questions all at once.

"Who are you? Where did you come from? Why are you here? What's your accent? Why are you here all alone? Would you like to join us? Do you want to climb with us?"

This was all music to my ears. "Why, of course I would!" Did I die and go to heaven?

Despite the fact that they were a gaggle of pretty girls, I was also starved for company my own age and had been spending a lot of time with older folks lately. The girls begged their chaperones to let me join them and they agreed, probably thinking that one boy wouldn't stand a chance against all of these girls. In fact, they were probably thinking they'd have to watch out for me since the girls were the bigger danger.

Off we went, laughing and chatting, and totally oblivious to the inspiring landscape around us. Uncle Hugh, who? He was completely gone from my conscience and memory while I was distracted by so much young femininity. I was just on a school outing with my pals. An all-female group of pals. All thirty of them mine for the day. Each one of them interested in ME, all clamoring for my attention!

Up and up we climbed, the steepness of the mountain having levelled out a bit, but the hiking still fairly strenuous. There were sections where you had to carefully climb up cliff faces, but I was having a blast and not even thinking of Uncle Hugh behind me and how much he'd have to struggle to get up. I loved it, helping all of the girls up, while they giggled.

Reaching the top of String's Edge, a narrow, knife-edge path with dizzying drop-offs on either side, we found a sign with a stark warning. It was a tribute to an unlucky hiker who had fallen hundreds of feet to his death. His dog stayed with his body until the search parties found him. Seeing that made us all realize how dangerous this hike could be.

We made the final ascent through a steep incline littered with large boulders and finally reached the summit. All of the girls flung themselves at the ground as the minders declared that it was lunchtime. They all started pulling lunch out of their packs and could barely eat through all of the chatter. "Jim, why don't you sit down here?"

"No, Jim, over here!"

"No, no, Jim, near us!"

My head was spinning; I'd never been so popular!

It was such a rush, and a big boost to my morale. "Wow! I'll never forget this," I thought to myself.

I ate my lunch and chatted away with the girls, completely forgetting about poor Uncle Hugh, who must have been worried and probably a little mad that I had disappeared. Eventually, he came into view and slowly plodded up through the boulders, obviously exhausted and looking disheveled and angry. "Jim!" he exclaimed, "I'm so glad you're safe. What would I have told your mother if something had happened to you up here?!"

Not wanting to look like a child in front of the girls, I shrugged him off and said, nonchalantly, "I'm fine Uncle Hugh, don't worry about me."

I sat down with him while he pulled out his lunch and started to eat, but then all of the girls suddenly shot up at a command from the chaperones. They were ready to hike back down the mountain!

I looked to them, then to Uncle Hugh, them, Uncle Hugh. I shot up and dove into the fray, yelling behind me, "I'll see you at the bottom!"

Uncle Hugh was left sputtering with a mouthful of food, not able to get a word out before I disappeared once more.

The descent was definitely easier and our young bodies made short work of it. We all bounded down the slopes and were at the bottom in no time. I painfully separated myself from the gaggle of girls, figuring that if I didn't wait at the bottom of the mountain for Uncle Hugh, then I'd really be in trouble. They all said goodbye, giving me hugs, handshakes, or pats on the shoulder. I really was in heaven!

Once the last of the girls departed, I ran to the camper and turned around to see if I could spot Uncle Hugh on the mountain. I couldn't see him anywhere. Suddenly, the realization of what I'd done dawned on me. I'd left this crippled old man who had done so much for me, alone! I was feeling awful, and I knew that he was going to be pissed.

How could I be so insensitive and rude, and after all he'd done for me? I didn't deserve this trip at all. I wasn't aware of the forces working behind the scenes in my brain, flooding me with teenage hormones that trumped logic, thought, and common sense. I was a marionette, unable to direct my actions and mostly helpless to the hormones that controlled the strings. I wasn't aware of any of this though and just felt awful. How could I make it up to Uncle Hugh?

I knew that by the time he made it down, he'd be dog-tired and in a foul mood, so I thought I'd have supper ready for him. I fried up some onions, peeled potatoes, and cooked up some ground beef. Uncle Hugh loved this meal. I also boiled some water, and when he finally came into view, huffing and puffing, I put on some tea – Earl Grey, his favourite.

When he reached the van, he collapsed into the lawn chair I had waiting for him, completely exhausted. He looked beat up and terrible, which served to make me feel even worse. I sheepishly thrust a cup of tea into his hands, telling him that I'd rushed down in order to have some tea ready for him. He took the cup, too tired to bother replying or digging at me for my obvious fib.

"Look," I said, "I made supper!"

His mood seemed to immediately lift when I brought him a full plate. "Oh, that's so nice of you, my boy!"

He said "my boy" when he was pleased with me, or feeling affectionate towards me, so that was a good sign.

We ate supper and downed a few more cups of tea and everything started to feel better. He confessed that he was very angry with me and disappointed that I'd left him, but that the cup of tea helped abate it. He was so tired, and cold, and thirsty, and that cup of tea was just what he needed. Gratification had helped heal his angry heart.

I had narrowly missed being in big trouble with this one, but I didn't gloat about it. I still felt very remorseful for what I'd done and tried to make it up to him by behaving extra well for the next few days.

The next morning, we continued our drive north to Hadrian's Wall, which was built by the Roman Emperor Hadrian in order to keep the Scots, known then as the Picts, out of the south. We walked along it until we reached a Roman temple and fort. Uncle Hugh told me that the Romans had conquered much of the known world, but they couldn't conquer the Scots and that's why they built the wall. They must have been impressive warriors!

On our way from there to Durham, we stopped in a little village called Blanchland. The village was quite quaint and held little of interest for me, but Uncle Hugh was smitten with the place. We spent a long time there, going through his rigamarole of taking pictures – testing lighting, adjusting settings, changing perspectives, fine-tuning the aperture, modifying the shutter speed, and who knows what else on that bloody camera. He was taking forever and I was quickly growing bored, but I was careful not to roll my eyes or sigh, as the Helvellyn mountain experience was still fresh in my mind.

We finally made it to Durham that afternoon and visited the Durham Cathedral, one of the finest examples of Norman architecture in the country. Durham was a beautiful city with lots of interesting history and architecture, so Uncle Hugh was in his glory, going all out with his instruction, acting like he was at a podium speaking to a large classroom of history students, even though it was just me there, trailing behind him.

This was our last day in England, as we were off to Norway the next day, so we made it a proper British night to remember. We stopped in a pub for a few beers, and then had a superb supper of fish and chips. It was a great way to end our British leg of the journey.

I really enjoyed England for its friendly people, pub culture, beautiful landscapes, architecture, and history. It felt a lot like home, but still different... comforting yet exciting, and a little bit strange.

Chapter 19

We decided to take a ferry from England to Norway, but the ship wasn't leaving until past noon, so we took our time in the morning, strolling around the campground a dozen times to stretch our legs. We departed and drove through the Newcastle tunnel to the docks.

Uncle Hugh said we had to cut down on costs, so he booked himself in 2nd class and me in 3rd class on the ship. After driving the camper onto the ship, which seemed more cruise ship than ferry, we were escorted to our rooms. Well, to Uncle Hugh's room anyway. He would be sharing the room with three other men, while the room I was to be in was shared by 50 men. He got a shower, bathroom, sofa, and all of the luxuries, while all I had was simply a chair. One uncomfortable chair, crowded in with the others, and access to a distant public washroom. Maybe this was payback for the mountain.

We grabbed some food in the cafeteria, where we met some very friendly Scottish people who invited us to the bar for a drink. We had a great afternoon with them, having several beers and then some whisky, laughing and joking the whole time. Eventually, we tore ourselves away from the bar and the gregarious Scots.

Probably softened up by the drinks and the fun afternoon, Uncle Hugh said he was feeling guilty about stuffing me in third class. He told me he'd make it up to me and instructed me to brush my hair, get cleaned up, put on my nice suit, and meet him in an hour.

When the time arrived, we met and headed up to the first-class restaurant on the top floor. On the way, he instructed me on how to behave, "Hold your head up high, keep looking forward, and don't speak. If we act like first-class passengers, they won't know that we aren't. I did my best Uncle Hugh impression, holding my nose in the air and trying to exude snobbery. With cool, haughty dignity, we marched right past the doorman, who never said a word. We were seated at a linen-covered table with crystal glasses, a high centerpiece, silverware that was actually silver, and ornate chairs, which we sat straight up in.

The waiter arrived and nodded, "Good day sirs."

Uncle Hugh was in his glory and acted all the English gentleman that he wasn't. Showing disdain for the waiter and emanating arrogance, he ordered the steak and lobster with a bottle of red wine.

When the waiter turned to me, I asked if they had hamburgers, and he replied, "Yes, sir, we do."

I ordered the hamburger, as they were my favourite and I'd been craving one. The waiter left and Uncle Hugh levelled furious eyes at me. I may as well have spat on the Queen. He began to berate me in his most boorish voice, "I bring you to this first-class restaurant and you have the AUDACITY to embarrass me and order a hamburger. I am ashamed of you James!"

I was quite used to his tirades at this point and was feeling a little bravery from the alcohol consumed that afternoon, so I boldly shot back, "You have some nerve, pretending that we're first-class passengers while you booked yourself as second and me, the lowly third-class. We are totally scamming the shipping company here, so who should be ashamed of who?! Don't you get so high and mighty on me, Uncle Hugh!"

It turned out to be a very cold meal, and I don't mean the food. Not letting my outburst spoil his dinner, he ate his steak and lobster, then ordered two desserts for himself, as well as sherry, liqueurs, and still more liqueurs. We ate so much that I'm sure they lost money on our ticket fares.

We waddled out of the restaurant, parting ways with a grumpy, "I'll see you in the morning."

I must have been quite the sight for all of the "commoners" in my dorm; a 14-year-old all decked out in a suit, long-haired, half in the bag, and looking totally out of place. I had a fitful sleep in the uncomfortable chair, dozing on and off for an hour at a time until the hangover crept in. Then I just sat in the chair feeling miserable and unable to sleep; dejected, hungover, lonely, homesick, and feeling sorry for myself. I just wanted to go home.

The next morning, I went and met Uncle Hugh, who never said a word about the night before. This was odd to me, as I thought that adults always wanted to rehash everything they thought you'd done wrong. Mystified, I went along with it, carrying on like nothing happened. I thought to myself that maybe I had beat him for once; maybe I had won this one?

We carried on like nothing had happened, chatting about what we'd like to see and do next. It was a pleasant morning which we spent on deck watching the seagulls floating over the dark rollers of the North Sea. The Scots from the day before spotted us and joined us and we all stood at the rail, letting the warm ocean breeze blow through our hair.

When Norway finally came into view, we immediately noted impressive craggy mountains and knew that we'd probably have to drive through them. I looked over at Uncle Hugh, whose face had gone ashen. This was going to be rough.

Reaching the port in Bergen, all of the passengers, including our Scottish friends, fled for somewhere dry as it began pouring rain. We made our way to the camper van and got in queue to drive it off the boat, which took quite some time. Driving away from the docks, we spotted a young woman walking by and stopped to ask if she knew the whereabouts of a campground. Luckily, she spoke English and directed us to one nearby, though it was tough to find due to poor visibility from the incessant rain.

Eating supper glumly, we decided to hit the sack early as the rain was depressing and we hadn't gotten much sleep the night before. We ended up sleeping in well past the time we were usually leaving in the morning, and awoke to the continuing pounding of the rain on our camper roof.

We decided to drive back into Bergen and see if there was anything worth visiting there, but quickly found that the driving rain made seeing through the windshield too difficult to pick anything out. We spotted a movie theatre on the main drag, so we decided we'd just stop and see a movie.

Uncle Hugh chose a movie without consulting me, and my eyes widened when I saw that it was rated R. They let me into the movie without question and I grew excited as non-stop scenes of violence, swearing, and nudity marched across the screen. I was enjoying the movie immensely, but Uncle Hugh, very much regretting his decision, was squirming uncomfortably beside me. I could tell exactly what he was thinking: "Oh dear me, how could I have brought a child to see something so bad? What have I done? What will his mother think?"

After the movie, he apologized profusely for bringing me in to see it, "I'm so sorry my boy, I hope you will forgive me!"

I eagerly accepted his apology, trying to not let on how titillated I was from having watched such a risqué film. I was still spinning with giddy excitement from it; compared to the last movie I'd seen at home, Willy Wonka and the Chocolate Factory, this was really something else!

For the rest of the day, Uncle Hugh remained pretty quiet and was very kind and polite with me. I was enjoying the change from the night before, but I had to admit that it did make me a tad uncomfortable.

We went to sleep again at the same campground, with the same rain pounding on the roof of the camper. Things were starting to feel claustrophobic and miserable, and we both muttered that we hoped the next day would be better.

Our wish apparently came true, since we rose the next morning to a bright shining sun. It's incredible how much better a sunny day can make you feel!

With lifted spirits we left the campground and nearby Bergen and began our Norway adventure. The first place we stopped was an old Viking Church called the Fantoft Stavkirke. It was a big building, made completely out of wood and was dark black. It was quite foreboding and looked nothing like the churches we'd seen anywhere else. We took a bunch of pictures, then carried on up the valley.

Driving alongside a fjord, we could see dozens of waterfalls cascading over the cliffs and falling hundreds of feet. Everywhere we looked the scenery was absolutely astounding; so clean and fresh and beautiful. We stopped early at a campground in Granvin, and woke early to another beautifully sunny day.

Driving along past lakes and rivers with towering mountains on either side, I decided that it had to be one of the most beautiful places I'd ever seen. The scenery seemed to pale though whenever we had to ascend a series of tight hairpin turns to make our way over or through mountain peaks. Though I didn't know much about the mechanics of a vehicle back then, I knew there was something wrong with Uncle Hugh's driving. When climbing up the switchbacks, he would roar the engine in second gear until it sounded like the entire van would explode, then, as he was going to change into third gear, he would let go of the gas. The camper would slow, on the edge of a stall, and he would switch gears. We then wouldn't have enough power or momentum to continue climbing and the van would struggle and slow even further. Uncle Hugh would respond by downshifting, causing the engine to roar, and he would do it all over again.

Once we got going again, it would be okay, but as soon as we approached one of those hairpin turns, he would slow down and start the whole process all over again. Of course, cursing and accusations would ensue, all directed at me as if I had anything to do with how he was driving the vehicle. I bit my tongue, knowing that any logic or defense on my part would only make it worse. All I knew was that I was glad we'd had the clutch changed before coming to Norway or else we may have been stuck in the middle of nowhere. It was a wonder we ever got through those mountain passes without tumbling over the sheer drops that lined the highway.

We finally made it through and drove into Vangsnes, where we took a ferry to a place called Hella, where it was cloudy and raining again. Tired of the rain, we opted to find a campground right away. We drove along a fjord called Sognefjord and found a campground near Stedje.

To our great surprise, people we had met from Australia, New Zealand, USA and England, including Victor and Donna and two couples Leanne and Glen, Kathy and Bruce from the free beach camping in Yugoslavia, who were all camping there.

We had a fabulous dinner together, recounting tales and telling stories over aquavit, a strong local spirit made from grain and potatoes that was quite good. After supper, we all went on a long hike up the side of the fjord, enjoying the scenery and the company of friends.

It turned out we were all heading in the same direction the next day, so we rolled out in the morning as a convoy, with our camper van at the head. Driving along the road, Uncle Hugh noticed another Stavkirke in the distance, so he signalled everyone to pull off down the dirt road and follow him. As we approached the church, it appeared that there wasn't an actual parking lot, only a rough driveway. Uncle Hugh pulled up right to the end of the driveway, which terminated in the grassy churchyard, in order to make sure that everyone could fit behind him.

As we drove to the end of the driveway, we felt the ground sink beneath us. Oh no. I got out to look and the van was sunk in a pit of mud, with deep tire ruts down half of the driveway. Everyone else had wisely stopped at the head of the driveway upon seeing us sinking in the mud.

Luckily there were many extra sets of hands to help, and we all got in front of the van, excluding Uncle Hugh in the driver's seat, and started pushing and rocking the van in an attempt to get it unstuck. Mud flew everywhere as Uncle Hugh revved the engine and spun the tires. At first it was kind of funny, but the mirth quickly subsided as everyone became slightly frustrated. Uncle Hugh just wouldn't follow directions. If someone directed him to drive slowly backwards, he would pop the clutch and spin the tires like crazy. If someone said come forward straight, he would turn the wheels left and right, making everything worse.

Finally, one of the guys had enough and motioned a sheepish Uncle Hugh out of the van. He climbed in and got the van free in short order, with everyone else helping to push. I don't think that churchyard had ever witnessed so much swearing in so little time!

Uncle Hugh was quite frazzled, and very embarrassed that he'd not only sunk the van, but that he couldn't get it out afterwards. Of course, he didn't actually want to admit that, so his grumbles seemed to imply that it was my fault, the church's fault, or maybe even the fault of our friends who helped get us unstuck; anyone's fault but his.

Whoever's fault it was in his mind, he no longer had much interest in showing off his knowledge about the church to our friends, so he tortuously backed up the entirety of the driveway while everyone patiently waited, then vroomed out back on to the road, throwing wads of mud behind him.

Leaving the church and its chewed-up driveway in our rearview mirrors, we headed on towards our original destination, a famous glacier in the area. The drive there would have been quite challenging for Uncle Hugh, as the roads were all gravel and very steep, but there were dozens of tour buses heading the same way, ascending incredibly slowly. Uncle Hugh happily settled in behind one of the buses, driving in second gear the whole time, while our friends behind us impatiently kept creeping to the left to try to catch a glimpse around the buses so they could pass.

We eventually arrived at the top, where there was a small boat waiting to take us across a body of water to the glacier. As we approached the glacier, my breath was taken away by the impossible blue colour that slowly filled my vision. Ice cold water spewed through a notch in the glacier, cascading down and tumbling through large rocks in its path, where it bubbled and frothed. What an incredible place.

We collectively decided to spend another night in the same campground as the night before, so we made our way back towards it. This time, one of the other guys quickly jumped to the front of the convoy as we left the parking lot and Uncle Hugh struggled to keep up with him the whole way back.

Back at the campground, the drinks started flowing and revelry ensued. Beer, wine, and aquavit accompanied a fantastic dinner, and we all stayed up late into the night having fun. It always amazed me that everyone treated me as an adult no matter where we went or who we met. There was no question of whether or not I should be drinking at the age of fourteen; if someone was grabbing a drink, they'd ask me what I wanted and get it for me. No one even mentioned my age, which was astounding, they just treated me like an adult and spoke to me as if I was the same age. I found this so empowering after a life of "being seen, not heard" at home with my parents, where everyone insisted on treating me like a child, and to be honest, made me act like one sometimes. How was I ever going to return home and relinquish my newfound adulthood to my parents and teachers?

The next day, we departed from our friends and continued on our journey. Over the next week, we continued north through stunning valleys, heart-stopping mountain passes, and breathtaking vistas. We crossed bridge after bridge and boarded ferries on the regular. We saw glaciers, mountain meadows, ominous

Viking churches, desolate landscapes above the tree line, and turquoise lakes and rivers that didn't seem to be a part of this world.

Everywhere we went, we easily found campgrounds to spend the night in, each crowded with tourists from all over the world. One such, near the town of Andalnes, was perched on the side of a mountain in a picturesque meadow. I raised our Canadian flag as was our custom upon arrival to proclaim that we were friendly Canadians and not Americans. After I rose the flag, a neighbour raised their German flag in what seemed like a friendly gesture.

This didn't sit well with Uncle Hugh though. He despised Germans, never forgiving them for the wars that they instigated. He glared at the German flag, cursing all Germans, and I watched his scowl deepen as a small group of harmless German teens started a soccer game in the road near us. This was his chance to get the bloody Germans back for everything they had done in the wars. Standing up suddenly, he pushed through the soccer players and marched to the camp office, where he adamantly complained that these delinquents, these, these hooligans, were making way too much noise while he was trying to take a nap. Neither of these things were true of course, but he pestered the owner of the campground until he acquiesced and came over to shut down the game.

Uncle Hugh sat back down in his chair, smug and gloating that he'd stopped those "Goddamned Germans" from ruining his day. The friendly neighbour, who'd raised his flag in response to ours, didn't look all that friendly anymore. I sat there with my head down, absolutely ashamed of what he'd done. I was thoroughly embarrassed by his actions and thought it was just rotten of him to have gone and ruined those boys' fun.

I was used to behaviour like this from him, but it didn't sit well with me, and I didn't know how to properly react to it.

Driving ever northwards, now through several rainy days, we finally made it to Trondheim, the very northern-most point of our journey. Trondheim was on the same latitude as Greenland and Baffin Island which blew me away when I traced it across a map. We stayed for a couple of days, taking advantage of the VW dealership there, repairing some gears and replacing a worn-out emergency brake.

While the camper van was being repaired yet again, we used the time to explore Trondheim, checking out the beautiful arched bridge, the fantastic Gothic Cathedral, the warehouse-lined river with its multitude of colours, the buzzing shopping district on cobblestoned streets, and Norway's largest university. It was a gorgeous town and we didn't begrudge the days spent there.

Once the van was repaired, we decided to spend the last night in a campground to save some money. Uncle Hugh shook me awake at 5:00 am, and we slipped quietly out of the campground without paying. I started to imagine that there were photos of us in campgrounds all over Europe with rewards for our capture issued by Interpol – $5000 reward for the capture of the Campground Bandits: Wanted Dead or Alive.

Utterly sick of driving on small and steep mountain roads, Uncle Hugh opted to hit the highway, which was fast but not too scenic. The freeway was modern and smooth and allowed us to arrive in Oslo only two days later.

While in Oslo, we strolled along the harbour, admiring the old warehouses, shops, and locals milling along the promenade. We visited the Edward Munch Museum as well as the Resistance Museum with its many

3D models of brave Norwegians fighting the occupying Germans and their valiant struggle to reattain their independence. We stopped in to see the 1694 Cathedral and the Town Hall, which was built in the Functionalism style of architecture, meaning it was designed purely for functionality and efficiency. This seemed to make a lot of sense to me, and I found myself admiring the Norwegian's wisdom.

We also visited Frogner Park with its Vigeland Sculpture Garden, where a single sculptor spent 20 years of his life creating 212 sculptures of bronze, granite, and cast iron, depicting all aspects of a person's life. Every sculpture was nude and dramatically realistic. It was very impressive and the weather cooperated with us that day, bathing the sculptures in rays of sunlight, which made them seem even more alive.

Norwegians are big on skiing, and we got to visit their huge ski jumping park. Since it was summer, it made for a strange sight – a massive man-made hill with a pond of water at its base.

To top off our visit to Oslo, Uncle Hugh had a great surprise for me which he led me to, giddy and giggling like a little girl. Oh. Another museum. He dragged me around the National Gallery, and we saw every single one of its 45,000 paintings, 900 sculptures, 17,300 drawings, and 25,000 prints, the most famous of which was Edward Munch's "The Scream". I was already empathizing with the tortured man in the painting and was ready to scream myself by the time we'd made our way through half of the museum. Uncle Hugh was very talented at stripping away any and all fun from a museum. I had certainly learned an incredible amount in our travels and had developed a real interest in history, art, and architecture, but these things needed to be savoured and enjoyed, not jammed down your throat until you felt like you were drowning in it.

I liked Oslo a lot and particularly enjoyed a dish of veal and pommes frites, which I ordered several times while I was there, but it was time to leave, as we still had a long drive before we reached our next country, Sweden.

Chapter 20

We took the freeway south from Oslo to Gothenburg, which took about 5 hours. Arriving in the Swedish city, we spent an enjoyable day visiting the downtown area with its historic buildings, beautiful fountain, art gallery, and shops. We stopped in a restaurant for dinner and ordered köttbullar, a delicious meatball dish, as well as some nice Swedish wine and some ginger snaps for dessert.

The next day, we took a ferry over to Denmark, successfully visiting three countries in two days. Driving to Copenhagen, the capital of Denmark, we parked the van on the edge of the city and took a bus into the downtown area. We ambled around for a while, admiring the city's core with its multitude of people.

Uncle Hugh always enjoyed people watching and had lots to say about this person or that person, and how they looked, dressed, walked, or talked. He never seemed to make the connection that WE would be the ultimate show for other people watchers – an older man with outdated clothes, a stiff hunched neck, and thick scowling eyebrows with a young, long-haired teen dressed in corduroy bellbottom pants following him around. I thought it was amusing and wondered if Uncle Hugh saw himself as the perfect, normal person who had the right to judge others he thought weren't equal to him.

We decided to go and visit Trivoli Gardens in the heart of the city, an amusement park that was touted as having something for everyone. Uncle Hugh was enamored with the fine architecture, the many beautifully manicured gardens, and the outdoor restaurants, while I was there for the rides. I especially enjoyed the bumper cars, which I rode three times, then I moved on to the roller coaster, which I rode over and over again until I could tell Uncle Hugh was getting visibly impatient. He pulled me away from the rides, saying that he wanted to see some of the shows before they sold out, and ended up bringing me to a comedy/ballet that had him clapping his hands giddily, and me wishing I was still on the roller coaster.

We were both still enjoying the park and we'd noticed lots of good-looking options for dinner, so Uncle Hugh suggested we eat there, enjoy the park some more, and then stay for the nightly fireworks. He had a hard time deciding which restaurant to go to and we wasted plenty of precious time stopping in the doorways and checking the menus while I impatiently bounced on my toes. Finally, he decided on Italian and we had a delicious supper of salmon in a garlic cream sauce with loads of bread, and some chilled white wine, which was a nice change from the usual red. We finished the dinner off with some great cannoli and a small glass of liqueur.

Everything was going nicely, until Uncle Hugh leaned in and whispered conspiratorially, "Now Jimmy boy, listen and follow my instructions. Don't say a word! And don't question what I'm telling you, just do it."

My heart started pounding and my mouth went dry as I intuited what he meant to do. I was feeling shocked and fearful and didn't want to comply.

"Now," he said, "You're going to get up like you're going to the toilet, but you're going to walk straight out the front door, nice and nonchalant-like. Just keep walking until you get to the Oriental Pagoda and I'll meet you there."

I opened my mouth to argue, but he held his hand out and said, "Go."

I did what he asked, standing up and attempting to casually walk out of the restaurant, though my legs were shaking and my palms were sweating profusely. I somehow made it outside of the restaurant and booked it towards the pagoda. I stood there for what felt like forever, wringing my hands and waiting for Uncle Hugh to show up, the whole time thinking that I was going to be stuffed into the back of a police car and thrown into a scary European prison.

He finally arrived, walking jauntily and ebullient with the pride and joy of his escapade. Grinning mischievously at me, he motioned down the street saying, "We'd better get out of here and back to the camper!"

"But what about the fireworks? And the rides? I thought we were going to stick around!"

Shaking his head, he started walking away and I realized the fireworks from getting caught for stealing might be too hot to handle, so I followed him quickly. We successfully made it through the exit of the park and marched up to the bus stop that would take us back towards the campground. It was a 30-minute wait for the bus and I could see Uncle Hugh's excitement beginning to wane as he paced back and forth, looking quite nervous.

I'm not sure if the term "dine and dash" had been coined yet back then, but I couldn't imagine doing anything like that and wondered what it was about Uncle Hugh that made him think it was okay. I guess it simply stemmed from his overriding cheapness, and he must have got a kick out of doing it too. He always seemed to think he deserved it and never spared a thought for the poor restaurant or campground owner who suffered as a result.

Once safely back at the campsite, he was humming and smiling to himself so much it nearly made me sick. He didn't seem to understand why I felt so shaken up and let me go to bed early without a word.

The next day, we took the bus back into town, did some banking, and went for a long stroll. We passed by the Tuborg Brewery, which had a sign out front offering brewery tours, so we went in on a whim. I'd never been in a brewery before and I found the entire process quite fascinating, as they led us through rooms of vats, tanks, and taps. At the end of the tour, there was a barroom where they were offering free Tuborg beers to everyone who took the tour. We each had two and Uncle Hugh was pleased as punch that he was able to get four free beers on top of a free tour.

We left the brewery and made our way to one of Copenhagen's many castles. This was the Kronborg Castle and was the inspiration for Shakespeare's Hamlet and so was quite notorious. The castle was not disappointing, possibly because I simply loved exploring castles, but I felt like this one was truly superb.

We ate supper in town again, and though I was nervous Uncle Hugh was going to pull another one of his hijinks, he behaved. He still left without leaving a tip though, which was no big surprise.

After dinner, we went to a circus that was travelling through town and I was having a great time, but started feeling quite ill. As it got worse, I let Uncle Hugh know and he suggested we head back to the campground. I went to sleep early and woke up with an awful cold and just feeling terrible. Uncle Hugh told me to stay in bed for the day and went into town on the bus alone. Returning around 2:00 pm, he asked me how I was feeling and if I'd be up for returning to Tivoli Gardens and going on some rides.

I was feeling a bit better, and was bored of looking at the camper ceiling, so I agreed and we got back on the bus and headed to town. I was worried about going back into Gardens and having the restaurant discover us, but Uncle Hugh didn't seem perturbed at all. It was like he had forgotten the entire thing, but I'm sure the restaurant hadn't!

Just looking at the rides gave me a wave of nausea, so instead, we sat and watched a few performances, including a concert. I was happy to just be sitting and not walking around, and I was having a hard time focusing on anything. Turned out, I was still quite sick.

Uncle Hugh said that he wanted to find some place for dinner that was cheaper, so he consulted his travel bible, "Europe on $5 a Day". We hadn't had a $5 day in Europe yet, but the book did list plenty of cheaper options. We chose one and made our way over there, giving the Italian restaurant from the other night a wide berth. Uncle Hugh seemed to be happy at the prices, but that good humour faded as soon as the food came out. It was awful!

Uncle Hugh was furious. He bitched about the book and how it led him astray by suggesting terrible restaurants, and he bitched about the restaurant itself, who dared serve him such garbage. I don't think the man had ever heard the old adage, "You get what you pay for."

The next morning, we broke down camp and drove the van into town. We visited the Resistance Museum and I was amazed at how determined the Danes were to break free from Nazi control. Photo and video exhibits showed men, women, and children working undercover in extremely dangerous situations to destabilize the occupying forces.

After the Resistance Museum, we visited the Royal Amalienborg Palace where the Queen of Denmark lived. I kept my eyes peeled the entire time, hoping to catch a glimpse of her, but she was nowhere to be found. The palace was magnificent; full of opulent furnishings and artwork that was "Fit for a Queen" as Uncle Hugh said, laughing at his own joke.

Before we were to leave Denmark behind us, Uncle Hugh insisted that I see the famous Little Mermaid statue, so we drove to the waterfront and walked along the promenade with other tourists. I spotted the statue about 100 meters away and then noticed a hovercraft zooming along over the water, racing towards it. I then saw a hydrofoil swiftly making its way towards the statue from the other side. I broke into a run, pulling my camera up and sliding in front of the statue just as the hydrofoil and hovercraft passed each other with the statue in the middle. I snapped a photo, hoping beyond hope that it would turn out. Back then, of course, you'd have to wait until you got the film developed to see the photos. Luckily, when I did eventually get them developed, I saw that I had caught the moment perfectly.

Uncle Hugh eventually caught up and asked what had come over me to charge off like that. I explained, and he praised my efforts, saying that he wished he had thought of such a thing so he could have gotten a photo of it. I laughed to myself, picturing the two vehicles racing towards one another and Uncle Hugh adjusting his aperture while the moment passed him by. Even if he were to replace the hovercraft and hydrofoil with a couple of slow-moving rowboats, he still probably would have missed it!

We made our way back to the camper and drove onto a ferry, which brought us back to Germany to a town called Lübeck. Despite it being in Germany, Uncle Hugh really liked Lübeck, as it was full of fine brick Gothic architecture. It had been bombed pretty extensively by the Allies but had mostly been rebuilt by that point.

We found a campground near town and ended up on a site next to a friendly older couple from England. They were having issues with a burnt-out generator and couldn't cook themselves supper, so we invited them over to our campsite. I ended up cooking and they mentioned how impressed they were with me that I would take on the task. They stated that they didn't know any teenager that would have done such a thing.

I didn't think that it was too big of a deal, as I often cooked and supper that night was a simple and regular meal in our rotation: spaghetti and meatballs. Despite the simplicity of the meal, I was feeling pretty proud of myself after all of that praise and was delighted when they kept offering me drinks from their cooler all night. Apparently, a teenager who could cook was a teenager who could drink. People are so funny sometimes.

The landscape flattened out as we drove from Lübeck through Hamburg, Bremen, and Oldenburg on our way to the Netherlands. Uncle Hugh was sure to take the time to let me know how flat and boring it was and how much it reminded him of Ontario (which is only flat in the south to be fair). Like always, I took his prodding personally, feeling like he was including me and everyone I knew with his derogatory comments. I don't know what Ontario had done to the man to make him continually disparage it and antagonize me with it, but I really came to resent him for it.

Before we knew it, we were crossing the border into Holland as we called it, though everyone calls it the Netherlands these days. We found a campground in Groningen, which was sandwiched between a few canals, which were loaded with colourful ducks. It was a beautiful campground and the owner let us know that we had arrived at the perfect time as the nearby town was having a festival.

Asking around, we discovered that the festival was celebrating freedom from Bernhard von Galen, the Bishop of Münster, a tyrant who terrorized the region 300 years prior.

After getting settled and raising the flag, we walked into town to find thousands of people enjoying rides, games, food booths, and kiosk bars. We jumped right in, playing a few carnival-style games, grabbing a beer at an outdoor bar, and sticking around to watch some fantastic fireworks later that night.

Everyone we interacted with was very friendly, particularly when they found out that I, and the cultural shapeshifter Uncle Hugh, were Canadian (oh, so now it's fine to be from Ontario?) "Canadian! Oh, we love Canadians," the people would invariably say. Canadians had liberated the Dutch from the Germans in WWII and they would forever be thankful. This made me feel great and proud to be Canadian and even more resentful of Uncle Hugh for masquerading as one.

The next day, we left Groningen and drove the backroads through Holland, crossing many canals and passing by countless windmills. The landscape was dotted with dairy cows, barns, farms, and the aforementioned canals and windmills and I thought it was absolutely beautiful, even if it was flat. Uncle Hugh must have thought so too, despite his earlier comments, as we stopped regularly to take photos.

We left the countryside for the freeway and drove out to Ijsselmeer dam, which is 29 kilometers long and contains Holland's largest lake, also named Ijsselmeer, which is over 1100 square kilometers. Once over the dam we searched fruitlessly for a campground for several hours, with lots of arguing and blame being settled on me for our failure to do so. Eventually, I spotted a sign pointing towards one and was soundly berated for not having seen one sooner and wasting so much time.

Arriving at the campground, I unpacked in silence, seething in anger and frustration. To make matters worse, the fuel cylinder ran out of propane while I was halfway through cooking dinner. Uncle Hugh refused to buy another cylinder as we only had a week left of our trip and he didn't want to end up with half a tank of unused fuel. Still, Uncle Hugh was mad that dinner was ruined and somehow managed to blame the fuel running out on me as well.

All of this criticism was very difficult for me to handle as a teenager and, not surprisingly, I didn't take it well. I didn't cry about it, but I was red in the face with frustration and deeply resented Uncle Hugh for saying such things, perhaps a little too much. I never understood why when adults got tired, they lashed out at their loved ones, saying things they didn't mean and hurting feelings. I took this senseless scolding personally and would often plot revenge in my mind.

We had no choice but to drive to town to find some supper at a restaurant there. Supper started out uncomfortably quiet, but after a few beers, Uncle Hugh suggested what seemed like a peace offering. He ordered a series of Dutch liqueurs for us, including jenever, oranjebitter, and some kopstootje and all of our evil feelings dissipated as we sipped on the strong liquor. Soon, we were back to chatting and planning for tomorrow's adventures.

We arrived back at the campsite in much better spirits and went to bed happy instead of mad. Just when I thought things were going to be better, Uncle Hugh awoke with a cold the next morning.

When Uncle Hugh was feeling sick, upset, or sorry for himself, he made sure that the world around him better be feeling the same way. Being sick or upset didn't stop him from doing anything, it just meant that whatever we ended up doing wouldn't be fun. How could you have fun with a walking thunderhead?

We drove to the outskirts of Amsterdam and luckily found a campground without any trouble. We took a tram into town and since he wasn't feeling all too great, he thought it would be a good time to sit back and enjoy a boat tour through the city's extensive canal system. This way he could simply relax without walking around or being active.

It was a great way to see the city, which hosted 160 canals, stretching over 100 kilometers, with more than 90 islands and 1500 bridges. The excessively narrow buildings lining the canals were impressive with their ornate facades and gables.

Uncle Hugh told me that the buildings were all so narrow because the taxes in Amsterdam were based on frontage dimensions, so the buildings ended up narrow, but very deep. I wondered what the staircases must look like inside, and how the houses could possibly be laid out.

I found Amsterdam to be a beautiful city, and as one person described, it felt like a storybook that came to life. Many others were enjoying the city from the water too, whether from tour boats like ours or from houseboats moored to the sides of the canals. The tour guide told us that there were over 1800 houseboats in the city, and they all seemed to be teeming with life.

Once the tour was over, Uncle Hugh complained that he was feeling even worse, so we went back to the campground and he climbed into bed. Bored, I left to walk around the campground and ended up running into a British couple who invited me over for a beer. We had a marvelous time swapping stories and telling tales until one of them asked me how old I was. When I answered 14, they both seemed taken aback and frankly embarrassed that they'd offered me alcohol. The conversation seemed to dry up after that, so I left for the camper.

I stayed very quiet all night and the next morning and Uncle Hugh slept in all the way until 10:00 am, which was quite odd for him. When he finally awoke, I made breakfast and washed up all of the dishes while he sat in his chair, staring at his Earl Grey.

Not wanting to miss out on the city even though he was feeling very ill, we took a tram into town again and slowly strolled through the streets, eventually coming across a large square that was hosting a flea market. Uncle Hugh sat down on a bench as I perused the vendor's kiosks, thoroughly enjoying looking through all of the strange items on display. I ended up purchasing a pair of wooden shoes for $3 that fit me perfectly as well as a box of cigars for my father and some small square purses for my sisters.

Uncle Hugh began feeling better and over the next few days we did all of the obligatory tourist attractions, including Anne Frank's house, which really left an impression on me, a few art galleries boasting original Rembrandts including his most famous work, The Night Watch, Rembrandt's home, the Van Gogh Museum, the Mauritshuis Museum with paintings by Vermeer, and also a museum full of modern art. I must have been slowly becoming a connoisseur, as I toured the museums with keen interest and even listened to Uncle Hugh's droning and extended renditions of their history.

I'd be remiss in not mentioning one wild night in Amsterdam. One afternoon in camp, Uncle Hugh suggested that we get dressed up and go into town for dinner and to enjoy the local nightlife. Little did I know that my worldly education was going to take an unexpected turn.

We had a fantastic supper of deep-fried herring, French fries, and beer, then went for a long aimless walk. As darkness descended, we found ourselves suddenly bathing in the glow of neon lights. They were everywhere, illuminating signs advertising "SEX" in large, foot-long English letters. I felt illuminated myself, never having heard of half the things I was seeing displayed in public. Explicit pictures holding nothing back accompanied the signs and lights, showing you what you could expect upon entering each establishment.

There were thousands of people milling in the streets, and just like we'd experienced in Greece, there were hundreds of American sailors in different stages of debauchery crowding the area and raising hell as they did.

Focusing on one group, Uncle Hugh suggested we stealthily follow them to see where they ended up. They stopped outside of each establishment, animatedly but good-naturedly arguing with each other over which one to go into and which show to see. The group loudly egged on their youngest member, who seemed to be not much older than me, to go in and get laid, and he seemed very reluctant to comply.

They kept pressing him and he finally confided that he was a virgin and didn't know what to do in the bedroom, which resulted in uproarious laughter from his friends. He finally agreed, but on the condition that they help pay, as he was short on cash and worried that he wouldn't get enough time. He was also worried that she'd know he'd never done it before. One of his buddy's put his arm around him and sagely offered some advice, "Man, just keep on pumping and she'll never notice the difference."

The scantily clad girls in the window echoed this and the whole group disappeared into the doorway. Not wanting to be caught spying, but invested in this little drama, we had drifted closer to them, ending up beside the windows with the prostitutes.

I never imagined anything like it in my life. Girls of all shapes and sizes, though most young and pretty, stood in the windows, wearing nothing but bras and underwear or sheer lingerie, all looking their sexiest and seductively offering good times to the passersby. We continued down the street, unable to tear our eyes from the hundreds of windows, all full of attractive women, calling out to people in the street.

"How do they all make a living?" I wondered aloud.

Uncle Hugh was either too embarrassed, or too entranced to bother explaining it to me. We returned to the area with the neon lights and found an outdoor bar. We sat down at a table facing the street and watched the spectacle of people going in each and every direction, and the antics of the sailors, who seemed to grow drunker by the minute. This whole experience felt like it belonged in a movie that I was still too young to see. The entire scene was unforgettable and thoroughly enjoyable, if a little overwhelming. I bet Uncle Hugh would never dream of telling my mother that he'd brought me here. Honestly, I never told my mother about it either.

As we left Amsterdam, Uncle Hugh's cold returned with a vengeance, which resulted in a foul mood permeating the van like a bad smell. We drove south as I navigated us (with plenty of criticism) through the Hague and then through Rotterdam. We jumped on the freeway and continued through Breda and into Tilburg where we decided to stop for the night.

Once again, we couldn't find a campground anywhere and had to stop at a gas station to ask for directions to one. I had to do all of the talking, as Uncle Hugh was too sick and miserable to be talking to humans by this time. I tried to follow the confusing directions given, but we just couldn't seem to find the campground. Once again, Uncle Hugh blamed me for this failure, becoming more irate with every passing moment.

We stopped again and asked some guys parked on the street if they knew of a campground nearby. To our surprise, they offered to lead us right there. They jumped into their car and led us right to the campground, which we'd somehow been circling for the last two hours. Uncle Hugh had been hesitant to follow them as he believed they may have been leading us into a back alley where they'd rob and kill us, but he was too weak and desperate to resist my reassurances. Encountering such nice and helpful people everywhere we travelled really gave me faith in the human race. Unfortunately, in the next few days, this faith would be shattered to pieces.

The campground was huge and very busy, but it had a great store and supermarket attached to it, which was perfect as we didn't feel like driving anywhere for food. I was able to purchase some bread, cheese, meat, and wine while Uncle Hugh lay in bed. After supper, he went right to sleep and I was left to my own devices again.

Bored, I wandered to the camp office lobby where I'd noticed a television while we were checking in. I sat down on a couch in the lobby and watched TV for a while. Eventually, I was joined by a 13-year-old girl named Paumi who lived at the campground. She told me that if I was still at the campground the next day, I should seek her out and we could hang out. I told her we were travelling back to Germany the next day so that I wouldn't be able to, but thanked her for the offer and said my goodbyes.

The next morning, Uncle Hugh was feeling so rough that he said he was in no condition to drive. He looked absolutely terrible and was so weak that he could barely make it to the public washrooms. I made him some tea and cookies in lieu of breakfast and he went back to bed. Twiddling my thumbs for a while, I decided to go in search of Paumi and see if she still wanted to hang out.

I found her in the camp office and she dragged me along for the day, playing checkers and watching the Olympics on TV. I had a great day with her, having lots of fun conversations which was nice after living with what was basically a grumpy bear with a sore tooth for so long. I went and checked in on the grumpy bear a few times, but he just groaned and complained about everything, so I inevitably found myself returning to my new friend to hang out. She found a radio and we sat on the floor in front of it, listening to Radio Luxembourg, which played modern music. This was a treat for me, as Uncle Hugh only listened to classical music, which I found boring and for old people.

The following morning, Uncle Hugh was well enough to get back on the road. He got up, showered, shaved, and got packed while I said goodbye to Paumi and we headed out. It was September 5th, which meant that we only had two more days before we flew home to Canada. I couldn't believe that it was coming up so quickly.

Uncle Hugh had intentionally stayed out of Germany as long as he could due to his intense hatred of the people and the country, but it was time to go back as we'd be flying out of Frankfurt. We left Holland, driving through Dusseldorf, Cologne, Bonn, and down to Koblenz, with Uncle Hugh finding something wrong with everything we drove past. It was too flat, the scenery was too boring, the buildings were too ugly, there were too many cars, the smog was unbearable, so smoggy you could barely see across the Rhine! The Goddamn Germans ruined everything they touched and could never be forgiven.

We stopped at a campground outside of Koblenz, setting up camp and raising the Canadian flag for the last time, as we'd be staying in a hotel for the last night in Europe before our flight. Uncle Hugh would be sending the VW camper van via cargo ship to his home in Oregon.

The campground was abuzz with the horrific news of the murders of the Israelis at the Munich Olympic village, and we were shocked to hear it recounted by neighbours while we ate supper. A terrorist group called Black September had broken into the village and taken several hostages. In the end, 12 innocent people were killed, plus 5 of the attackers. Being in Germany during this awful event really put it right in our faces, and we were deeply touched by it. It would take some time before my faith in humanity was restored.

Between the disturbing news, Uncle Hugh's lengthy illness, and the fact that our trip was coming to an end, we were feeling pretty down in the dumps. Instead of celebrating six months of travel and our very last night of camping, we sat around the radio all night, listening grimly to the news. It felt like the funeral of a close relative rather than a joyous occasion.

The next day, we drove the final leg of our journey, arriving in Frankfurt before noon. We returned to the VW dealership where they had agreed to make shipping arrangements for the camper. We packed all of the gear as tightly as we could in the storage compartments, returned all of our personal items to our suitcases, and Hans, that same nice man from the beginning of the trip, drove us to a hotel close to the airport.

We checked in, stowed our luggage, then walked to a nearby restaurant. Uncle Hugh was feeling much better now, and he was actually quite pleasant. I was unsure of how he was feeling internally. Was he happy our trip was over? Disappointed? Maybe happy to return to an existence not plagued by the presence of a teenager?

Outwardly, he seemed a little sad and wistful while we reminisced about the trip, retracing our path and dwelling on the highlights. There was laughter and even some tears as we went through all of our recent memories. It all seemed surreal to me as we summarized all of the places we'd been, all of the cities we'd visited, all of the people we'd met, and all of the adventures we'd had on our journey. It really was unbelievable that we'd travelled thousands of kilometres through eighteen different countries, and 3 continents, all in a little VW camper van.

He, this crippled old man with a stiff neck (in more ways than one), vastly overeducated, opinionated, biased, prejudiced, and eccentric as all hell, and me, this strangely dressed, long-haired, wet-behind-the-ears, teen who didn't know anything of the world outside of his humble home, and who somehow survived the six month and seven-day journey that was at once challenging and fascinating, with a man he didn't even know through worlds he didn't even know existed. What a long, strange trip.

September 7, 1972

Arriving at Frankfurt airport, we were surprised to see all of the people and the long line-ups. We soon realized that Germany was on high alert due to the terrorist killings at the Olympic Village. I guess we were still naïve in a pre-terrorism-paranoid world, but we'd be schooled quickly and ruthlessly. Upon entering the security area, we were forced to go through metal detectors repeatedly, and then I was taken to a little curtained booth, where I was told to spread my legs and put my hands on the wall. Shaking and not knowing what was going to happen, I was frisked and patted down thoroughly by a large and grim woman who must have been an ex-pro heavyweight wrestler.

I wobbled out of the booth on shaky legs, happy to have only been given a pat down, however thorough. Uncle Hugh and I slowly advanced through the airport being put through humiliating experience after humiliating experience. We were both feeling flustered and out of our element.

We finally boarded the plane and then sat there on the runway for well over an hour before the captain spoke over the loudspeaker saying that all of the luggage had been boarded, but that a few passengers were missing and couldn't be located. We were told we'd have to de-board and pick up our luggage from the runway to a chorus of moans from the passengers. He warned us not to miss any of our luggage, as anything left behind would be suspect and blown up as a potential terrorist threat.

Wow. What an end to our trip!

We were scared and being herded around like cattle. We eventually re-stowed our luggage and made it back onto the plane, scared like everyone else that we'd be blown up or hijacked. Finally, we were given clearance for take-off. It was an unnerving experience, something we'd never had any life training to deal with. Luckily, the plane never blew up and we landed safely in Toronto eight hours later.

My parents were waiting for me in the airport and seeing them, I realized that it really was the end and things would be going back to "normal". The thing was, I was no longer the same person after this trip, and I didn't know if I'd ever be able to fit back into "normal" again.

THE END

www.ingramcontent.com/pod-product-compliance
Lightning Source LLC
Chambersburg PA
CBHW071314090426
42738CB00012B/2701